Microfinance and Public Policy

The International Labour Organization

The International Labour Organization was founded in 1919 to promote social justice and, thereby, to contribute to universal and lasting peace. Its tripartite structure is unique among agencies affiliated to the United Nations; the ILO's Governing Body includes representatives of government, and of employers' and workers' organizations. These three constituencies are active participants in regional and other meetings sponsored by the ILO, as well as in the International Labour Conference – a world forum which meets annually to discuss social and labour questions.

Over the years the ILO has issued for adoption by member States a widely respected code of international labour Conventions and Recommendations on freedom of association, employment, social policy, conditions of work, social security, industrial relations and labour administration, among others.

The ILO provides expert advice and technical assistance to member States through a network of offices and multidisciplinary teams in over 40 countries. This assistance takes the form of labour rights and industrial relations counselling, employment promotion, training in small business development, project management, advice on social security, workplace safety and working conditions, the compiling and dissemination of labour statistics, and workers' education.

Microfinance and Public Policy

Outreach, Performance and Efficiency

Edited by

Bernd Balkenhol

© International Labour Organization 2007

First published in 2007 by
PALGRAVE MACMILLAN
Houndmills, Basingstoke, Hampshire RG21 6XS and
175 Fifth Avenue, New York, N.Y. 10010
Companies and representatives throughout the world.

ISBN-13: 978–0–230–54702–5 hardback
ISBN-10: 0–230–54702–8 hardback

and

International Labour Office
CH-1211 Geneva 22, Switzerland

ISBN-13: 978–92–2–119347–0 hardback
ISBN-10: 92–2–119347–0 hardback

PALGRAVE MACMILLAN is the global academic imprint of the Palgrave
Macmillan division of St. Martin's Press, LLC and of Palgrave Macmillan Ltd.
Macmillan® is a registered trademark in the United States, United Kingdom
and other countries. Palgrave is a registered trademark in the European
Union and other countries.

This book is printed on paper suitable for recycling and made from fully
managed and sustained forest sources. Logging, pulping and manufacturing
processes are expected to conform to the environmental regulations of
the country of origin.

A catalogue record for this book is available from the British Library.

A catalog record for this book is available from the Library of Congress.

10 9 8 7 6 5 4 3 2 1
16 15 14 13 12 11 10 09 08 07

Printed and bound in Great Britain by
Antony Rowe Ltd, Chippenham and Eastbourne

Contents

Part I Introduction

Part II Conceptual Framework

v

List of Tables

List of Figures and Boxes

Figures

Boxes

List of Abbreviations

ASA	Association for Social Advancement
BNDA	National Bank for Agricultural Development
BRAC	Bangladesh Rural Advancement Committee
CAME	Centro de Apoyo al Microempresario
CGAP	Consultative Group to Assist the Poor
CVECA	Caisses Villageoises et d'Epargne et de Crédit Autogérées
CYSD	Centre for Youth and Social Development
DEA	Data Envelopment Analysis
FCFA	Franc CFA (monetary unit in the West African Economic and Monetary Union)
FONDEP	Foundation for Local Development and Microcredit Partnerships
FSS	Financial Self-Sufficiency
GIAN	Geneva International Academic Network
GNI	Gross National Income
GNP	Gross National Product
IGVGD	Income Generation for Vulnerable Group Development
ILO	International Labour Organization
IMF	International Monetary Fund
MBB	*MicroBanking Bulletin*
MDG	Millennium Development Goals
MECREF	Mutuelle d'Epargne et de Crédit des Femmes
MENA	Middle East and North Africa
MFI	Microfinance Institution
MIS	Management Information System
MIX	Microfinance Information eXchange
NAC	Number of Active Clients
NBFI	Non-Banking Financial Institution
NGO	Non-Governmental Organization
OSS	Operational Self-Sufficiency
PAC	Access to Credit Program
PRSP	Poverty Reduction Strategy Paper
RDP	Rural Development Programme
SEF	Small Enterprise Foundation

SERCOTEC	Servicio de Cooperación Técnica
SHG	Self-Help Group
SML	SHARE Microfin Ltd
SUR	Seemingly Unrelated Regression
UBN	Unsatisfied Basic Needs
USAID	United States Agency for International Development

Acknowledgements

This book is the result of team work over three years. It was initiated by the Social Finance Programme of the ILO in 2001, following discussions around a paper I had originally presented at the annual conference of the Verein für Socialpolitik in 2001 in Heidelberg. The book presents the findings of a survey of microfinance institutions carried out under the joint responsibility of the University of Geneva, the Geneva Institute of Development Studies (IUED), Cambridge University and the International Labour Office (ILO). The field work and meetings would not have been possible without the generous financial support of the Geneva International Academic network (GIAN), the European Commission (AIDCO), the Ford Foundation and the ILO.

The individuals representing these institutions in our joint effort deserve recognition for their sustained commitment, both as leaders of the partner institutions, Flavio Comim, Daniel Fino, Yves Flückiger, Renata Serra and Jean Michel Servet, and as representatives of donor agencies, Frank de Giovanni, Randall Harbour, Koen de Lange and Georg Matzner.

Several conferences and workshops were held from 2003 onwards to plan for this book, prepare for the questionnaire-based surveys and agree on a common framework for analysis. The work brought together microfinance practitioners, academics and representatives of donor agencies. Fabrizio Botti, Milasoa Cherel-Robson, Florent Song-Naba, Isabelle Hillenkamp, Laura Leoncini, Jean Claude Luvini and Almoustapha Moumouni were instrumental in bringing this to a successful conclusion.

Those who carried out the surveys, mostly postgraduate students preparing their doctoral degree, also deserve a special word of appreciation.

Microfinance institutions are constantly being solicited with requests for data and surveys. The managers and staff of the MFIs interviewed were prepared to receive our reviewers and openly discuss all issues – even delicate ones – related to their outreach to poor clients and financial performance. They deserve a special word of thanks and recognition.

I also would like to acknowledge the contribution to the survey design by Diana Barrowclough and Yannis Berthouzoz at the start-up stage of the project.

Very much appreciated were the suggestions and moral support of Thorsten Beck, Frank de Giovanni, Yousra Hamed and Jonathan Morduch.

Last but not least, I owe a special word of thanks to my assistant Nalina Ganapathi, who helped navigate us through several narrow straits.

BERND BALKENHOL

Social Finance Programme
International Labour Office

Foreword

Globalization in finance has largely failed to translate into better access to finance at the level of villages, inner city areas and working-class areas. Between 70 and 80 per cent of the active population in low-income countries and a smaller percentage of the population in high-income countries are excluded from vital financial transactions. This is a paradox: it is precisely the majority of wage earners, pensioners, people on welfare and the working poor that need affordable loans, savings, insurance and payment services to stabilize their household finance in order to make a more or less decent living.

The appeal of microfinance is that it seeks to respond to this need in a market-conforming manner, in other words: microfinance institutions price their services at real costs and become – after a few years – fully independent of donor or government subsidies. This ambitious goal has indeed been met in a number of well-documented cases. However, there is growing evidence that not all – and probably the vast majority of institutions – can reach a scale of operation that allows them to finance themselves. Given the public goods produced by microfinance, that is, additional or stabilized incomes, social integration, empowerment of marginalized groups, employment and social protection, there is a case for policy in support of microfinance institutions.

The contribution of this book to the debate on the role of the state and public policy in microfinance is that it defines criteria for meritorious microfinance institutions that are – not yet – financially self-sufficient. The key concept developed here is efficiency. The contributions in this book show that efficiency is a necessary but insufficient condition for full financial sustainability. Thus there is room and space for public policy.

Given the key role that the financial market plays for employment, social protection and decent work, in November 2005 the ILO adopted a strategy on social finance. One of the key areas of intervention for the ILO is action research on policy issues: this book describes the topic and methods that the ILO – led by our Social Finance Programme – intends to work on in the future, in partnership with the World Bank, academia and other partner agencies, and through networks like Consultative Group to Assist the Poor (CGAP).

José Manuel Salazar-Xirinachs
Executive Director
Employment Sector
International Labour Office

Notes on Contributors

Bernd Balkenhol heads the ILO Social Finance Programme. He served as advisor to central banks in Africa on policies in support of microfinance institutions and SME financing. He holds a PhD from Freiburg University and an MA from Fletcher School of Law and Diplomacy (Medford, MA). He lectures regularly at the Geneva Institute of Development Studies (IUED) and the University of Geneva. His publications deal with informal finance, collateral and property rights, savings and credit cooperatives, small enterprise finance, remittances and related subjects.

Thorsten Beck is Senior Economist in the Finance and Private Sector Development Team of the Development Research Group of the World Bank. He has published numerous academic papers on financial sector issues and is co-author of the *Making Finance Work for Africa* flagship report and the forthcoming *Policy Research Report on Access to Finance: Measurement, Impact and Policy*. His country experience, both in operational and research work, includes Bangladesh, Bolivia, Brazil, China, Mexico, Russia and several countries in sub-Saharan Africa. He holds a PhD from the University of Virginia and an MA from the University of Tübingen in Germany.

Fabrizio Botti is a research fellow at LUISS University of Rome. He recently received his PhD in History and Theory of Economic Development from the LUISS University of Rome. He participated in a research project on Women and Microfinance in the Mediterranean Countries for the UN International Year of Microcredit in Italy, the main results of which were published in the Society for International Development (SID) journal *Development* in 2006.

Milasoa Cherel-Robson is an economist working on poverty, food security and microfinance. Most recently, she has served as Deputy Director of the International Guarantee Fund in Geneva. She holds a Maîtrise from the Université de la Reunion, France, and an MA in International Economics from Sussex University in the UK, and is currently finishing a PhD at the Institute of Development Studies at Sussex University. Her research focuses on vulnerability to food insecurity, looking at spatial factors, policy processes and household coping strategies in Madagascar.

Flavio Comim is a development economist. He is a fellow of St Edmund's College, University of Cambridge. His areas of interest and publication include human development indicators, the capability approach, poverty measurement, microfinance, social capital, poverty and environment links, and sustainable consumption.

Amadou Diop has an MA in Economics and Finance from Orléans University and an MA in Development Studies from IUED, Geneva, where he is now completing his PhD. His research interests lie in microfinance and poverty reduction in West Africa, with particular focus on Mauritania. He is also involved in teaching the masters programme at IUED, including a seminar on 'the social development challenge', which looks at the interface between inequality, exclusion and human development.

Yves Flückiger has held the position of Full Professor of Economics at the University of Geneva since 1992 and that of Vice-President of the Swiss Competition Commission since 2003. He teaches labour economics, industrial organization and public finance at the University of Geneva. He has written numerous books and articles published in international journals, including *The International Trade Journal, Economics Letters, Journal of Econometrics, Journal of Income Distribution, The Oxford Bulletin of Economic and Statistics, Swiss Journal of Economics and Statistics* and *Economie Appliquée.*

Yousra Hamed is a researcher and a microfinance expert in the Social Finance Programme of the ILO. She holds a PhD, an MA in economics from Université Paris XII, and a BA in financial management. Her research interests and publications are related to the informal economy, the financing and development of microenterprises, and microfinance and the MENA region. Before joining the ILO, she taught economics and finance at the universities of Le Maine and Reims (France). She also worked as a consultant and researcher with NGOs (PlaNet Finance, MMM) and a consultancy firm.

Isabelle Hillenkamp investigates alternative economic practices in Latin America from a socio-economic perspective. Over the last five years, she has spent 16 months in field studies in Bolivia and Mexico. Her contribution to the analysis presented in this book is based on a two-month survey of two microfinance institutions in rural and urban Mexico in the framework of the GIAN project. She is currently working on her PhD thesis on the social and solidarity-based economy in the Bolivian town of El Alto and is an assistant lecturer in development economics at the Graduate Institute of Development Studies in Geneva.

Giovanni Ferro Luzzi holds the position of Assistant Professor at the University of Geneva, in the Department of Political Economy. He has also been a consultant for the ILO and the OECD. His main areas of research are applied labour economics, income distribution and discrimination.

Saâd Filali Meknassi is a research fellow in the University Mohamed V of Rabat (Morocco) and adviser in microfinance and corporate social responsibility. Since 2002, he has collaborated on many projects with the ILO and the World Bank. He is also member of many NGOs, notably the Moroccan chapter of Transparency International.

Vito Sciaraffia Merino is a civil engineer and a medical doctor from the University of Chile where he completed both degrees simultaneously, graduating with distinction. In 1992, he obtained his MBA from the University of Illinois. Dr Sciaraffia is the Director of the Institute of Health Administration at the University of Chile and also works as a director advisor and consultant to the Chilean Government as well as numerous multinational corporations and organizations. He has participated in various international conferences and seminars and published numerous articles and papers in the fields of economics, medicine, international trade and health administration.

Jonathan Morduch is Professor of Public Policy and Economics at Wagner Graduate School at New York University. His research focuses on financial access, global poverty and international development. Morduch chairs the United Nations Steering Committee on Poverty Statistics and belongs to the United Nations Advisors Group on Inclusive Financial Sectors. He is the co-author of *The Economics of Microfinance*. He has taught on the Economics faculty at Harvard University, and has held fellowships or visiting positions at Stanford, Princeton and the University of Tokyo. Morduch received his PhD in Economics from Harvard and his BA from Brown.

Justyna Pytkowska is a researcher at the Microfinance Centre for Central and Eastern Europe and the New Independent States (MFC). She is in charge of several market research projects carried out in the CEE/NIS region, among them the annual mapping of the supply side of microfinance. She is a co-author of the 2002 CGAP publication *The State of Microfinance in Central and Eastern Europe and the New Independent States* and its annual updates. She also manages demand studies for microfinance services among low-income populations, has worked in the coordination of development projects run by Land O'Lakes, providing technical assistance and training to Ukrainian agribusinesses, and assisted an ACDI/ VOCA project in implementing grain warehouse receipts in Poland.

Renata Serra is currently a lecturer at the Center for African Studies, University of Florida. She was previously lecturer and Director of Studies in Economics at Wolfson College, University of Cambridge, during which time she started to collaborate on the GIAN/RUIG project Microfinance and Public Action. She has a PhD in Economics from the University of Cambridge, and she has carried out research and consultancy work in a number of African countries.

Jean-Michel Servet has held the position of Full Professor of Economics since 1990 and that of Professor at the IUED, Geneva, since 2003. His research deals with microfinance, solidarity-based economics, development and history of economic thought. In 2002 he created the microfinance research programme at the French Institute of Pondicherry (India). He has published numerous journal articles on microfinance, in *Tiers Monde, Savings and Development, Revue économique, Techniques financières de développement* and others, as well as several books (*Banquiers aux pieds nus*, Odile Jacob, 2006; *Exclusion et liens financiers*, Economica, 2003). He has also co-edited the *Oeuvres économiques complètes of Auguste and Léon Walras* (Economica).

Anton Simanowitz has worked in the field of microfinance since 1997 as manager, trainer and researcher. He is currently Director of the Imp-Act Consortium, based at the Institute of Development Studies, at the University of Sussex. *Imp-Act* is an international consortium that supports and promotes the management of social performance in microfinance, providing practical lessons for practice and for public policy. Prior to moving to the United Kingdom, he headed the Development Department of the Small Enterprise Foundation, a poverty-focused MFI in South Africa.

Anatoli Vassiliev received his MA in Econometrics from Université Catholique de Louvain, Belgium, and his PhD in Economics from University of Geneva, Switzerland. His work focused on applied statistics in the areas of labour and environmental economics, evaluation of efficiency, and clinical research. His research was published in *Swiss Journal of Economics and Statistics, Socio-Economic Planning Sciences, Fertility and Sterility*, and *Swiss Journal of Sociology*. Since 2005, Anatoli Vassiliev has been a quantitative credit risk analyst at UBS in Zürich.

Sylvain Weber holds the position of Teaching Assistant at the University of Geneva, in the Department of Political Economy. He has worked and published on various topics, including unemployment, poverty and microfinance. He is now preparing a PhD thesis on human capital depreciation. The study contained in this book was completed while working in the Geneva School of Business Administration, University of Applied Sciences of Western Switzerland.

Part I
Introduction

1
Efficiency and Sustainability in Microfinance

Bernd Balkenhol
International Labour Office

1.1 Promise and achievements

More than many other development strategies, microfinance, that is, the provision of financial services to the poor on a sustainable basis, sets high expectations. It is supposed to help attain – more or less directly – several of the Millennium Development Goals adopted by the United Nations in 2000. Microfinance should enhance access to education, health services, water and social services. In addition, it should extend and deepen the market, pushing out the frontier of the financial sector (von Pischke, 1991), pioneering where commercial institutions do not (yet) dare to tread. Such positive externalities are rarely associated with other poverty-reducing strategies. Above all, microfinance institutions are expected to be able – ultimately – to pay for themselves. After just a few years of start-up support, they should in principle become fully self-financing.[1] The question is: is that actually happening?

It is true, over the past 20 years there has been a spectacular proliferation of microfinance institutions (MFIs):[2] at the end of 2005 over 3000 MFIs were reported to be operating worldwide, serving over 113 million poor families,[3] raising at least US$40 billion in small deposits and distributing US$50 billion in small loans. Within five years (1999 to 2003) MFIs in West Africa, for example, overtook banks in their client outreach, offering services to 25 per cent of the active population compared to the 8 per cent reached by banks (PASMEC, 2005).

Microfinance is not just promises; there is evidence of positive impact. There can be little doubt that MFIs reach the poor and help them to better cope with risk, to take advantage of income-generating opportunities and to reduce their vulnerability (Paxton, 2002). While this impact may be less spectacular than many had hoped for, on the whole, millions

3

of the poor would be worse off without microfinance. In comparison to alternative development strategies, microfinance certainly has not done badly at all. As far as outreach to the poor and tangible impact on incomes is concerned, microfinance has delivered. But this is not the whole story.

The promise of microfinance is also to achieve a positive impact on poverty via institutions that are fully financially self-sufficient, meaning that they can survive without any subsidies. This is unusual for anti-poverty strategies which one tends to associate with endless and substantial resource transfers. Microfinance is different: it claims to be able to cater to the needs of the poor operating on pure market principles. Of course, it is generally admitted that at the start of a microfinance scheme some public money is required and even for a transition period until the institution has reached market maturity; but there is a broad consensus in microfinance circles that, with time, subsidies should phase out. Poverty outreach and financial sustainability are thus the twin goals that make up the essence of microfinance, placing it somewhere in the middle between welfare schemes and commercial banking.

'Full financial sustainability' or 'financial self-sufficiency' is defined as a ratio of adjusted operating revenues to adjusted operating expenses (financial, administrative, provisions), where the adjustments show whether or not the institution could cover its costs if its activities were unsubsidized and if it had to raise capital at commercial rates. These adjustments call for some complicated calculations that many MFI managers may not have the time to carry out; or they may be reluctant to disclose failure to have reached full financial self-sufficiency, the hallmark of the best MFIs. Whether for lack of capacity or unwillingness, the fact is that only very few MFIs report audited and verified figures.

The *MBB* (*MicroBanking Bulletin*), a database to which leading MFIs report voluntarily, and the only source of information displaying financial performance data of microfinance institutions worldwide with a consistent methodology, shows in its April 2006 issue that of 302 MFIs reporting to it, two-thirds (209) were indeed financially self-sufficient. One could conclude then that the promise of microfinance can be fulfilled, that it is possible to cater to the poor and yet make a profit sufficient enough to cover the relatively high costs of carrying out financing activities in this market segment. Compared to the total sample of 302 MFIs these financially self-sufficient MFIs tend to be older (eight years and more), larger in terms of clients and loan portfolio and use individual lending techniques (Table 1.1).[4]

To have 209 out of 302 MFIs reporting voluntarily is not bad at all, particularly if one takes into consideration that all MFIs reporting

Table 1.1 Selected indicators for a sample of microfinance institutions, July 2003 (per cent, unless otherwise indicated), comparing all MFIs with financially self-sufficient MFIs

	All MFIs	Financially self-sufficient MFIs
Institutional characteristics		
Age (years)	8	10
Average assets (million US$)	7.9	14.5*
Institutions (number)	124	66
Offices (number)	19	17
Financing structure		
Capital/asset ratio	42.7	40.4
Commercial funding liabilities ratio[1]	44.1	76.0*
Deposits to total assets	12.3	16.4
Gross loan portfolio/total assets	70.9	73.1
Outreach indicators		
Active borrowers (number)	15,553	22,841
Percent of women borrowers	62.9	61.9
Average loan balance per borrower (US$)	532	621
Average loan balance per borrower/ GNP per capita	54.3	66.4
Voluntary savers (number)	3,345	6,019
Average savings balance per saver (US$)	269	258
Financial indicators		
Return on assets	0.1	5.7*
Return on equity	2.3	14.6
Profit margin[2]	0.3	19.4
Operating expense/Loan portfolio	29.4	22.2
NPLs (overdue >30 days) to gross loans	2.8	2.5
NPLs (Overdue >90 days) to gross loans	1.5	1.5

Notes: The sample of MFIs comes from the *MicroBanking Bulletin*. It is obtained by voluntary participation of MFIs worldwide, and therefore vulnerable to self-selection bias. Participating MFIs are benchmarked, and the information may be used by investors, donors and other service provides. A more detailed description can be found at http://mixmbb.org.
[1] All liabilities with 'market' prices in per cent of average gross loans.
[2] Net operating income/financial revenue.
* The value of financially self-sustainable differs from the total sample at the 1 per cent significant level.
Source: MBB, 2003.

to the *MBB* appear to improve in their financial performance from 2001 to 2004, even those that manage to cover their costs only with *unadjusted* operating revenues. Still, a few hundred success stories do not make up for the thousands that do not report to the *MBB*, and whose success or failure to phase out subsidy dependence remains unknown.

The *MBB* is one of the principal publications of the MIX (Microfinance Information eXchange, Inc.). While the *MBB* has fairly rigorous reporting requirements there are other MIX data facilities that put the threshold somewhat lower. The 'MIX Market', notably, lists all the microfinance institutions that report to it, ranking them by a five-diamond system according to data quality and disclosure. Here the data on financial self-sufficiency are not adjusted: the MIX Market reports 'operational self-sufficiency' (OSS). OSS values exceeding 100 per cent signal that operating revenues cover and exceed operating expenses, regardless of whether or not their capital and staff costs are subsidized. There is no distinction here between institutions that are heavily subsidized with substantial and long-term credit lines at concessional rates and other MFIs receiving a one-off donation of office furniture and computers. Operational self-sufficiency is the very minimum in performance that one can expect from an MFI: if an MFI cannot break even with external support and fails to get closer to the break-even point over time, then it has a problem.

This applies to over 259 MFIs of the 640 that report to the MIX Market as of December 2006; and even the 381 institutions with operational self-sufficiency in excess of 100 per cent may not be able to do without subsidies: an OSS value of, say, 140 per cent means that the institution manages to generate a comfortable margin, but whether this is largely or just marginally due to heavily subsidized refinancing facilities cannot be determined.

While the MIX Market population may be three times the number of MFIs that report to the *MBB* and thus be somewhat more representative, it is still just the tip of the iceberg of thousands and thousands of known MFIs that report to neither database, and, if one goes by the reports of the Microcredit Summit, even this may not capture the universe of all microfinance institutions worldwide.

The lack of reliable information puts donors and government on the spot. How can they withdraw from an anti-poverty strategy that they had helped to start up and which should become ultimately self-financing if the extent of continued subsidy dependence is not known? Not only are the data lacking, but the performance indicator 'operational self-sufficiency' is itself confusing, as it lumps together what is being earned by the MFI's own loan operations and what it received as subsidies.

In 1995 the donor community arrived at a straightforward consensus that all MFIs should finance themselves after seven to ten years.[5] Indeed, some do (which, by the way, has not stopped some of their donor partners continuing to subsidize them). Others have not, and their number by far exceeds the success stories. The seven to ten-year transition period is over now, so donor agencies and governments are beginning to ask themselves what conclusions they should draw:

- Are MFIs that continue to be subsidy dependent simply slower at arriving at full financial sustainability or structurally unable to meet the target?
- Financially self-sufficient MFIs have more assets, clients and staff; they use more credit lines and take deposits. Since the successful MFIs appear to be larger than the less successful MFIs, could it be that the failure to become fully financially self-sufficient is due to the lack of scale economies?
- If it is scale that determines whether and how an MFI can combine poverty outreach and financial performance, social and financial goals, why is it that some MFIs do not grow faster? Is it the local context or is it poor management of the MFI?

It is also possible that the norm of seven to ten years was simply unrealistic and this could go some way to explaining the high proportion of apparent underachievers in terms of financial self-sufficiency. The time limit may have made sense for MFIs in a particular region with particular market characteristics, say South Asia, but not globally. It could also be that the norm of full financial self-sufficiency after seven to ten years has induced managers of some MFIs to make decisions that are actually detrimental to the goal they are after, such as excessively pushing the growth of the loan portfolio at the expense of their mission and the quality of their loan portfolio.

If failure to become financially self-sufficient is not due to poor management but to contextual factors and to a market with a low client density and limited absorption capacity of debt, then the financial performance of an MFI cannot be interpreted in isolation of its context. While all MFIs pursue the twin goals of poverty outreach and financial self-sufficiency, they combine these two goals differently. This means that the, say, 90 per cent of apparent 'underperformers' cannot be measured against the standard of the 10 per cent of performers, just on the basis of their *financial* performance.

In a first step towards differentiation, the *MicroBanking Bulletin's* peer group and benchmarking methodology classifies MFIs by region, loan portfolio size, institutional type (member-based or not) and target market. This adjusts for regional and other variations in the entire MFI universe. Theoretically, the differentiation by peer groups and setting of meaningful relative benchmarks could be pursued indefinitely, since no two MFIs are really alike: they differ by delivery methodology, institutional maturity, accessibility and competitiveness, even within the same country.

Assuming that the set of characteristics currently used by the *MBB* and MIX represents a meaningful degree of differentiation between types of MFIs, another question arises: how can one apply financial self-sufficiency as a criterion of performance to those MFIs that *choose* to position themselves more towards the 'social' end of the continuum between poverty outreach and financial sustainability? Poverty-focused MFIs set their priorities differently and may want to take more time to reach full financial sustainability than other MFIs that attach a higher priority to full financial sustainability. Just as it would not make sense to measure commercially viable MFIs primarily or exclusively in terms of their poverty impact, so it is obviously debatable to use financial self-sufficiency as the primary performance criterion for more poverty-oriented MFIs.

There has to be a balance in the measurement of advancement towards these two goals, taking into account the plurality of MFI types and missions. After all, donors and governments also position themselves differently on the continuum between pure market prescriptions and state interventions.

To recognize the multiple combinations possible between poverty outreach and financial performance is one thing, to transform this into a practical principle guiding decisions on subsidization is another. Donors and governments face several challenges:

- The information about subsidy dependence is available only for a few hundred MFIs.
- The most commonly used indicator of financial performance, operational self-sufficiency, can be misleading as it lumps together genuine operating net revenue with transfers.
- Scale economies are fundamental for a successful combination of social and financial goals; but local markets do not always allow such scale economies.
- There are MFIs and MFIs: some may have made a deliberate decision to achieve full financial self-sufficiency as rapidly as possible even if

this is at the expense of poverty outreach. How should donors accommodate the multiplicity of mission goals and their combinations in the microfinance industry?

There is a puzzling variety of MFIs out there, some regulated and others not, many multi-purpose NGOs, others cooperatives, banks or non-bank financial institutions, a few very large and many others with barely a few thousand clients. To be even-handed in their decision to continue, discontinue or start funding support, governments and donors need to be able to discriminate between different types of MFIs and different operating environments. At present this is not possible. What a donor can do – at least for those MFIs that produce statistics on social and financial performance regularly – is to distinguish between MFIs of varying degrees of financial self-sufficiency, or to rank MFIs by the extent to which they reach many very poor clients. However, whether a given MFI is doing as best as it can *given the circumstances* can only be determined on the basis of a criterion that transcends social and financial performance.

What donors need is a criterion that captures all possible combinations of poverty outreach and financial performance, since profitability in isolation is not a reliable yardstick for performance measurement of MFIs, which are constrained profit maximizing institutions. A criterion that encompasses both financial and social dimensions of microfinance is efficiency. It is equally applicable to commercially viable MFIs and not yet financially self-sustaining MFIs that seek more immediate poverty reduction. This book argues that it is possible and fairer to base the performance measurement of MFIs – and hence entitlement to continued donor and government funding – on their efficiency relative to other MFIs sharing the same mission and operating in comparable contexts. Efficiency allows donors and governments to base their decisions on overall achievement in both dimensions, financial and social.

1.2 Efficiency in the microfinance literature

Efficiency relates quantities and costs of inputs and outputs. A firm is efficient if it maximizes the quantity/price of an output for given quantities/prices of inputs; alternatively it is efficient if for a given quantity/price of output it operates with the least quantity or least costs of inputs. Efficiency is not an entirely unfamiliar concept in microfinance. The Microfinance Consensus Guidelines (CGAP, 2003), which provide donors and MFI practitioners with a common framework for measuring performance, present nine ratios for efficiency/productivity.

Two of these relate an output to another output (value of loans disbursed to total number of loans disbursed), two other ratios relate the number of active borrowers/clients to an input, that is, the number of loan officers/ staff. Four ratios relate operating expenses (or a subset of these) to an output (average gross loan portfolio) or to the number of active borrowers/ clients. One ratio is singled out as the 'most commonly used efficiency indicator for MFIs', and that is operating expense/average gross loan portfolio or total assets.[6]

The definition of 'efficiency' in the microfinance literature has evolved considerably.[7] The first issue of the *MicroBanking Bulletin (MBB)* of 1997 does not mention efficiency at all. The notion 'operational efficiency' appears for the first time in the 1999 *MBB*. The *MBB*'s fourth issue of 2000, dedicated entirely to 'efficiency in microfinance', proposes two indicators of efficiency: administrative expenses/average loan portfolio and yield/ average loan portfolio.[8] In 2001 yield/portfolio is dropped as an indicator of efficiency and the ratio 'administrative expense/average gross loan portfolio' is split up into two (staff and other administrative costs), as shown in Table 1.2.

From 2005, the set of efficiency indicators appears to have finally settled with five measures (Table 1.3). The only change compared to earlier exercises is that the *MBB* now also adjusts the gross loan portfolio and the number of active borrowers; there is also now an indicator relating adjusted operating expense to the adjusted average number of loans.

The efficiency ratios presented in the Donor Consensus Guidelines and the *MBB* are input/output ratios, using the outputs 'loan portfolio' and 'borrowers'. Other outputs (savings accounts, other financial services) are not considered, nor inputs such as total liabilities, long-term debt and so on. Given the differences in costs, volume and fungibility of financial resources (equity, soft loans, market loans and deposits), it would be interesting to add these inputs to the calculation of efficiency ratios.

Table 1.2   Efficiency indicators in the *MBB*, sixth edition (2001)

Efficiency		
Total administrative expense/loan portfolio	Administrative expense + in-kind donations/ Average gross loan portfolio	(%)
Salary expense/Loan portfolio	Administrative expense + in-kind donations/ Average gross loan portfolio	(%)
Other administrative expenses/Loan portfolio	Administrative expense + in-kind donations + personnel expense/ Average gross loan portfolio	(%)

Table 1.3 Efficiency indicators in the *MBB*, tenth edition (2005)

Operating expense/Loan portfolio	Adjusted operating expense/Adjusted average gross loan portfolio	(%)
Personnel expense/Loan portfolio	Adjusted personnel expense/Adjusted average gross loan portfolio	(%)
Average salary/GNI per capita	Adjusted average personnel expense/GNI per capita	(%)
Cost per borrower	Adjusted operating expense/Adjusted average number of active borrowers	(x)
Cost per loan	Adjusted operating expense/Adjusted average number of loans	(x)

The way efficiency is defined and efficiency ratios are constructed has direct implications for the performance measurement of MFIs. The choice of the denominator, for example, changes rankings amongst MFIs: in Latin America, FIE, Los Andes and FONDESA achieve high efficiency values because of large average loan sizes, whilst two WWB affiliates in Colombia come out best when measured by borrower/staff ratios (von Stauffenberg, 2002).

Efficiency measurement in microfinance calls for techniques that can be applied to performance measurement both of profit-maximizing and constrained profit-maximizing or public service units, such as data envelopment analysis (DEA) or similar linear programming techniques.

1.3 Efficiency: the concept

Microfinance is not the only sector using 'best of class' or 'best practice' concepts. In banking, manufacturing or not-for-profit organizations, measures are being used to determine how close a given firm comes to the efficiency frontier (Berger and Humphrey, 1997). Given the diversity of objectives of MFIs, ranging from very pronounced poverty focus all the way to quick commercialization, non-parametric approaches such as DEA seem to be in principle more suitable (see an application in Chapter 6).[9]

In 'frontier efficiency' the performance of an average firm is expressed as economies in input use that it could achieve if it produced on the frontier instead of on its current location. A value of 0.79, for example, signals that a MFI could save on 21 per cent of inputs, such as loan officer staff time, if it operated on the frontier. The value can also be expressed as a percentage inefficiency, in this case 27 per cent: (1–0.79)/0.79.

DEA-based studies of the efficiency of banks, insurance companies and other financial institutions by Berger and Humphrey (1997) come up with findings of interest to the performance measurement of MFIs:

- Cross-country comparisons have limited value because of differences in the regulatory and economic environment which should be controlled for (as is done in Chapter 6). This is reflected in the fact that MFIs in the same country share similar ranges of spread.
- In banking, market power is significantly associated with lower deposit rates and higher loan rates, after accounting for efficiency differences, but it has little effect on profits. This should have an interesting resonance in microfinance with institutions that are not profit-maximizing units, but where competition is gradually obliging MFIs to take a critical look at deposit mobilization and remuneration and pricing of loans.
- How outputs are specified and how the range of outputs is determined makes a difference to efficiency; especially whether deposits are counted as an output or as an input. As most MFIs see deposit-taking as a service their clients expect them to provide, it may be appropriate to include deposits (number of accounts or total deposit volumes) as outputs. This is not the case in the Consensus Guidelines, the *MBB* nor the Micro Rate/IDB Technical Guide.
- There is no strong evidence that the legal form, ownership and organizational form make much of a difference to efficiency. This could be an aspect in which microfinance differs from banking, given its labour-intensity and associated agency problems and the widespread use of clients in the loan appraisal, monitoring and enforcement process.
- Broadening the range of products and services seems to reduce cost efficiency: this would probably also be the case in microfinance but has so far not been empirically shown.

The confusion between efficiency and financial sustainability may partly have to do with the use of ratios to measure efficiency. Financial performance is easier to observe, which may have biased the construction of ratios in favour of financial aggregates, rather than the combined social and financial outputs that are the trademark of microfinance. DEA, by contrast, uses multiple inputs with multiple outputs to construct *best practice* cost and production frontiers. The qualification of a particular variable as 'input' or 'output' depends on one's interpretation of what finance is all about: in the intermediation model the input 'deposits' is transformed into an output 'loans'; in the production model (Nieto, Cinca and Molinero, 2004) deposits are seen as an output – a financial service – produced by inputs such as labour, financial resources and information technology and communication (ITC) equipment.

The interest in applying DEA to MFI performance measurement lies in three particularities that fit the real-life situation of MFIs. First, DEA requires that the entities whose performance is assessed relative to each other must be homogeneous, that is, 'use the same resources to procure the same outcomes albeit in varying amounts' (Thassoulis, 2001, p. 21). This is meaningful in an environment where credit-based NGOs compete with other types of MFIs such as savings and credit cooperatives. DEA also seeks to single out performance drivers that the management of a firm can influence, separating controllable from uncontrollable variables. This makes sense in microfinance because of important differences in market and regulatory contexts: some countries have interest rate ceilings, others not; some prohibit deposit-taking, others not; some governments are actively involved in retail microfinance, others stay out. Thirdly, DEA accommodates the fact that a unit uses several inputs and produces several outputs: measurement takes into account whether the output mix is modified as a result of an increase or reduction in input uses. Again, considering the modifications over time in product range and use of different kinds of labour and capital that one finds in microfinance, this is an appealing feature of DEA as a measurement tool of efficiency.

The application of DEA by Nieto, Cinca and Molinero (2004) on 30 Latin American MFIs shows that the level of efficiency achieved by a particular MFI depends on the specification of the input and output variables chosen. Some MFIs score high on efficiency because of superior technical efficiency or productivity values (number of loans per loan officer), others score high because of the maximization of revenues for a given level of operating expense, that is, because of the efficient use of financial resources (allocative efficiency). Differentiating the observed MFIs by legal status also brings out different efficiency rankings. If one allows for scale effects by integrating or leaving out the output variable 'gross loan portfolio', yet another ranking of MFIs emerges.

Nieto, Cinca and Molinero's DEA application uses the number of credit officers and total operating expenses as indicators of inputs, whilst outputs are measured by the number of loans outstanding, the gross loan portfolio and the income from interest and fees. These two inputs and three outputs can be combined in 21 possible variable specifications. The finding is that no MFI is efficient under all specifications. The way variables are specified thus determines the ranking and efficiency status of individual MFIs: 'there is no single path to efficiency in MFIs' (Nieto, Cinca and Molinero, 2004). The MFI WWB Popayan is nearly on the efficiency frontier in terms of number of loans per loan officer, whilst another MFI, FINDESA, is the relative best in terms of optimizing interest and other operating revenue per unit of operating expense.

The advantage of a DEA application over ratio analysis for efficiency measurement in microfinance is that it integrates all possible interrelationships between the factors of production in microfinance.[10]

1.4   Applicability of efficiency concepts in microfinance

The business of microfinance can be seen from two angles: one can see it as the transformation of certain inputs into certain outputs; one can also see microfinance as the intermediation of surplus holding units and deficit units. In the first case efficiency is a matter of maximizing output quantities or revenues with given inputs, or minimizing input use for a given quantity of outputs. In the intermediation perspective efficiency in microfinance is signalled by the spread, that is, the difference between what MFIs pay for their resources and what they charge for their services. Data collected for this book (see Section 1.6 for more details) show that the spreads in microfinance are high, generally 20 per cent and more, with only around a quarter falling just below 20 per cent.[11]

In microfinance, efficiency is thus a matter of technical transformation of inputs (staff, funds) into outputs (loans, other services). Such 'technical' efficiency measures include ratios such as the number of clients per loan officer or staff. In our sample of 45 MFIs, eight have ratios of more than 400 clients per loan officer, and two of less than 100, whilst the bulk (35 MFIs) have between 100 and 400 clients. Looking over the five-year period 1999 to 2003, 35 MFIs made improvements in the ratio, but in ten MFIs the ratio dropped.

Measures of allocative efficiency show whether output prices have been maximized for given input prices (loan officer wages, interest paid on credit lines) or alternatively whether input prices have been minimized for a given output price. Most of our sample 45 MFIs remain more or less within a certain range of operating expenses over time, though at very different levels. In Viet Nam the three MFIs reviewed have consistently low operating expenses because they do not pay for physical infrastructure and staff expenses as part of their operations are taken care of by the state. By contrast even large MFIs such as CARUNA and FDL in Nicaragua or CACTRI and San Roque in Bolivia show consistently high levels of operating expenses.

MBB data show that MFIs generally do act on and modify input and output prices to improve their technical and allocative efficiency, though within certain constraints. MFIs that focus on the very poor and engage in very small transactions set their interest rates high compared to other, mixed portfolio MFIs (interest rates in the range of 35–37 per cent on average as opposed to a range between 20 and 26 per cent on average), unless constrained by interest rate ceilings (Christen, 2000). These poverty-oriented MFIs charge relatively high interest rates, but also seem to pay modest salaries; their staff members are as productive as staff in other MFIs; still, these MFIs do not seem to attain full financial sustainability. There can thus be a situation where an MFI is efficient technically and in allocative terms under market constraints, but not fully financially sustainable. This discrepancy between efficiency and financial sustainability in real-life MFIs confirms the need to highlight efficiency as a neutral and higher-order performance criterion.

There are good reasons why MFIs that serve very poor clients often appear to charge higher interest rates than MFIs catering to a more mixed clientele. As in commercial finance, microfinance has high fixed production costs; MFIs with a portfolio of many small loans carry higher unit costs, as their clients may often live in inaccessible locations and need more interactions. These poverty-focused MFIs would have to raise the interest rate even higher, near the level of usury rates, to ensure full financial sustainability. By choice or by imposed regulation, MFIs may not want nor be able to do that. Yield maximization is not always a reliable indicator of efficiency in microfinance since, as we have seen, many institutions are unable to move upscale (Morduch, 2000).

Inversely, according to *MBB* data, financially sustainable MFIs can afford to charge comparatively modest interest rates, because they face lower financial and administrative costs catering to easier market segments. The question is whether these administrative costs are lower because of good management or because of context-related factors such as population density, a higher debt absorption capacity, a more homogeneous clientele, the acceptance of group liability and more competition in factor markets. As MFI are *not* profit-maximizing entities per se, ratio analysis alone relating input and output quantities and costs cannot reveal the drivers of efficiency. However, it is precisely this sort of information that donors and governments need to be able to make an informed decision on whether or not to subsidize an MFI that is not yet self-financing but efficient, or to cut off support to another MFI that is not yet self-financing, but inefficient.

According to *MBB* data the most commonly used efficiency ratio in microfinance, operating expenses related to average gross loan portfolio, is much higher in financially unsustainable programmes than in sustainable programmes (51 per cent compared to 24 per cent) (Christen, 2000). This can be due to several factors: it could be the result of inefficient management failing to compress costs or expand the loan portfolio; but it could also be due to a limited debt absorption capacity of clients, scarcity of qualified loan officers, low client density, lack of competition and so on: contextual factors.

To understand the determinants of the classical efficiency indicator in microfinance, that is, operating expenses/average gross loan portfolio, it helps to look at its three main drivers: average loan balances, staff costs and staff productivity.

Average loan balance

Average loan balance (expressed as a percentage of GDP) is a common poverty indicator: it reflects the debt absorption capacity of clients and the MFI's poverty focus. When an MFI decides to set itself up in a particular location, it cannot always freely vary its clientele. The average loan balance in this location may be too low for compressing administrative expenses, but this is a deliberate choice on the part of the MFI: it may want to stay within this market niche and serve the poor. Such an MFI cannot be labelled 'inefficient' only because its average loan balances are small. Within any given market segment, some MFIs can be efficient and others not: average loan balance alone is an indicator that has nothing to do with efficiency.

Staff costs

The second driver of operating expense is staff costs. Salaries and other labour costs reflect supply and demand in a particular labour market for a given level of skills, experience and trustworthiness. Of course, it is possible that an MFI carries high staff costs because it failed to search the market of loan officers sufficiently, but high staff costs could also be the result of scarcity of skills and experience. Hence it is more meaningful to compare the wage rates paid by MFIs facing similar local labour markets and using similar delivery techniques, that is, production functions, as illustrated in Table 1.4. The lower ratio of wages to GNP per capita in poverty-focused MFIs is not a reflection of inflated pay rates or

Table 1.4 Wages/GNP per capita

	MFI average	Poverty focused MFIs
Individual	4.9	2.4
Solidarity	6.7	5.4
Village banking	5.1	4.7

Source: Christen, 2000.

Table 1.5 Staff productivity (clients/loan officer)

	MFI average	Poverty focused MFIs
Individual	99	159
Solidarity	127	135
Village banking	186	199

Source: Christen, 2000.

unsatisfactory staff productivity. In fact, poverty-focused MFIs appear to pay lower wages per head and have comparable or even higher levels of staff productivity (Christen, 2000) (Table 1.5). Their high level of operating costs is due to other factors, rooted in different production functions.

Staff productivity

Staff productivity is the third driver of administrative costs. It is determined by organization and management but also depends on location and delivery methodology: MFIs in rural areas using an individual client approach are likely to show lower staff productivity than MFIs operating in urban areas with a mix of group lending and individual lending. Staff expenses are higher if transactions are small and frequent, as they require the same staff-time in screening, negotiating, controlling and monitoring larger transactions. Cost-reducing delivery techniques, such as joint liability, cannot be applied systematically, because they are not universally accepted: they may work wonders in Bangladesh, but not necessarily elsewhere. Moreover, there is less scope for risk diversification in rural markets than in others, and this affects provisions for bad debt – and thus yield.

One also needs to differentiate between loan officers that are regular, paid staff and those that are volunteers. The Caisses Villageoises in Mali, for example, relied on volunteers for up to two-thirds of total staff. As competition increased with other MFIs in Mali, the Caisses Villageoises found it difficult to retain these volunteers and were obliged to recruit salaried staff. This drove up operating expenses and affected adversely its compliance with financial performance benchmarks.[12]

The three main drivers of efficiency in microfinance (average loan balances, staff costs and staff productivity) are thus only partly under the control of MFI managers. They constrain pricing at full cost and they also constrain the compression of costs. Put differently, pricing financial services at fully cost-covering levels is not feasible for *all* MFIs.

1.5   Efficiency versus financial sustainability

Can MFIs that are unable to charge fully cost-covering interest rates be automatically considered 'inefficient'? Poverty-focused MFIs are not avoiding pricing their services so as to cover their costs: MFIs that focus on the very poor and engage in very small transactions particularly tend to set their interest rates relatively high; compared to average MFIs they also tend to have the highest staff productivity in their respective regions and delivery techniques and compressed staff pay (Christen, 2000). In terms of allocative and technical efficiency they seem to operate already fairly close to their efficiency frontier. They appear to have pushed managerial efficiency to the limit and few options remain to obtain full financial sustainability, other than raising the average loan size. In other words, they may have no choice but to go up-market.[13]

Cases such as Bancosol in Bolivia illustrate that MFI managers can choose to modify their production function (by switching from group liability-based loans to individual and collateral-based loans). The result is a relative realignment of the MFI's mission, between poverty outreach and financial sustainability, but not necessarily a radical departure from its social goals.

Emphasizing or de-emphasizing financial sustainability versus poverty outreach can be the choice of the managers and owners of the MFI. It can also be the result of pressure by donors. Donors may wish to see a better financial result, or, to the contrary, donors may want to see more focus on the very poor. If management follows these instructions, then the production function of the MFI (namely range and nature of products and services, mix of financial and non-financial services, requirements for collateral, group vs. individual loans, but also use of data processing and transport technology) changes, which means that its efficiency norms – technical and allocative – change as well.

Joint liability, a technique of microfinance delivery, is a case in point. Production functions in microfinance differ in their collateral requirements and the scope for externalizing transaction costs to clients. Joint liability is popular with more poverty-focused MFIs because it suits very poor clients without any assets whatsoever. KAXA Taon, an MFI in Mexico with 3000 clients, used to be such an MFI. It started with joint-liability based lending until, under donor pressure to improve financial performance, it introduced individual lending in 2002. Group-based loans declined from 100 per cent of the total loan portfolio in 2001 to 58 per cent of total loans outstanding in 2003. At the same time, average loan size – a rough indicator of poverty focus – increased from 485 pesos in 1999 to 3165 pesos in 2003. While no tangible guarantee had been required for a group loan, it became a requirement for individual loans. The financial result improved from a deficit of 37,789 million pesos in 2000 to a surplus of 41,065 million pesos in 2003.

Similarly the CVECA Sissili in Burkina Faso, with 17,000 clients/members in a mainly rural environment, came under pressure from diverse donors in 2002 to improve its financial performance. The MFI announced that it would set itself a target of at least 70 per cent operational self-sufficiency. To that end it opened branches in urban areas catering to better-off clients, largely wage earners in the public sector. The MFI declared its continued commitment to rural operations. It hoped that the change in the production function would compensate for losses incurred in operations in rural areas.

These examples suggest that efficiency and financial sustainability are distinct dimensions of institutional performance in microfinance. In a perfect market and contextual environment it probably makes sense to equate efficiency with yield and operating costs relative to the loan portfolio; but in a market where most operators are not profit maximizers, financial sustainability fails to fully capture performance. Two, not uncommon, scenarios illustrate this. In the first, an MFI operates in an environment that constrains scaling up and leads to prohibitively high cost-covering interest rates, and at the same time also constrains further reductions in staff and non-staff costs. A second scenario is where a fully financially sustainable MFI continues to receive grants and subsidies, although they are no longer needed; in fact such a financially self-sufficient MFI could actually be technically inefficient compared to its peers.

Both scenarios show that in the longer term, it may be better for the growth of a competitive and undistorted microfinance market in developing countries that donors and governments look beyond financial performance and poverty outreach and consider more systematically a dimension that has so far been largely overlooked: efficiency. Admittedly it is easier to read the bottom-line financial results of an MFI than to go through the pains of separating endogenous from exogenous drivers of operating expenses; but donors need to better understand this difference and appreciate how it influences the rationality of their decision to start, continue or discontinue specific forms of grants to individual MFIs, their networks and associated support institutions.

1.6 Structure of the book

The book draws on a survey of 45 MFIs, carried out in the framework of a joint project under the Geneva International Academic Network (GIAN), involving the University of Cambridge, the University of Geneva, the Institute of Development Studies (IUED) and, as coordinating agency, the ILO. Details are given in Annex I. Some of these MFIs perform well financially, others reach large numbers of very poor people, and a few manage to do both at the same time. The relative best performers are listed on the MIX, but most are not. In fact, most MFIs surveyed are probably representative of the larger population of MFIs in that they still struggle to get up to scale and combine their social and financial objectives, and they still depend on outside support.

The book is organized in five parts, including this introduction. Part II sets the stage and builds the conceptual framework; Part III presents four methods of empirical analysis, while Part IV applies these methodologies to specific regional contexts; Part V concludes, with policy recommendations.

In the chapter that follows, Chapter 2, Diop, Hillenkamp and Servet open Part II with a critical examination of the ambiguous links between access to finance and poverty reduction. In Chapter 3, addressing some of the reservations voiced by the previous authors, Comim takes Sen's 'capability perspective', arguing that intangible changes can be attributed to access to finance, beyond material improvements.

Having explored through these two chapters the relevance of microfinance to poverty reduction, we need to examine whether all kinds of institutions are equipped to deliver: whether in some types of MFIs and under some external constraints a microfinance institution may need to sacrifice financial performance for poverty outreach, or, inversely, need to move up-market to guarantee positive financial returns. In Chapter 4, Simanowitz examines the conundrum of the trade-off between social and financial objectives and how it can be managed practically.

In the concluding chapter of Part II, Chapter 5, Morduch addresses the role of the donor in microfinance and introduces the notion of 'smart subsidies'. As positive spreads are perfectly compatible with substantial financial exclusion or the failure of new institutions to emerge and innovate in order to capture the demand for small-scale finance, there is a case for corrective action by public authorities. Morduch argues that government measures can be meaningful and effective, and can be designed in such a way as to avoid negative externalities.

Part III moves from theory to practice, presenting different methodologies for the empirical measurement of efficiency in MFIs. Because of the variety of goal combinations in the space between poverty reduction and profitability it is a real challenge to measure performance. In Chapter 6 Flückiger and Vassiliev present the DEA method, considering microfinance as a production function and the optimality of input use and output pricing. Using empirical data concerning over 40 MFIs in Peru, they show that efficiency can be measured in relation to one MFI ('best of class') that demonstrates the relative best combination of inputs and outputs.

Financial institutions can be treated in the same way as any other firm, producing goods and services with a given input mix, but the efficiency of financial institutions, including MFIs, can also be interpreted as the transformation of financial resources from surplus-holding units (depositors, investors) into deficit units (credit-taking firms and households). This financial intermediation model is implicit in Chapter 7 by Beck, which looks at efficiency in finance from the macroeconomic and sectoral point of view, focusing on spread as the key indicator of efficiency in finance.

Hamed explains in Chapter 8 how an application of multivariate analysis to the 45 countries in the GIAN survey leads to the determination of four clusters of MFIs that differ in the combinations of poverty outreach, financial performance and efficiency. The findings show that efficiency and financial results are distinct dimensions of performance. According to Hamed there are five drivers that position an MFI on the socio-financial space: location, legal form, scope for externalization of transaction costs, method of staff remuneration and delivery technique (group vs. individual loans, collateralized vs. uncollateralized loans). That leaves the precise location of an MFI relative to its peer leader to be determined. In an application of factor analysis, Ferro Luzzi and Weber demonstrate in Chapter 9 that it is possible to present graphically the location of MFIs as clusters, the relative best performers and the distance of any given MFI in a cluster to that relative best performing MFI.

Part IV presents four case studies that illustrate the variety of exogenous variables bearing on the precise position of an MFI on the poverty–profitability continuum. The Mali case by Serra, Botti and Cherel-Robson (Chapter 10) deals with the consequences of subsidy dependence despite impressive growth and an encouraging policy and regulatory environment. The case of Morocco, presented by Meknassi in Chapter 11, is instructive for the probably unique combination of government support, commitment by the commercial banking sector, scale and pronounced poverty focus. The setting is entirely different in Eastern Europe and Central Asia (Chapter 12 by Pytkowska) where most MFIs are involved in lending to microenterprise activities to the exclusion of anything else. Finally, Chapter 13 (by Sciaraffia Merino) presents a unique application of an auctioning system to subsidies in microfinance. The Chilean PAC initiative offered *ex post* grants to commercial banks that could provide evidence of having given a micro-loan to an eligible microenterprise. Evaluations appear to show not only that this method was less costly to the taxpayer than alternative measures of getting credit to microenterprises, but also that a substantial proportion of these clients graduated into the banks' regular portfolio: an illustration of a 'smart subsidy'.

While the social value of microfinance is recognized by donors and governments, these same are reluctant to lend support to MFIs indefinitely. Part V examines both the importance of efficiency for donor agencies in their decision-making and the effects of public policy on the efficiency of MFIs. Chapter 14 (by Balkenhol) sums up the argument and identifies the implications for managers of MFIs, governments and donors. It calls on the donor community to focus on efficiency as the fundamental performance criterion so as to be able to encompass different degrees of social and financial missions in the large universe of MFIs.

Notes

1 'Poverty outreach and financial performance can be attained simultaneously' (Christen et al., 1995).
2 Some estimates put the total number of institutions at 1500, with 54 million clients; the World Bank's Sustainable Banking with the Poor Inventory refers to 1000 MFIs that have a minimum of 1000 clients and started operations before 1992; the Microcredit Summit Campaign lists 2931 MFIs serving over 80 million clients as of end 2003; Mosley refers to 7000 institutions. Schrieder and Sharma put the figure at 7000 (1999, p. 67); see also Lapenu and Zeller (2001, p. 10).
3 Microcredit Summit Campaign: State of the MCS Report 2006, p. 2.
4 *MBB*, Issue 12, April 2006, p. 47.
5 According to the 'Guidelines for the Selection and Promotion of Financial Intermediaries for MSE Finance', adopted in 1995 by the international donor

community and later by the Consultative Group to Assist the Poorest (CGAP), a donor consortium. These pink book norms have recently been replaced by a less rigorous target in the 'Donor Guidelines on Good Practice in Microfinance' (CGAP, 2004a).

6   The Consensus Guidelines warn that this indicator may lead to misinterpretations: 'MFIs that provide smaller loans will compare unfavorably to others, even though they may be serving their target market efficiently ... ; likewise MFIs that offer savings and other services will also compare unfavorably to those that do not offer these services.'

7   This section has benefited from thoughtful contributions by Yousra Hamed.

8   In an article in the same *MBB* issue, Todd Farrington (2000) proposes three efficiency indicators, the administrative expense ratio (as Christen), the number of loans per loan officer (Christen considered this as one of three drivers of operating expense together with wage costs and staff productivity) and the ratio of loan officers to total staff (not used by Christen). By contrast, Farrington does not consider yield/portfolio as an indicator of efficiency.

9   See Charnes et al. (1994) for an overview of DEA theory, methodology and applications.

10 In the words of Nieto, Cinca and Molinero (2004), ratios are 'only consensus indicators'.

11 Further analysis is required to explore the spread of MFIs with the spread in banks of the same environment, as well as the spread of MFIs in rural environments and others. The relation of spread with market power also needs to be explored further.

12 As one MFI staff member commented, 'initially it was normal for everyone to work for the community without being paid; unfortunately lately the competition with other NGOs that pay their staff is making things more difficult for the CV. As a result many cashiers who had been trained by our extension service leave and work in other NGOs where they get better wages. [...] These NGOs also compete with unrealistically low interest rates, because they get a lot of funding from donors' (GIAN survey questionnaire response, translated from French).

13 According to Christen (2001, p. 16) seven out of nine leading MFIs in Latin America, for example, saw an increase in their average real outstanding loan balance as a percentage of per capita GNP from 1990–99, remaining, though, still below poverty parity. Only two (Procredito Caja de los Andes and ADEMI) ended up with a portfolio that was clearly no longer poverty focused.

Part II
Conceptual Framework

2
Poverty versus Inequality

Amadou Diop, Isabelle Hillenkamp and
Jean-Michel Servet
Institut Universitaire d'Etudes du Developpement

2.1 Introduction

Poverty reduction and microfinance are generally referred to in the same breath by microfinance institutions (MFIs) and by the organizations supporting them at the international level, through multilateral or bilateral cooperation or through large private foundations, or nationally. In national strategic poverty reduction plans, microfinance is the preferred means of achieving the Millennium Development Goals. It is usually presented as a package of financial services for poor people that aims chiefly to enable those people substantially to improve their lot in life. Of the various poverty reduction instruments, microfinance is considered one of the most promising, in particular because it can be used on an unprecedented scale thanks to its supposed capacity rapidly to become self-sustaining. Let us start by briefly defining the two terms in the equation: microfinance and poverty.

Today, microfinance is no longer limited to microcredit. The term is used to designate low-cost, short-term financial products for people thought not to have access to *traditional* services. In addition to individual and group loans, these products comprise savings services and, increasingly, the cashing of cheques, payment orders, micro-insurance, loan guarantees and the transfer of remittances from abroad. In the case of loans, the proven technique of joint surety means there is no adverse selection of borrowers unable to provide material collateral. Microfinance, in the form of community banks or village funds, aims to establish self-managed groups of people able to meet their own credit needs thanks (in part) to the group's savings and the relations of trust that exist in primary societies. This group approach does not preclude individual loans, which in fact seem to be growing in number. In 2002, one of the pioneer MFIs, Grameen Bank, stopped lending money to micro-groups of joint borrowers, a means of providing credit that had proved successful, and opted instead to promote individual loans. These various financial services are intended for people who are 'unbankable' but not necessarily *poor*: in many countries, only a limited sector of the population has access to the traditional banking system, and the potential market for microfinance is all those who are 'excluded' from it; in other words, several hundreds of millions of people around the world.

Poverty reduction, for its part, has been an integral part of development paradigms for the past 15 years at least. It emerged as a World Bank objective in the 1990 *World Development Report*. Ten years later, *attacking poverty*[1] had become the main goal of the World Bank's development work. This slow process of maturation resulted in the adoption in September 2000 of the Millennium Development Goals by the United Nations Member States. The first goal, specifically, is to reduce by half the proportion of people living on less than one dollar a day in low and middle economies between 1990 and 2015.[2] The other goals, which concern education, gender equality, child mortality, maternal health, HIV/AIDS and the environment, can be considered to be either specific aspects of poverty, which is a multidimensional phenomenon, or factors thereof. They are indicators that can be calculated for every country, no matter what the level of per capita income, so long as it has a reliable statistics service, and poverty as an issue is therefore not limited to the developing countries. Even the richest countries have pockets of poverty, large and small. Moreover, microfinance is not exclusive to low or middle economies and countries in transition; indeed, the ILO has conducted a comparative study of microfinance in industrialized countries (Canada, France, Germany, Ireland, United Kingdom and the United States).[3]

The present study discusses microfinance in developing countries. Microfinance can serve to reduce poverty in a number of ways: loans for productive activities, better distribution over time of resources and spending, empowerment. The first thing to note is that, notwithstanding optimistic statements based on success stories, there is little data for gauging the overall contribution of microfinance, in all its forms, to poverty reduction, especially if the negative effects (segments of the population on which microfinance had a negative impact)[4] are taken into account as well as the positive. There are a growing number of studies of the impact and effects of microfinance, but few of them explain the different effects microfinance has on the poor and less poor, or the dynamics of those effects.[5] It is not rare for the profile of the clients or members of an MFI to change substantially over time, usually for the benefit of the less poor, and in most cases this is not because the poor have become richer and thus changed category. This may or may not be the result of a deliberate policy on the part of the institution.[6] It prompts us to consider briefly how poverty is defined and measured, on the one hand, and the extent to which microfinance may even increase inequality, on the other.

Indeed, we shall see that, except in specific situations where the external conditions were favourable, offering financial services to the poorest of the poor is not compatible with the general objective of MFIs to achieve financial independence (Morduch, 1999a).[7] Indeed, the hypothesis of such an inverse relationship or trade-off has serious consequences on microfinance support policies. It justifies the demands made by MFIs for public or private subsidies beyond the start-up phase to which it was initially thought the subsidies could be limited. The GIAN study aims to provide empirical evidence for this hypothesis on the basis of data collected on a large scale.

The purpose of this chapter is to shed light on the conceptual link between microfinance, poverty and inequality, in order to facilitate the subsequent reading of the GIAN survey's findings. It starts by presenting the definitions and measurements of poverty. The subsequent section takes a critical look at the different ways in which microfinance can help reduce poverty. This is followed by a review of the links between poverty and financial performance. The last section concludes with an analysis of the limits of microfinance as a means of reducing poverty and how it relates to alternative objectives such as greater equality and financial inclusion.

2.2 Defining and measuring poverty

Poverty was long defined as the lack of sufficient material means to ensure biological subsistence as determined by the research of nutritionists. This definition was accepted until the 1970s, when the concept of 'basic needs' gained currency. In the ILO report to the World Employment Conference in 1976, the concept is presented as encompassing two aspects: the minimum conditions of private consumption for a family, such as food, housing, some items of furniture and equipment, and clothing; and the essential services furnished by and for the community, such as drinking water, sanitation, public transport, health care, education and cultural facilities and centres (ILO, 1976). Basic needs are therefore no longer limited to subsistence in the physiological sense, rather, it is specified that they are to be considered in a context of economic and social development.

As the concept of poverty was expanded to cover basic needs, the multidimensional nature of poverty gained credence and is now largely accepted.[8] However, opinions differ on the number and nature of those dimensions. For example, social groups in some countries claim that the absence of birth control, greater vulnerability to disease, political under-representation and lack of free time should also be recognized as indicators of poverty. Other authors have discussed the correlations and relations of cause and effect between dimensions. The result is recommendations for poverty reduction strategies that are also multidimensional or *global*. The Millennium Development Goals also acknowledge the multidimensional nature of poverty, in that they refer to different aspects of poverty that are considered to be interdependent.

In addition, reflection on the concept of *relative* poverty has led some researchers[9] to cast doubt on the absolute nature of poverty on which most studies are predicated. Their criticism is two pronged: first, it requires a variety of resources over time and in space to satisfy one and the same need; second, whether or not needs are constant is debatable. To those who assert that *basic* biological needs do exist, they point to the constructed nature of those needs. The anthropologist Marshall Sahlins (1976) analysed the paradoxical wealth of so-called primitive societies, made possible by their limited material needs.[10] This approach in turn raises two further questions: one, poverty is experienced subjectively and thus varies from person to person, thereby complicating the possibilities for quantification and comparison;[11] two, since the way one experiences poverty is a function of the 'living standard' of the society as a whole, the needs deemed to be essential gradually expand as the society's standard of living rises. This relative poverty casts the discussion in terms of inequality.[12]

One final aspect of poverty that is gradually – but probably insufficiently – being taken into account has to do with its close link with vulnerability.[13] A dynamic analysis of poverty reveals that the most underprivileged are also those who are most exposed to the various risks of life and have the fewest means of coping. Vulnerability is reflected in the fact that the poorest are more prone to fluctuations in income and find it difficult to spread that income over time in such a way as to meet essential needs at all times. This chronic poverty was increased by the so-called neoliberal policies that have prevailed in many countries since the 1980s.

The growing recognition of vulnerability is to be understood in the broader context of the large-scale paradigm shift in social policies that occurred in the past 20 years or so. The view of a homogeneous population uniformly exposed to the risks of life, which saw the emergence of the principle of social security for all, has been replaced by that of people facing mounting burdens who are the victims of determinism (Cunha, Leresche and Vez, 1998; Lautier, 1999). This change of view has logically been accompanied by the desire to have these vulnerable people, and only them, benefit from social policies, whether in the form of compensatory assistance or of programmes such as microfinance.

The fact that poverty is hard to define inevitably has repercussions on how it is measured,[14] which is key to assessing the contribution of instruments such as microfinance to poverty reduction. The number and nature of the dimensions to take into account and the way they are combined in what is usually a scaled indicator must be determined. A choice has to be made whether to measure *effective* or *potential* poverty, depending on whether it is the effective satisfaction of needs or the potential income or monetary outlays for goods and services to satisfy them that is observed. The measurements may also be *indirect* or *direct*, depending on whether they are based on income (indirect) or spending (direct).

Two methods are widely used to measure poverty, in some cases for international comparisons: the poverty line method and, to a lesser extent, the unsatisfied basic needs methods.

The poverty line method consists in comparing the income or spending of a household or person with a threshold (the poverty line) that corresponds to the monetary cost of a number of goods and services considered to be indispensable to the household or person's reproduction. It serves to calculate the *incidence* and *depth* of poverty,[15] and therefore measures potential poverty, directly or indirectly. The needs included vary, the only common item being a shopping basket of the basic foodstuffs needed to survive, the exact content and monetary value of which are estimated for a given context. Variations of the method take account of the other dimensions of poverty, which are based on an explicit determination of needs, or on the contrary, infer their monetary value by observing the proportion of income or spending of a control group selected because what it spends on food is equal to the cost of the basic shopping basket.[16]

The poverty lines of one and two dollars per day (in international 1985 prices converted to local currencies in order to ensure parity in purchasing power) defined by the World Bank, and generally applied to the least advanced and middle-income countries respectively, have been established as the yardsticks for measuring poverty internationally.[17]

Although approximate in nature, poverty lines can be used to make international comparisons and frequently serve as references for the poverty levels with which MFIs operate.

The unsatisfied basic needs (UBN) method directly observes the extent to which basic needs are or are not met. It measures *effective* rather than potential poverty, and is significantly different from the poverty line method. Like the latter, the difficulty with the UBN method lies in defining what constitutes a *basic* need.

What these different methods show, and what is important when discussing microfinance as a means of reducing poverty, is the special position of monetary income among the other established dimensions of poverty, which are hard to gauge. The method that compares the poverty line with income, the most frequently used, implicitly supposes that monetary income provides purchasing power and therefore covers all basic needs. There is thus a gap between the theory or thinking on the multidimensional nature of poverty, on the one hand, and the method's application in practice, on the other. The existence of that gap also reflects the somewhat overweening ambition to have the concept of poverty encompass almost all aspects of development. No matter what the case, the effective application of poverty measurements is based on an economic view in which inadequate material means are considered to be the reason people have limited or no access to education, health care, basic utilities like water and electricity, decent housing and so on. Monetary income thus becomes *the* strategic variable on which to act. Yet the fundamental cause of not just insufficient income but also little or no access to education, health care, decent housing and so on is often discrimination and processes of marginalization, which in exceptional cases are identified as the cause of the problem and combated as such. In addition, these monetary measurements classify the poor as extremely poor, fairly poor or living on the poverty line, without any social analysis. The main tenet is that they are excluded, discriminated against, or marginalized for economic reasons, whereas it can be demonstrated to the contrary that exclusion begets poverty. Because there is no social analysis, the 'poor' all tend to be lumped together, with no understanding of the fact that even within poor populations there exist discrimination and pecking orders. Enabling segments of the population living just beneath the poverty line to improve their plight may give them the means of reinforcing their domination and exploitation of those who are even poorer and thus worsen the poverty of the most needy. This is one of the risks of microfinance we shall emphasize.

The failure to analyse the processes of exclusion and the tendency to focus on poverty are reflected in the fact that even a financial organization such as the World Bank does not list degrees of banking and financial exclusion as an indicator of poverty. Public policy-makers consider financial services as means and not as needs within the context of the growing 'financialization' of contemporary societies.[18]

2.3   How microfinance can help reduce poverty

In the face of what is seen to be the inadequate income of a segment of the population, the alternative is to distribute income support or to support the creation of income-generating activities. Microfinance is considered to be able to help reduce poverty in various ways, on which there is not necessarily a consensus.

The first question – the type of population that should benefit as a priority from microfinance services – opposes those who believe in the ripple effect and those who believe that MFIs should directly target people according to poverty lines. For the former, microfinance is intended to provide microcredit and thereby to strengthen the productive activities of the less poor, whose consumption is thought to create jobs and thus provoke a ripple effect that has positive repercussions on the entire local population, in particular the most needy. Transaction costs are thus lower than if the MFI provided its services directly to the poorest. This solution is said to promote the MFI's financial efficiency, allowing it to expand its services and thus reduce poverty on a large scale.

Many observers remain unconvinced by this strategy, however, not only because it reinforces existing local hierarchies and inequality and therefore the mechanisms of domination, but also because redistribution by the creation of jobs or consumption does not necessarily benefit the poorest. There is also the exacerbation of felt needs and relative deprivation.[19]

Another school of thought prefers MFIs to target the poor directly, no matter how difficult or costly.[20] Identifying the poorest among the poor implies the existence of consequential information systems. Convincing the poor to become the beneficiaries of a microfinance service usually requires an effort and therefore involves greater 'transaction costs'; given the difficulties faced by the poor, it is relatively more difficult to keep them as clients or members of an MFI than other kinds of clients.[21] Some people use this argument to explain why MFIs working with the poorest segments of the population are not bound by usury rates and can charge much higher interest rates. The service they provide to the most needy is said to justify the fact that the poor have to pay much more for credit. It is a strange form of social justice that has the most underprivileged paying more. The demand to waive interest rate ceilings can also justify the payment of a subsidy to compensate higher transaction costs. It is a neoliberal vision of society that tips the scales.

Those who believe in targeting the poor clearly hold sway in the microfinance world, and within that group, a second question arises: how the poor are 'targeted'. This question draws a further line between the defenders of one or the other type of approximation. Many MFIs are content to target women, in the belief that the discrimination and inequality they suffer, especially in their homes, make them on the whole poorer even than men.[22] Although it greatly facilitates targeting, the roughness of the approximation raises numerous questions and again reflects an economic view of social relations and identities. No account is taken of the obvious inequalities between women and hence of the mechanisms of domination that inevitably fall into place, especially in groups of women providing joint collateral, or of the various strategies employed by men, notably husbands or other family members, to profit from the loans granted to the women by the MFIs.[23]

Working on the basis of statistical observation means ignoring the reality that inequalities exist between social and family groups. The general category 'women' itself is made up of extremely disparate units representing as many social groups who suffer gender inequality in what may be radically different ways and to varying degrees of intensity. It is one thing to say that women are poorer than men; it is quite another to assert that a woman's income within the household is less than that of the man and that in a given cultural context her management power and ability to use resources independently and enjoy personal property rights vary. It only makes sense to assert the poverty of women when speaking, for example, of single mothers raising their children without a father or family support. In all other cases, women are spouses, common-law wives, mothers, sisters, nieces and daughters, granddaughters and great-nieces, cousins within the family group to which they belong, and there are differences of income and power between them. Women benefit from those differences. Giving preference to women as a general category and masking other forms of belonging allows the educated, urban, privileged elites to maintain a position of dominance, more over women from underprivileged sectors than over the male elites with whom they *de facto* share power, albeit from a subordinate position. Gender-based claims are thus often redirected for the benefit of the dominant classes. This in no way negates the fact that the female half of the family tends to be the dominated and in some cases exploited half.

Other techniques of targeting the poor give priority to the 'rural environment', where poverty rates are higher overall than in urban areas. This manner of targeting is also open to severe criticism. To equate the rural population with the poor population, even if the statistics show that per capita income in some areas is particularly low, does not mean that the MFI's clients are automatically the genuinely poor members of that population. Where the MFI's clients or members represent a limited proportion of the local population, they may be the rich or most powerful and microfinance may be part of their power-building strategy of domination. It is interesting to note from this point of view that more loans are taken out for commercial or transport activities than for agricultural projects as such. It has also been observed that in rural areas with a high number of migrants the proportion of clients is higher among the families with one or several migrants than among those with none.

MFIs working in urban areas can choose from among those areas with the highest levels of unsatisfied basic needs, if an indicator of that kind is available and sufficiently accurate. Taken separately, each of these established indicators is insufficient, and the MFIs can only target their clients effectively by combining several indicators and employing staff with good local knowledge.[24]

Looking beyond these controversies and difficulties, several theories on how the various financial services provided by MFIs help reduce poverty merit further explanation. The main idea underpinning the promotion of microcredit *for the poor* is that the inability to invest is the principal block to productive activity. At the level of the individual, microcredit is intended to allow the individual to invest so as to increase productivity and hence income, thus enabling him or her to repay the interest and the capital and perhaps to start saving. There are other anticipated benefits, in particular better nourishment and thus health (and productivity), a long-term rise in the level of education and the *empowerment*[25] of the beneficiaries.[26] In some cases, however, it is not, for example, the enrolment rate, but rather the rate of child labour that goes up, especially among girls called on to perform the household tasks that mothers no longer have time for because microcredit has given them income-generating work. These young household helpers may be members of the family or come from poorer families. It is symptomatic of MFIs and the national and international organizations that support them that they are much more interested in the supposed poverty of women than in the exploitation of children. Numerous microcredit projects have resulted in an increase in child labour.

The idea of insufficient resources for investment is part of the 'vicious circle' theory of underdevelopment, which was presented in particular by R. Nurske in *Problems of Capital Formation in Underdeveloped Countries* (1953) and according to which insufficient savings, the consequence of which is the inability to invest in productive activities, constitutes the main factor of underdevelopment.[27] After the acknowledged failure of state subsidized credit policies in the 1970s, microcredit appeared as a fresh solution to an old problem, all the more so as shrinking state resources tightened the public purse. While the United States had indebted themselves by providing subsidized loans that were financially unsustainable, microfinance claimed a high-cost recovery rate. While state institutions had suffered from low repayment rates, many MFIs boasted of record recovery rates (which nevertheless require close scrutiny).[28] While in most countries subsidized credit had benefited only a limited number of companies, usually the best established, many MFIs have claimed that their services are intended for the most destitute (AMUCCS, 2000; Mestries Benquet and Hernández Trujillo, 2003). This is possible thanks to group lending methods (joint surety among small groups of joint borrowers or community banks and village funds) that, unlike individual loans, do not require material collateral.

There is nevertheless room for doubt. The 'vicious circle' theory of underdevelopment has, let us remember, itself been criticized. It is today common knowledge that there once were and still are savings, or rather surplus productive activity, in many developing countries. These savings may nevertheless be placed on international capital markets by financial institutions, used for collective consumption or for prestige spending,[29] or confiscated by certain agents rather than reinvested in productive activities as they should be under the theory of optimal allocation of resources. As such, microcredit cannot be understood as a mere stopgap for insufficient domestic savings, and its use to create (or strengthen) productive activities are open to debate. Indeed, MFIs have admitted difficulties in monitoring the use of the loans they grant and several recent studies have demonstrated that relatively few micro-loans are effectively used to generate productive activity. In the Bolivian textile sector, a study by J. Samanamud Ávila and colleagues showed that microcredits were usually used to reinforce an existing activity and not to create a new one (Samanamud Ávila, Alvarado Portillo and del Castillo Villegas, 2003).[30] The overall difficulty of following up and accounting for microfinance as a principal factor in the creation of businesses serves to heighten these doubts. Statistics on the number of micro-businesses founded are only meaningful when accompanied by the number of bankruptcies, which is rarely the case in practice. And how can we be sure that a business was created *thanks* to a micro-loan and not to a combination of other factors or even another form of financing?[31] Numerous studies show that loans are highly fungible.

In fact, some scholars promote the use of micro-loans for purposes other than to finance entrepreneurship. M. Goldberg and M. Motta show, for example, in the case of Mexico, that certain kinds of microcredit could be used to finance the renovation or construction of housing (Goldberg and Motta, 2003). This is particularly important for urban poverty reduction in countries, especially, but not exclusively, in Latin America, where shanty towns and squatter settlements are a major social problem in urban areas.

In the transition towards expanded microfinance, the role of financial services other than microcredit in poverty reduction, is gaining recognition. The savings services offered by MFIs, for example, are now seen as a means of securing savings and of encouraging the poorest to save more and more systematically.[32] In comparison to traditional forms of saving (from the purchase of an animal to participation in a tontine fund), *formal* savings in an MFI offers the advantage of greater liquidity and higher returns thanks to the interest paid (Campos, 1998).[33] The build-up of savings can be seen as one of microfinance's most promising contributions to reduced vulnerability of the poor, in that it offers a means of compensating earnings fluctuations. The same holds true for micro-insurance, a financial service that is, as yet, relatively little developed by MFIs, but for which demand is strong and which is likely to grow once a system of reassurance has been established for the large-scale compensation of the risks covered. Generally speaking, relatively new microfinance services such as the transfer of migrant remittances, cashing of cheques or payment orders all have an important role to play because they offer greater security for the financial operations of the most vulnerable segments of the population.[34]

2.4 Poverty reduction and financial performance

In addition to the difficulty of targeting the poor, MFIs are also called on to achieve a balance between poverty reduction and positive financial performance. In this section, we will look at how increased risk and high transaction costs can result in a trade-off; we will then consider the consequences of such a trade-off and what the role of subsidies might be.

Transaction costs are all the costs to be assumed by MFIs to allow the operation to take place. These costs include, among others, fixed costs, personnel costs, transportation costs, costs incurred to obtain administrative documents and so on. In the case of a poor clientele, these costs rise very quickly. Such people generally live in areas where access is difficult and which are sorely lacking in infrastructure and services. Consequently, completing any administrative formality means a costly trip. This can prompt MFIs to set themselves up in areas where infrastructure is relatively more developed.[35] Three factors can explain the high cost of transactions if MFIs wish to reach a poor clientele: small loan amounts, the location of poor people and the method of joint groups.

By definition, the loan amounts granted by MFIs to their clients (namely poor people) are low. However, the fixed costs involved in delivering such loans remain high; this is all the more pronounced if MFIs seek to target the poorest people (Greely, 2003).

The difficulty of reaching certain areas also involves costs for MFIs wishing to offer their services to poor clients. It is very tempting for MFIs to neglect such clients living in hard-to-access areas (in some cases, the employees of the credit institution must walk long distances or use animal transportation). In fact, not only are transaction costs high, as we have already seen, but recovery costs can also be prohibitive. An additional problem is the risk of theft during fund transfers.

The joint liability method originated at the Grameen Bank and has proved to be the most appropriate in terms of credit to target poor people. Bearing in mind the virtual impossibility for the poorest people to provide material collateral for loans, the technique of joint surety provides a solution to this problem, as long as the borrowers are not incited to present themselves as being collectively insolvent subsequently and the groups really exist and are not just front companies. It is presumed that the pressure the group puts on each member will encourage him or her to repay the loans when they mature. This loan technique requires regular meetings (weekly or monthly) to collect the repayments. Furthermore, the sums paid at these meetings can be derisory in relation to the constraints placed on the credit grantor and on the clients in terms of attendance time and opportunity costs. For example, these meetings can significantly increase the work or the time devoted to the association (this can be observed in examples of MFIs in Niger and Burkina Faso which have the status of mutual benefit associations or cooperatives).

All the costs generated by these obstacles constitute an additional constraint for MFIs and weaken their financial performance. This implies a trade-off, which raises the question of balance between targeting poor people and seeking to uphold the financial performance of the MFI. For MFIs, financial performance is generally contradictory to their objective of combating poverty (Morduch, 1999a).[36] Examples of MFIs that have achieved a balance between targeting poor people and achieving good financial performance are exceptions and they should consequently be recognized as cases that have benefited from unusual circumstances (a high level of literacy, high population density, efficient means of transport and communication, the potential for the marketing of products, a high percentage of migrants bringing in outside revenue, positive developments in old credit structures, forms of government intervention, specificities of intervention sites, etc.) rather than their approach being seen as one to be simulated. Therefore, they cannot be applied just anywhere or at any time. Furthermore, donors put pressure on the institutions they support to become financially autonomous. This has led some MFI administrators to focus on financial performances which are easier to measure. And, with the accounting tools currently available, it is easy to evaluate the financial situation[37] of an MFI.

However, it is more difficult to calculate the contribution of MFIs to poverty reduction as specific objectives vary from one institution to another,[38] from one site of implantation to another, and so on. 'The period of consolidation and the move towards the perpetuation of MFIs have focused attention on issues of financial and institutional viability' (Lapenu et al., 2004). Currently, the evaluation of the participation of microfinance in poverty reduction is less elaborate than the evaluation of the financial performance of MFIs. Some microfinance organizations maintain, nevertheless, that they achieve a balance between satisfactory social impact and financial soundness. If these experiences show that despite high costs and risks it is possible, in certain conditions, for an MFI to target truly poor clients, it would be advisable to study the specific conditions that enabled it to do so to ascertain to what extent they could be reproduced and to understand how it can be possible to reduce poverty effectively. One of these conditions appears to be the possibility for an MFI to have access to subsidies.

Some MFIs surveyed recognized that subsidies were indispensable for them to go on targeting the poor. This does not only mean external subsidies, but also internal ones within the MFI (cross-subsidies). In this study, we will limit ourselves to external subsidies. It is clear that some subsidies are needed to start up MFIs. These generally take the form of fixed assets which, more often than not, consist of computer equipment. In some cases, the MFI uses these subsidies to cover operating costs for a certain time or to supplement their credit funds or guarantee commercial loans. This type of subsidy is not controversial. In fact, as long as the subsidies are used during the start-up phase (which donors increasingly want to shorten), they are generally not questioned.

Criticism relates to the permanent or ongoing nature of some subsidies which, in theory, allow MFIs to reach vulnerable or poor clients. Actually, as we mentioned on the issue of trade-offs, a number of quite exceptional conditions need to combine for an MFI to serve truly poor populations while at the same time achieving a good financial performance. At this juncture, it is useful to note how difficult it is for MFIs to obtain these subsidies. It appears that public donors seem to attach more conditions than private donors to the subsidies they give. Charitable foundations, in particular, seem more liberal. Furthermore, a variety of donors brings additional stability to the MFI. It is clear that if the subsidies come from a single donor (or a very small number of donors) the risk of it (or them) withdrawing increases the financial vulnerability of the MFI. MFIs appear to have recognized this and most of them seek to diversify their sources of subsidies and, as far as possible, subtly combine public and private donors.

As we have already seen, it is difficult for most MFIs to succeed in associating poor clients and financial balance. It is consequently very tempting for some MFIs to select their clients and members. Targeting the most profitable or least costly clients and members allows the institution to achieve a better financial performance. In this way, by only dealing with clients and members selected from among the least poor, the MFI can generally reduce its risks[39] and limit its transaction costs. In the majority of cases, the targeting is not explicit but is a result of how the institution operates. The institution might claim to be targeting poor people, but an in-depth sociological or anthropological study would reveal a gap between claim and reality.

2.5   Can microfinance reach the poor?

Do MFIs have the capacity to reach the poorest? By concentrating on poverty, do they not run the risk of neglecting certain harmful side-effects caused by growing inequalities? This will lead us to a discussion of which social objectives are desirable for microfinance.

There can be two reasons why it is difficult to reach poor clients: there is no MFI active in the area where the poor people are located; despite the presence of an MFI, the poor cannot have access to the services on offer.

Absence of material collateral, insufficiency and irregularity of income, exposure of activities to climatic conditions, geographic distance and low population density all explain the relative absence of MFIs in rural areas. But as an MFI administrator in Niger explained: without resources from urban centres, it would be impossible to maintain operations in rural areas. Urban customers often seem more appealing to MFIs seeking good financial performance. It is in towns that one generally finds a majority of public or private sector employees, and of educated micro-entrepreneurs. These appear to be the best qualified to manage a microenterprise. Conversely, rural areas are, for the most part, characterized by the narrowness of markets, which restricts prospects for productive entrepreneurship. In some regions, the reasons stopping MFIs from being set up are of a practical nature: difficult access or difficulty for promoters to communicate with local populations owing to a language barrier, for instance.

Even with the presence of an MFI truly poor families may be or are perceive to be excluded from access to finance: there may be a difficulty in joining or leaving. Some barriers to entry are virtually insurmountable for a fringe of the poor population. Because poor people are not part of a network, they might not be informed that such a mechanism exists. This lack of information can be due to illiteracy or to marginalization caused by ethnic or racial discrimination. In addition, their entrepreneurship capacity is rather limited and their empowerment appears insufficient.

Furthermore, departures, be they voluntary or forced, can explain why truly poor people are neither members nor clients of MFIs. These departures can be explained by institutions having a policy of creaming-off their clientele and choosing the 'good clients', or the departures might be decided by the clients themselves. Voluntary departures are seen in particular in cases where the mechanism makes provision, at the end of a cycle, for further loans of sums higher than those in the previous period. In this case, the members or clients who are not interested in these new loans will leave; in general, it is the poorest segments of the population who have the most limited investment opportunities. These voluntary departures can also be seen when there is a change in the system of loans, for example, when the MFI decides to go from group credits to individual credits. In this case, if material collateral is required, the clients or members who are not in a position to provide it, leave. It is invariably the poorest segment of the clientele which finds itself unable to provide this collateral.

Forced departures are due to defaults in the repayment of loans, compulsory savings payments or insurance contributions. They can be explained by an illness affecting a member of the family, an animal that dies and that must urgently be replaced, a ceremony (birth or death, leading to unexpected expense). Such events generate unforeseen expenses for the family and can compromise their ability to meet their financial obligations vis-à-vis the microfinance organization and repay their debts, which in turn leads to them being excluded from the system. This likelihood affects the poorest families which, in addition, have less social capacity to be able to negotiate such situations.

2.6   The harmful side-effects: increased disparities

Some effects of microfinance can lead to a deterioration in the situation of a segment of poor people, although it is supposed to attenuate or even globally reduce poverty. Three effects can contribute to an increase in disparities: over-indebtedness, excessive attention paid to micro-entrepreneurship and the financing of high loan amounts using the savings of the poorest. There is a high risk of microfinance actually accentuating income disparities in this way.

The remarkable expansion of microfinance and the widespread appearance of MFIs offering a range of services (savings, credit, insurance, cashing of cheques, funds transfers, foreign exchange, etc.) have contributed through microcredit to the over-indebtedness of some populations. There have even been instances of cases of non-repayment ending up endangering the system as a whole.[40] This was above all due to consumer credits granted by the MFIs. Taking into account the interchangeability of credits, it is often difficult to distinguish between production credit and consumer credit. Loans serve, then, as a way of managing resources to bridge the gaps.

In Benin, for example, it is the phenomenon of *la cavalerie*[41] which is blamed. This process consists of a client going to various MFIs to contract loans to repay other loans taken out with other MFIs. Clients thus enter into a dangerous borrowing-repaying cycle which makes them increasingly vulnerable. Hence the support for national programmes for the compilation and exchange of data on borrowers (developed in Latin America, in particular).

In Africa, some mutual networks clearly state their wish to go beyond the stage of financing survival towards support of entrepreneurship. This is the case, for example, of the RCPB, which states that its network is already at this level, its clients include enterprises and, furthermore, it is developing financial services beyond loans and savings. The support provided to these entrepreneurs is often to the detriment of the poorest people. The fact is, developing an entrepreneurial activity showing financial surpluses requires the acquisition not only of technical equipment, working capital and seed capital, while waiting to establish a clientele, but also of a set of skills, particularly management and marketing skills. It is clear that the poor rarely have such indispensable resources for the smooth operation of a microenterprise. Consequently, the clients increasingly targeted by these microenterprises are small traders or craftsmen, often already established. Microfinance generating productive development relates more to existing enterprises than to enterprise creation, strictly speaking. The accumulation is found more in these units than in life-sustaining self-employment activities.

A particularly pernicious effect seen in the savings and credit activities of MFIs is the financing of the least poor by the most poor. In some cases, the least poor are considered at the local level as elite. When regulations permit, savings collected from the poor can be recycled by the MFI to grant loans for the development of micro-entrepreneurial activities or for the investments of public service employees. In a number of networks, a proportion of one to ten can be seen between the number of savers and the number of borrowers. Certainly, as we have seen, savings correspond to a need of the poorest, but investments made by the wealthiest using the savings of the poorest contribute to broadening income disparities within the population.

Beyond the alleviation of poverty microfinance could also have alternative objectives, attenuating the negative externalities mentioned above. The question of poverty is, generally, raised by MFIs on the basis of indicators of material insufficiencies. MFIs thus take the level of loans[42] as being one indication of the social make-up of their clientele. A low level would imply poor clients. But poverty can also be understood as a consequence of inequalities, particularly social, legal and cultural inequalities, as well as the complex processes of discrimination that lead to marginalization and exclusion (Servet, 2006). Just as ethnic, racial, regional and religious discrimination explain why some populations encounter difficulties in gaining access to water, health care, education, economic opportunity and public administration, they also explain the obstacles that restrict some people in their access to financial services.

MFIs seem to be increasingly involving themselves in the reduction of inequalities, often driven by product innovation. Following the example of insurance against the risks related to illness, death or the loss of property, these new products protect populations against certain types of vulnerabilities. Some MFIs propose transfer services in areas with migration, which can help protect in emergencies. Microfinance services can provide original and innovative responses to reduce the effects of inequalities, but if limited to microcredit it cannot – except in exceptional conditions – be a low-cost panacea to reduce social inequalities and eradicate poverty.

Notes

1   From the title of the 2000–01 *World Development Report*.
2   In other words, from 27.9 per cent of the global population in 1990 to 14 per cent in 2015.
3   See the summary prepared by Bernd Balkenhol and Isabelle Guérin.
4   For example, in the case of debt overload and decapitalization, or of an insurance policy under which unpaid premiums lead to a loss of benefits.
5   A fair number of impact studies have been carried out by people with a vested interest in showing the positive contribution of microfinance to poverty reduction so as to maintain subsidies. It is thus hardly surprising that some studies are not as thorough as might be hoped.
6   A microfinance institution can attract less poor clients by changing the conditions of access to its services (usually by moving from group lending to individual loans) or by introducing operating rules that oblige the poorest to leave the institution voluntarily or to be excluded from it.
7   In his benchmark article, Morduch postulates that, contrary to earlier mainstream theories that microfinance institutions could reduce poverty while attaining financial independence (a win-win situation), the two objectives are usually contradictory.
8   See, for example: World Bank (2001); J. Boltvinik (2003, pp. 453–65); UN-HABITAT: *The Recife Declaration*, International Forum on Urban Poverty (Recife, 1996); P. Townsend (2003, pp. 445–52).
9   In particular, P. Townsend (2003) and J. Boltvinik (2003).
10   M. Sahlins (1976).
11   For an interesting discussion on this issue see R. Anker's paper on the ILO website http://www.ilo.org/public/english/bureau/integration/download/publicat/4_3_378_wp-72.pdf (suggestion owed to David Kucera).
12   A criticism made by A. Sen (1983) in defence of the concept of absolute poverty (without denying that needs may change).
13   Vulnerability is one of the development indicators calculated by the World Bank for its *World Development Report*. It is defined as the present probability of becoming poor or poorer in the future.
14   The rest of this chapter refers to absolute poverty, as poverty considered from the relative point of view leads to qualitative analyses and does not allow for the desired quantitative measurement.
15   The *incidence* of poverty refers to the percentage of people in a given population whose income or spending is below the poverty line; this measurement is usefully supplemented with that of the *depth* or *intensity* of poverty, which is calculated as the average gap in terms of the poverty line, and constitutes an indicator of the mean distance from the poverty line.
16   The proportion of total income that the control group spends on food determines the Engel coefficient, which is used to calculate the poverty line

by means of the formula: poverty line = cost of the basic shopping basket / Engel coefficient. The control group can also be chosen so as to have an income that is slightly higher than the basic shopping basket. In that case, for reasons of data availability, the decile of the population whose income is above that cost is usually chosen. These approximations call for careful scrutiny, because a small variation in the Engel coefficient can have a considerable effect on poverty incidence and depth.

17 The poverty line of one dollar per day was selected for the 1990 *World Development Report* (the first to contain statistics on poverty) 'because it is typical of poverty lines in low-income countries' (World Bank, 2005, p. 68). It is still used today and in 1993 corresponded to $1.08 in international prices.

18 On this aspect of financialization and its definition, see J.-M. Servet and I. Guérin: 'Introduction', in *Exclusion et liens financiers* (Exclusion and financial links), report of the Walras Centre 2002 (Paris, Economica, 2002).

19 The idea that the creation of wealth by one group in no way impoverishes other groups, indeed indirectly enriches them, is debatable from the point of view of relative poverty. Overall, the idea is based on a pacified concept of social relations that denies the existence of hierarchies between people.

20 This is the approach implicitly adopted in the GIAN study, which looks at how MFIs target the poor, the difficulties encountered in keeping them in the portfolio and the possible changes in method that could reveal a shift in the target group.

21 The last section of this article discusses these difficulties in detail.

22 Another argument frequently cited is that women are more likely than men to spread the benefits of loans to their families, especially their children.

23 On this subject, see I. Guérin (2003).

24 In the GIAN study, a combination of indicators was used to assess the relative level of poverty of the MFI's members: the MFI's geographical location, targeting techniques and credit methods (group or individual lending); percentage of members who are women, the members' professional status, their ability to read, write and calculate.

25 *Empowerment* refers to three types of power: *power to*, meaning the individual or collective ability to create; *power of*, which refers to the capacity to claim rights or interests through collective action; *internal power*, which is understood as the capacity to accept oneself the way one is and to respect other people's differences. In all three cases, the capacities acquired are not necessarily obtained to the detriment of others, which is a fundamental difference with the traditional model of domination, or *power over* (J.-M. Servet: 'Performances, impacts et effets des organizations de microfinance' (forthcoming).

26 The explanation given by the MIX Market of the way in which microfinance helps reduce poverty puts it in a nutshell: 'Experience shows that microfinance can help the poor to increase income, build viable businesses, and reduce their vulnerability to external shocks. It can also be a powerful instrument for self-empowerment by enabling the poor, especially women, to become economic agents of change' (The MIX Market, *How does microfinance help the poor?* http://www.mixmarket.org/en/how_microfinance_helps.asp).

27 Daniel Fino quite relevantly points out that overall the so-called poor countries do not suffer so much from insufficient investment resources (their

banks often have too much liquidity) as they do from the inability to assess risks and the scarcity of relay institutions; hence the importance of establishing guarantee funds.

28   This opposition between public institutes and MFIs is deeply ideological, given that the world's biggest MFI, the BRI in Indonesia, which has nearly 30 million clients, is a former public development bank that has just started the process of privatization.

29   Although it is rarely recognized as such by standard economic theory, prestige spending is often a form of long-term investment based not on merchant logic but on reciprocity.

30   The field survey carried out in El Alto showed that textile micro-businesses were created using personal savings and loans from family members. Microcredit was used during periods of strong demand and to reproduce the productive cycle.

31   This question raises another, that of the fungibility of financial resources. Loans are not always used at the time and for the reason indicated when they were taken out, but this does not mean that the borrower is acting in bad faith.

32   Most group lending methods provide for a gradual build-up of savings along a well-established schedule and use the level of savings to calculate the maximum amount of credit to be granted. However, the moralistic side of these techniques, which are intended to 'teach the poor to save', are hard to overlook. See on this subject the work of P. Campos (1998) on Mexico, which shows that, contrary to a widely held myth, most poor Mexicans save part of their earnings.

33   At the level not of savings but of the institution, the availability of savings enables the MFI to finance its credit portfolio more independently (to have less recourse to external refinancing) and in some cases to extend its services to more people. Admittedly, however, since most loans are taken out by the poorest, it is their savings that often end up subsidizing loans to the less poor (differential asset-liability rate).

34   It is common knowledge that international transfers of migrant remittances using informal channels often occur at exorbitant cost and excessive risk.

35   Nimal Fernando shows that in India 70 per cent of MFIs are located in two provinces in the south where economic infrastructure is the most developed. See Nimal A. Fernando (2004).

36   See also Flückiger and Vassiliev, 2004; Servet, 2006.

37   Furthermore, financial performance indicators for MFIs have been harmonized: the technical instruments of the Consultative Group to Assist the Poor (CGAP), Micro Rate and the Inter-American Development Bank, 2003.

38   On this question, see the multidimensional character of poverty.

39   The less poor offer greater guarantees of repayment and the average amount of their operations is higher (Servet, 2006).

40   See SOS Faim, 2002.

41   The word comes from *cavaler*. This is when a client rushes around after credits, in other words, he or she enters a vicious circle of taking out one loan to repay another, and so on.

42   It is true that the level of loans is an easy indicator to record and that one can compare the loan amounts among institutions.

3
Poverty Reduction through Microfinance: A Capability Perspective

Flavio Comim
Cambridge University

3.1 Introduction

The importance of assessing the impact of microfinance schemes on poverty reduction cannot be overestimated. Poverty reduction is the *raison-d'être* of microfinance. It is because other forms of finance are not usually accessible to the poor (due to high transaction costs, the poor's lack of collateral, etc) that microfinance has been explored as a possible solution to poverty reduction. But it is more than that. The assumption underlying this argument is that poverty is partly explained by lack of economic opportunities and that microfinance can provide a *sustainable path* towards viable surviving economic strategies. Therefore, microfinance can be important not only because it can lead to poverty reduction but mainly because it promotes, in a non-patronizing and decentralized way, economic alternatives to the poor that are in principle more sustainable (permanent) in the long-run. Microfinance can be compared with other poverty reduction initiatives based on paternalistic concessions (e.g., basic income programmes) that are a priori unsustainable in the long-run because they are dependent on a continuous inflow of resources.

However, the evaluation of the poverty outreach of microfinance initiatives is permeated by controversies in the literature. First, the general positive impact of microfinance on poverty reduction is not widely accepted. Many authors such as Morduch (1998) or Copestake et al. (2005) have expressed concern with 'mission drift' in microfinance schemes. Secondly, a consensus seems to have been built about the lack of depth of outreach in microfinance schemes. As Halder and Mosley

(2004, p. 404) put it, 'the general tendency is to accept the 'microfinance is for the not-so-poor' critique'. Thirdly, the acclaimed impact of microfinance on the promotion of women's autonomy has proved to be non-robust (see, for example, Ehlers and Main, 1998; and Kabeer and Noponen, 2005). Fourthly, negative impacts of group loans on individuals' well-being have raised doubts about their efficacy vis-à-vis individual loans (Navajas et al., 2000). Finally, the proposal of assessing the *wider impacts* of microfinance (see, for example, McGregor et al., 2000, or Zohir and Rock, 2004) has brought into perspective an overlap of different dimensions that are rarely compared among alternative proposals.

A crucial issue that has not been fully explored by the literature concerns the handling and evaluation of different dimensions for assessing the poverty outreach of microfinance schemes.[1]

The main objective of this chapter is to probe into the concept of poverty outreach and impact of microfinance.[2] It is divided into four parts. The first part explores the main issues in the impact of microfinance on poverty. These set the context for the second part, which describes in more detail 'the positive mechanisms' of microfinance schemes. This is complemented by the third section, which presents 'the negative mechanisms' that prevent the poor from benefiting from these schemes. Fourthly, an argument is put forward for seeing poverty, in the context of microfinance, as 'capability deprivation'. Finally, some implications for empirical work are explored. In particular, it is suggested that the whole issue of trade-offs between sustainability and outreach might be seen differently when poverty is looked at from a capability perspective.

3.2   Who are the poor? What are the issues?

Diversity is not an undesirable analytical category in itself, provided that it is well-understood. For this reason we should not see with (a priori) disapproval the large variety of designations used to categorize 'the poor' (and the non-poor). Different taxonomies to classify the poor have been proposed.[3] These taxonomies follow, in general, two basic principles of separation between different classes of poverty. The first principle is based on the depth of poverty. Unsurprisingly, this has been a common theme in the literature and alternative classifications of poverty attempted to evaluate the impact of microfinance according to the intensity of poverty among the poor. The second principle focuses instead on the idea that some types of poverty do not compromise the agency aspect of the poor. Thus, concepts of 'the economically active' or 'the working' or 'entrepreneurial' poor refer to a potentiality enjoyed by some groups among the poor that can be particularly important for their participation in microfinance schemes. These principles emphasize the issue of thresholds in separating different groups of people in society. They are relevant for targeting social policies and prioritizing the welfare of some groups.

Mission drift

As argued by Halder and Mosley (2004, p. 403), 'Failure to reach the poor, never mind the poorest of the poor, has been a recurrent criticism of microfinance since its takeoff in the early 1990s'.[4] As much as this remark characterizes an important apprehension revealed by current analyses, it is important to note that the debates on whether the general impact of microfinance schemes on poverty reduction is minimal or significant are not only about impact. More importantly, these debates are about the best routes to reduce different types of poverty. As claimed by Matin et al. (2002), it might well be that the 'poverty escape through credit' route is inappropriate for some targeted groups.

In this case the problem is not simply about 'mission drift' but about the sort of financial services that might be appropriate for tackling different kinds of poverty. Navajas et al. (2000, p. 343), when analysing the poverty outreach of five microfinance schemes in Bolivia, argued that the lenders 'reached the richest of the poor and the poorest of the rich much more than they reached the poorest of the poor. This does not necessarily mean that they did a bad job'. This suggests that concern should be directed to different microfinance services and their relative impact, moving away from a 'yes-no' assessment of the poverty impact of microfinance.

Lack of depth

There is robust evidence in the literature that the poorest are least likely to benefit from microcredit (e.g., Hulme and Mosley, 1996). Whereas some programmes fail to target those living in extreme poverty (they do not think about the poorest of the poor when defining their eligibility criteria), others simply do not succeed in bringing the poorest on board, either because of problems of self-exclusion of the poorest or through lack of sustainability of their participation. As a result, as suggested by Copestake, Bhalotra and Johnson (2001, p. 86), 'recipients of microcredit tend to be bunched around the poverty line, but with more above than below it'. One important limitation of this 'lack-of-depth' argument is that it classifies the poor based only on income criteria. This means that if the incomes of the poor do not rise, programmes cannot be considered 'successful'. However, one might wonder about other non-income effects that might arise from poor people's involvement in microfinance schemes. A different approach is needed to arrive at the 'lack of poverty depth' conclusion, taking into account not only unidimensional quantitative measures but multidimensional qualitative elements.

Impact on women's autonomy

In qualitative terms, one of the most important well-established results of the impact of microfinance schemes is empowerment of women (see Zohir and Matin, 2004). However, it has also been suggested that 'women's empowerment is not an automatic gain' (Kabeer and Noponen, 2005, p. 28) and that 'positive gender effects cannot always be taken for granted' (Sharma, 2000, p. 2). Further, there are studies, such as Ehlers and Main's (1998, p. 426), which argue that 'in general, microenterprise produces a host of latent consequences that are ultimately more damaging than productive for women'. Whatever the views that different proponents might hold, there is a consensus about the contribution given by women to family welfare and how it is strategically relevant for microfinance institutions to target women as a means of promoting human development. One might argue that assessing the impact of microfinance schemes on women's well-being is not a trivial task because it involves the handling of different incommensurable dimensions (such as earning capabilities, self-respect, autonomy, group solidarity, etc). Once again, conclusions based only on an investigation of *before-and-after* income profiles, due to microfinance interventions, could provide, at best, a partial picture of the outreach and impact of these interventions.

Wider impacts

There is a general consensus in the literature that the poverty impact of microfinance schemes cannot be reduced to an analysis of the direct impacts on households, given that there is a range of indirect impacts to local economies that should also be taken into account. The key point, as argued by Mosley and Rock (2004, p. 485), is that different types of impact 'potentially convey *externalities to poor non-borrowers which do not appear in a conventional poverty impact assessment*' [original emphasis]. However, as noted by McGregor et al. (2000, p. 3), 'the wider impacts of microfinance are notoriously difficult to identify or assess'. As a result, different assessments end up employing different *informational spaces*[5] in evaluating the poverty impact of microfinance. Problems of comparability could also arise in defining direct and indirect causation effects based on different dimensions. A natural question to be asked concerns the choice of criteria for electing broad areas of impact. Without a robust definition of poverty, the election of different criteria might lead to incommensurable assessments and more confusion on the analysis of poverty outreach of microfinance schemes.

These four issues taken together suggest that an investigation of the impact of microfinance operations on the poor should address the problems of relative impact of different financial services; multidimensionality of poverty; and choice of informational spaces for evaluation. These three are obviously related. The choice of informational spaces should be based on a scrutiny of properties of different dimensions of poverty in relation to microfinance. These properties should follow from a conceptualization of poverty that proves more reliable than other alternatives. Based on these dimensions and properties, it is then possible to assess the relative impact of different financial services on different 'poverties'.

3.3   Positive mechanisms

The classical mechanism through which small loans could help reduce poverty is given by investments in microenterprises (income generation). Microfinance loans provide new contractual structures with more accessible eligibility criteria (for instance, no collateral requirements and lower transaction costs) that could target poor individuals or groups. Whatever the case, the classical mechanism assumes a certain managerial capacity by the poor (often based on the idea of self-employment). It is based on the implicit assumption that poverty is partially caused by a lack of resources that entrap individuals into a vicious circle of poverty. Thus, for instance, microfinance (microcredit) can help small farmers to increase their productivity with new investments and subsequent increase in their food production. By doing so, farmers can improve consumption and well-being. The classical mechanism is complemented by a broader view that links food and income security to other channels of financial security. As suggested by Meyer (2001), access to financial services can also increase the risk-bearing potential of poor households, reducing the cost of self-insurance (individuals with greater economic security can afford riskier investments) as well as smooth consumption, helping with coping strategies due to weather variations, medical expenses, investment in education and social occasions. An important addition to the classical mechanism comprises investment in human capital, increases in schooling or health motivated by microfinance.

Other positive mechanisms can be detected by taking into account the 'wider' impacts, separating the economic impacts from the social (or institutional) impacts. A simplified taxonomy, based on Mosley and Rock (2004), Zohir and Matin (2004), McGregor (2000), suggests three classes of wider impacts:

* *Economic impacts*: through the operation of labour markets (where non-borrowers are employed by borrowers, employment and wages might rise), capital markets (private moneylenders lower their interest rates to compete) or lowering of price of goods (due to an increase in supply). This might also involve building social assets and reductions in vulnerability.
* *Social impacts*: through a promotion of social capital between different networks of individuals (even non-borrowers can enjoy positive externalities created by an increase in social capital) or change in social attitudes and practices (for instance, related to family planning – e.g., increase in the use of contraceptives – or a fairer intra-household distribution of resources) or individuals' capacity to cope with crises. Thus, social impacts occur whenever microfinance can change the ways in which individuals are socially related. For this reason, sometimes changes in gender relations could also be considered as a social impact.
* *Political, institutional and cultural impacts*: through the development of civil society structures or improvements in the links between public reasoning (including systems of beliefs) and participation and the State's accountability.

One of the most celebrated positive mechanisms has been through women's access to credit. A wide range of poverty impacts, from raising household income to improving the nutritional status of children, has been acknowledged and/or corroborated by several studies (e.g., Hulme and Mosley, 1996, or Khawari, 2004). The main justification for targeting women in microfinance schemes is based on their very low opportunity cost (as a result of discrimination in labour markets) which provides great incentives for them to comply with payments and dedicate effort to (usually) new activities. More importantly, lending to women is instrumental in improving household welfare. As put by Rahman (1999, p. 69), 'The hypothesis is that women's priority is to invest their earnings in their children, to be followed by their spending on other household necessities.' So, the multiplier effects are higher when loans are disbursed to women in groups or individually. Evidence suggests that impacts are even stronger when microfinance is based on group methodologies (see, for example, *Imp-Act*, 2003).

A variety of tools has been developed to identify and to systematize the different scales of poverty impacts mentioned above. Each tool focuses on a set of particular dimensions:

- *CGAP Poverty Assessment*: This is based on a comparison of poverty scores between targeted and control groups that are contextualized within national poverty incidence indicators. Single poverty indicators are derived by using principal component analysis (see CGAP, 2004c). Copestake et al. (2005) extended this methodology towards 'poverty correlates'.[6] By using observable household characteristics that correlate well with levels of income, it is then assumed that one can reliably infer the poverty status of individuals.

- *Prizma Poverty Scorecard*: This is composed of eight non-monetary indicators, such as education, residence, employment status, family size, consumption of meat, consumption of sweets, household assets (such as colour TV or CD player) and possession of a family vehicle. Scorecards are then used to determine the relative and absolute poverty of participating households. Although not strictly based on monetary indicators, these measures focus on an assessment of living standards of the poor (see for instance *Imp-Act*, 2003).

- *Index of Fulfilment of Basic Needs*: This focuses on four characteristics of households; namely housing, education, access to health services and access to public services (Navajas et al., 2000). Each dimension consists of clusters of observable proxies for access to public services, such as source of water, presence of an indoor toilet, access to electricity and type of fuel used to cook food. As with the Prizma Poverty Scorecard, it is multidimensional and it avoids direct relation to income as an informational space. And yet, it is interesting to note that most variables refer to a form of resource.

- *CASHPOR Housing Index*: This is a quick assessment method based on a classification of houses according to three characteristics; namely size, physical condition, or building and roofing materials. Gibbons and Meehan (2006, p. 6) illustrate the discriminatory powers of this index, noting how 'poor households tend to live in medium-sized houses with reinforced mud walls of between five and eight feet in height and having a permanent roof of used tiles. The poorest households live in small huts with mud walls of less than five feet with an impermanent roof of thatch.' Despite some general critiques that the Housing Index might be exposed to bias, its simplicity is remarkable.

- *Freedom from Hunger*: This consists of a set of methods that aim to assess absolute poverty. It distinguishes four food security scales (food secure, food insecure with hunger, moderate hunger, severe hunger), exploring the universal aspects of 'behaviors that consistently characterize the phenomenon of food insecurity and hunger, such as anxiety that food or money may be insufficient, the experience of running out of food without money for more, substituting fewer or cheaper foods, and reduced food intake, i.e., fewer and smaller meals' (*Imp-Act*, 2003, p. 9). Similar to the other tools, Freedom from Hunger stresses the importance of resources as an indicator of well-being. In this case, the emphasis is justified on the grounds of concern with absolute poverty.[7]

3.4   Negative mechanisms

Many mechanisms might prevent the poor from enjoying the benefits of microfinance. Evans and colleagues (1999) classify *barriers to participation* into two groups, namely 'programme-related barriers' and 'client-related barriers'. In the first group, they include insufficient supply of microcredit, high membership requirements, peer group expectations and institutional incentives. In the second group, they stress the role of insufficient resources, ill-health or vulnerability to crisis, a female head of household, lack of education, and individual and household preferences as mechanisms that could prevent the poor from participating and/or not benefiting from microfinance. These factors could be combined cumulatively, for instance when programme officers push repayment targets and go for more creditworthy groups (institutional incentives) and these further self-select the 'more reliable' among them (peer group expectations).

As Copestake, Bhalotra and Johnson (2001, p. 91) noted, under these circumstances the main impact of a group lending approach might be the simple shift of costs (screening, monitoring and enforcement costs) to clients. A similar situation is also characterized by Rahman (1999), who argues that debt-burden might create anxiety and tension among borrowers. As Rahman pointed out (1999, p. 68), 'At the level of grass-root credit operation, bank workers and peer group members inflict an intense pressure on borrowers for timely repayment, rather than working to raise collective responsibility and borrower empowerment as originally envisaged by the [Grameen] Bank.' The operation of loans by bank workers might be easier under microfinance, since the poor would sometimes deprive themselves of available resources in order to avoid humiliation or moral coercion.

Greeley (2003b) provides a classification according to which poor households might be underrepresented because of systematic programme exclusion or self-exclusion, or, in group models, exclusion by borrowers, as discussed above. Rahman (1999) addresses the issue of 'unintended consequences' of microfinance in cases in which women, forced to stay in the loan centre, disrupt household chores, generating tension and violence in the household. Due to already established power hierarchies, for instance 'in a situation where a woman pays off her outstanding loan but does not receive the subsequent new loan according to established practice (which is very common in the study area), she faces serious consequences of verbal aggression of physical assault from her spouse or male relatives' (Rahman, 1999, p. 73).

The poor might not welcome borrowing for many motives, characterizing self-exclusion. Whereas some features are related to the economic environment in which they live, others are associated with their individual reactions (such as attitudes towards risk). Mosley and Rock (2004, p. 474) contrast the behaviour of better-off individuals with poorer individuals, arguing that the latter are 'by direct observation and by the imperative of survival more likely to favour 'protectional' strategies which protect their livelihoods, involve minimal levels of risk and as a consequence also offer minimal levels of yield'. 'Protection' is seen as a major component of survival strategies. It is not only the fact that transaction costs might be higher to the poor, but also that their condition of poverty raises a different range of concerns and values.[8]

Risk aversion under conditions of deprivation is a rational behaviour that provides a homogeneous and continuous scale across different income levels. One can easily mathematize a relation between income levels and behaviour towards risk. Informational asymmetries stimulated by lower educational levels also provide a homogeneous and monotonic scale where behaviour can be assessed quantitatively according to particular control variables. However, it is interesting to note that poverty and poverty depth are associated with qualitative changes in behaviour that are rational, but discontinuous within different survival strategies. Evidence shows that 'the marginalisation and vulnerability of very poor people means that they often do not have the self-confidence to come forward on their own initiative' (*Imp-Act*, 2003, p. 6). Therefore, the most important precondition for the operation of the classical positive mechanism of microfinance (via business investments and income generation) seems to be absent in principle or taken for granted in the formulation of microfinance policies. The proposed solution is, in fact, the problem to be solved: how to foster initiative and confidence in the poor, when objective deprivation conditions suggest strategies that rationally point towards isolation, apathy and risk-aversion.

In general, most impact assessments of microfinance programmes (as seen above) are based on a resource view of well-being that does not confer any particular role to 'informational spaces' of agency, autonomy and choice in evaluating people's advantages. In particular, when examining the issue of poverty *depth*, most taxonomies simply view it as 'less of a common unit'; for example, resources or income. The 'space' of 'autonomy' comprises many features that are also important for an assessment of microfinance outreach. Issues of participation, power, self-confidence, initiative, independence and empowerment, among others, are quintessentially issues related to autonomous behaviour. They are also at the root of the 'capability approach'.

3.5   A capability perspective

In comparison to other value-based approaches, the capability approach (see, for instance, Sen, 1992 and 1999, and Nussbaum, 2000) includes in its informational space not only opulence, utilities, primary goods, rights, but also functioning and capabilities that individuals and groups have reason to value: valuable things that people are able to do.

This element of autonomy, as argued above, has been consistently raised in the microfinance literature. For instance, Copestake, Bhalotra and Johnson have noted that 'Microcredit is also consistent with a shift in thinking towards promotion of self-help and against welfare dependency' (2001, p. 81). Halder and Mosley report how microfinance has produced 'important improvements in *autonomy and social status* of the ultra-poor [original emphasis]' (2004, p. 404). Mosley and Rock (2004) show how married women expressed a sense of greater autonomy after gaining financial independence.

The capability approach acknowledges a pervasive human diversity in the characterization of individuals. There are many sources of diversity between human beings, from which Sen (1999, pp. 70–1) identifies as the most important those concerning:

- personal heterogeneities (e.g., levels of education, age, health status, etc);
- environmental diversities (e.g., political, related to the physical environment);

- variations in the social climate (e.g., local culture, norms, social capital);
- differences in relational perspectives (e.g. hierarchies, job-relations); and
- distribution within the family (e.g., concerning the equality of distribution of resources, fairness, prioritization).

As individuals are diverse, their capabilities cannot be measured solely in terms of the resources that they have available or over which they have command but need to be assessed also in terms of what they are capable of doing and being with these resources. The consequence of human diversity can be seen not only in the variation of income-*earning* ability of individuals but also in their income-*using* ability (Sen, 1999). Sen has stressed the degree of ability that individuals have in transforming resources in valuable functioning. This lesson seems to be fundamental to the debate on the poverty outreach of microfinance schemes.

Standard measures of poverty (based on one dollar a day or headcount measures) emphasize the use of resources as indicators of human well-being. Sen's argument about 'pervasive human diversity' provides the main justification for rejecting these measures as good proxies for assessing the impacts triggered by microfinance initiatives. Resources can be translated into different sets of functioning and without a proper analysis of control variables (sources of diversity), it is difficult to conclude that equal levels of resources are conducive to similar levels of well-being. Alternative measures based on living standards are surely an improvement, because they are multidimensional. The meaning of having one dollar a day may be very different for different people. Survival strategies and entrepreneurial behaviour depend not only on resources but on people's levels of education, self-confidence and autonomy.

Capabilities have an *intrinsic* and *instrumental* value. Capabilities are intrinsic when they are valued independently of their consequences. Capabilities are instrumental when they are valued dependent on their consequences. It is common to find capabilities that present both intrinsic and instrumental value. For instance, education is both important per se and relevant for its consequences in terms of labour productivity, health, and so on. Similarly, the financial service provision to the poor might be important for its intrinsic value, as argued by Matin et al. (2002).

From a capability perspective, poverty is a multidimensional deprivation of basic capabilities, lack of autonomy, weak agency, absence of choice and weak self-confidence. From a microfinance angle, poverty can be seen as lack of initiative and entrepreneurial skills, dependence and apathy. The poorest of the poor, quite often, live in isolation and the potential for building social capital and group lending ties might prove difficult. The challenge of microfinance is not simply to provide income for the poor, but allow conditions for them to develop their autonomy.

The trade-offs between outreach and sustainability is rooted in the fact that lending to the poor usually involves higher transaction costs due to the small size of loans and difficulty in accessing the poor. Features such as lack of collateral or aversion to risk do not help in forecasting *ex-ante* positive repayment rates. Gibbons and Meehan (2000, p. 4) feel though, that there is 'no necessary medium to long-term trade-off, as even among the poorest loan clients average loan size tends to increase considerably over the years, as clients prove their ability to repay and consequently have access to larger and/or multiple loans'.

Notes

1 'There is confusion about the concept of poverty, which can be grasped through different dimensions such as income, basic needs, capabilities or social exclusion, and different magnitudes like absolute and relative poverty or depth of poverty. This confusion has deepened since there is more dissatisfaction with income-based measures and multidimensional definitions have become more widely adopted' (*Imp-Act*, 2003, 6).

2 The logic of this investigation is corroborated by Mosley and Rock's (2004) acknowledgment that impact assessment depends on the particular concepts and measures used to estimate poverty.

3 Among them we could mention, for the sake of illustration, the following terms used in the literature to assess the poverty outreach of microfinance schemes: (i) 'moderate' vs. 'extreme' poverty (Khandker, 1998); (ii) the 'hard-core' poor vs. the poor (Hashemi, 1997); (iii) the 'middle' poor, the 'upper' poor and the 'core' poor (Hulme and Mosley, 1997); (iv) the 'economically active' poor (Robinson, 2001); (v) the 'near-poor' and the 'not-poor' (Remenyi and Quinones, 2000); (vi) the 'destitute', the 'extremely' poor, the 'moderately' poor, the 'vulnerable' poor and 'the ultra-poor'; (vii) the 'vulnerable non-poor', the 'working-poor' and the 'entrepreneurial' poor (Mosley and Rock, 2004); (viii) the 'economically-active' poor (Copestake, Bhalotra and Johnson, 2001); and (ix) the 'new' poor and the 'traditional' poor (*Imp-Act*, 2003) – to name just a few.

4 For instance, Chowdhury, Mosley and Simanowitz have referred to 'The experience that microfinance typically does not reach clients well below the poverty line' (2004, p. 292).

5 An 'informational space' refers here to a class of information that is considered to describe the well-being status of individuals. Examples of informational spaces include 'resources', 'primary goods', 'rights' or 'capabilities', among others.

6 As defined by Copestake and colleagues (2005, pp. 708–9), 'A poverty correlate is a household characteristic that reliably captures much of the variation in

income across different households.' The objective of poverty correlates is to estimate income poverty when data about income might not be very reliable.

7 The list could be extended with further references to other tools, such as the Participatory Wealth Ranking (PWR) or Detailed Geographic Targeting (PRADAN), but the principles used by these different tools would be very similar (i.e., they are based on non-monetary, multidimensional measure of living standards of the poor), allowing for some idiosyncratic variations (like the inclusion of environmental considerations in PRADAN's Geographic Targeting). For more on those tools, see *Imp-Act* (2003). A variety of selection criteria serve as proxies to inform the elaboration of eligibility standards. As pointed out earlier, the great majority of these criteria is resource-based.

8 Halder and Mosley (2004, p. 401) summarize the most important mechanisms, based on their case study with BRAC. Major reasons for not wanting a loan were fear of debt management due to their very small and uncertain cash flow which can be used for repayment. The other reason, as perceived by the beneficiaries, was that they do not have the capacity to cope with the risk of any investment which may ultimately create more debt. Many of the beneficiaries claimed, incorrectly, that they were not eligible to receive loans; they also alleged that 'unpleasant treatment' of defaulters by NGO staff also caused a spill-over effect among potential borrowers.

4
Achieving Poverty Outreach, Impact and Sustainability: Managing Trade-offs in Microfinance

Anton Simanowitz
Institute of Development Studies, Sussex

4.1 Introduction: combining social and financial objectives

There is a widespread belief that the social and financial objectives of microfinance operate in opposition to each other. This chapter questions the assumption that trade-offs between financial perform-ance and social impact are inevitable and fixed, and provides a framework for increasing performance towards social objectives in even the yield-orientated microfinance institutions (MFIs). This is in contrast to the earlier 'win-win' vision of MFIs which rapidly reach scale and outreach bringing about positive impacts on large numbers of the world's poor people, whilst at the same time becoming finan-cially self-sufficient and therefore no longer dependent on external funding.

As the 'win-win' vision of microfinance is difficult to achieve in prac-tice, there has been a tendency over the past years to emphasize the financial rather than the social objectives of microfinance. In a situation where donor support is linked to strictly applied timetables for the achievement of financial self-sufficiency, the very future of most MFIs depends on the realization of these goals. However, sustainability is in no way an end in itself: it is only valued for what it brings to the clients of microfinance.

There is a growing recognition that social performance – the effective translation of an MFI's social mission into practice – should be given equal prominence. At the core are questions about the trade-offs and choices combining financial with social objectives:

- *Which social objectives?* MFIs commonly seek to develop microenterprises, reduce poverty, reduce gender inequality or improve social equity. These objectives relate to who the MFI works with and the design of the programme to achieve these ends.
- *Who is served?* The decision about which people an MFI will work with (micro-entrepreneurs, poor people, women, excluded groups) relates directly to the social objectives. Decisions relating to outreach may result in operational challenges for the MFI. For example, more remote, marginalized or very poor people may be particularly challenging and costly to serve.
- *What kind of services?* Experience in working towards an MFI's social objectives may reveal opportunities for improved products or services that will lead to increased impacts. Again these may have implications for operational costs and efficiency, for example a more holistic and intensive (and expensive) intervention may achieve greater impact.
- *What level of financial viability?* Operational experience may point to possibilities for increasing financial performance. For example, a focus on clients who require larger loans, are geographically close and require little support is likely to achieve good financial performance, but may compromise both the social objectives of outreach to particular client groups and their impact.

Debates about the potential for microfinance to achieve social as well as financial goals are, however, hindered by a lack of information, in particular on social performance. Lack of information reinforces the tendency to go towards what is measurable and available in financial statements. Most MFIs respond more to financial than social signals and become more focused on achieving their financial rather than their social objectives. This chapter outlines some of the parameters that affect the nature of trade-offs between social and financial objectives in microfinance based on the experience of the *Imp-Act* programme, with a network of 30 partner organizations working together to improve both their individual performance towards their social mission as well as maintaining financial objectives. Five MFIs are discussed: SEF in South Africa, PRIZMA in Bosnia-Herzegovinia, CYSD and SHARE in India, and BRAC in Bangladesh. Each organization is committed to working towards maximizing the fulfilment of its social objectives, within the constraints of its chosen approach and context. They represent a range of approaches – from individual lending to solidarity groups and self-help groups, from minimalist to holistic, and from financially self-sufficient to subsidy dependent.

The following section examines the nature and extent of trade-offs. This is followed by a review of the techniques available to MFIs to manage their social performance. The final section looks into the implications for the microfinance industry's reporting on social performance and the justification of subsidy support for this purpose.

4.2   Trade-offs

Can MFIs achieve both social and financial performance?

To what degree have MFIs to date been successful in achieving a viable balance between social objectives – in particular poverty outreach and impact – and sustainability? Data from the *MicroBanking Bulletin* show that financially self-sufficient institutions working with very poor populations 'had a higher average financial self-sufficiency, adjusted return on assets and adjusted return on equity than the overall averages for the 66 institutions combined. In other words, the low-end institutions outperformed the overall sample of institutions reporting to the bulletin. It is possible to reach very poor people and be financially self-sufficient.'[1] This finding is supported by Woller and Schreiner who, analysing a sample of village banks, find that 'contrary to widespread beliefs, the empirical examination finds a robust positive relationship between financial self-sufficiency and depth of outreach' (2002, p. 4), that is, organizations working with poorer clients are more likely to be financially self-sufficient. This suggests that in certain circumstances a balance can be achieved and that there is no inherently inverse relationship between depth of poverty outreach and financial performance.

However, overall the answer is mixed. Certainly many MFIs have achieved financial self-sufficiency whilst also effectively serving poor people (Daley-Harris, 2003; Simanowitz with Walter, 2002). Looking more in depth at the social objectives a more complex picture emerges. Relatively few MFIs achieve significant depth of outreach; most reach clients who are just above or below the poverty line (moderately poor and vulnerable non-poor), rather than in the 'very poor' group significantly below the poverty line.[2] 'Mission drift' led to a polarization of views within the microfinance industry. Some view a lack of information about the poverty status of MFI clients as the primary barrier to effective depth of outreach and call for the development of cost-effective poverty assessment tools and financial incentives for MFIs to deepen their outreach. Others believe that market mechanisms will ensure that microfinance reaches those who can be cost-effectively served, and that targeting of poorer clients will lead to market distortions.[3]

In actual fact, the targeting of women shows in the majority of MFIs a possible 'win-win' situation in the pursuance of social and financial goals.[4] Targeting of women may achieve social benefits whilst at the same time increasing operational efficiency. For some MFIs the targeting of women is not premised on social objectives, but is for practical reasons – they are seen as more reliable in terms of loan repayment. However, women also tend to be poorer than men and more financially excluded, and many MFIs target women to increase their likelihood of creating positive impacts on the lives of their clients and their families.[5] Therefore an MFI that aims for 'gender outreach' in addition to or instead of 'poverty outreach' should score well on both social and financial performance.[6]

Understanding the nature of trade-offs

The fact that a balance can be achieved does not imply that it can be achieved in all contexts. In most operating environments the situation is unlikely to be so straightforward, and, as demonstrated by the data from the MIX, the relationship is clearly not linear. Within a certain set of parameters – defined by the MFI's operating environment, objectives and capacity – what balance can be achieved between objectives, and what would be the impact of giving greater emphasis to one objective over another?

It is essential to question how much the nature of the trade-offs described can be modified or compensated for by changes induced by MFI management or through the external environment. The central question is how much innovation and increasing efficiency can modify the nature of the trade-offs and increase the range of possible options.

No two MFIs operate in the same environment. The performance of an MFI is affected by a range of internal variables including staff education levels, staff incentives and management, working culture of the MFI, national salary norms and unionization, range of services provided, and resources spent on non-financial services and targeting. External factors include the regulatory environment, infrastructure and communications, security, population density, client education levels, market opportunities, clients' ability to productively use credit, client vulnerability to crises and shocks, and cultural factors including local norms and sanctions.

An MFI such as the Association for Social Advancement (ASA) in Bangladesh, which operates in a skilled but low-salaried labour market and works in densely populated areas, can charge lower interest rates than SEF in South Africa, where high wages and low population densities create a more difficult environment for balanced financial and social performance. Table 4.1 compares the operating environments of ASA and SEF, focusing in particular on how population density can affect loan officer portfolio, and the huge variation in the operating costs where average loan sizes are similar, but staff costs are hugely different.

Balancing social and financial objectives in programme design[7]

What can be achieved as social outcomes depends on both context and an MFI's objectives. The nature of poverty differs and the strategies necessary and costs incurred in addressing poverty vary. For example, SHARE is well adapted to the relatively high-potential area in India in which it operates, where there is a level of economic activity which allows for both growth in client livelihoods and rapid expansion of the microfinance model. It does not necessarily reach the poorest clients in its State, and certainly not in the country.

By contrast, CYSD, another MFI in India, applies a holistic approach to poverty reduction, and sees microfinance as one part of an intensive intervention designed to strengthen the livelihoods of the poorest. CYSD is a promoter of Self-Help Groups (SHGs), and aims to build the capacity of these groups to sustainably manage their own savings and credit in the future. The programme is intensive and achieves significant impacts on the relatively small numbers of clients.[8] CYSD works in one of India's most impoverished States, Orissa, and chooses to target remote and inaccessible 'tribal' communities. Many of their clients have few linkages to the monetary economy, and therefore have little potential to

Table 4.1   Factors affecting financial performance in different contexts

	SEF, South Africa	ASA, Bangladesh
Population density	42/km^2	949/km^2
Borrowers per loan officer	257	414
Average loan size	US$125	US$130
Average loan officer salary	US$250	US$95/month
Ratio salary/loan size	2	0.73
Effective interest rate	65%	25%

Note: US$ figures approximate due to exchange rate variations.

Sources: www.sef.co.za; ASA annual report 2003; World Bank development indicators (2003); Microfinance Network statistics, 2002.

productively use large amounts of credit. The intensive nature of CYSD's work, high operating costs and low economic potential of many of its clients means that CYSD is not able to operate in a financially sustainable way. It depends on donor support. However, this is a chosen strategy, not the result of poor management, and justified because of the depth of outreach and scale of impact.

PRIZMA, SEF and BRAC modified their approaches, adapting to their respective circumstances. PRIZMA in Bosnia-Herzegovina initiated a series of changes to ensure that the organization was better tailored to meet the needs of very poor people in terms of its services, staff incentives, and overall leadership and culture. These changes improved targeting, and also saw gains in financial performance by addressing the problem of client exit. It better positioned the organization in a highly competitive market. In PRIZMA's case there has been no net trade-off in terms of financial performance. As the approach is focused on excellent financial performance, it therefore gives little scope for more intensive or costly interventions. Poverty in Bosnia is a recent phenomenon resulting from war, and therefore PRIZMA is not facing the problem of chronic poverty which is prevalent in much of the developing world.

Small Enterprise Foundation (SEF) in South Africa found that conventional methods of achieving poverty outreach, such as offering small loan sizes, did not prevent the non-poor from becoming clients. A new, poverty-targeted programme was established, providing additional support for client motivation, business planning and ongoing business support. SEF has found that on balance, the poverty-focused programme is more costly to operate. The use of a poverty-targeting tool is costly, but it also allows for a better understanding of the needs of the clients reached, it builds staff motivation and serves to promote the work of the programme, which in turn allows for greater numbers of clients to be reached. SEF's experience also demonstrates that poverty focus can lead to positive and negative impacts on financial performance. SEF found that working with poorer and more vulnerable clients means a greater potential for client failure and the need for greater support from staff, but this is in part balanced by the greater loyalty of poorer clients leading to lower arrears and drop-out rates.

BRAC in Bangladesh uses a 'credit plus' approach, integrating a range of non-financial services.[9] BRAC's mainstream microfinance programme, the RDP (Rural Development Prtogramme), is financially self-sufficient. However, relative to local measures of poverty, the RDP excludes a significant proportion of very poor people. This led to the development of a separate grant-based programme, the Income Generation for

Vulnerable Group Development (IGVDG) Programme, designed to address the needs of very poor people by providing an integrated mix of food assistance, training and access to credit.[10] Further research on the position of the 'ultra poor' and the reasons for their exclusion from the IGVDG led to the launching of another experimental programme.[11] Both IGVDG and the programme for the ultra poor rely on subsidies. However, some of the very poor people supported through grants are potential future clients for the mainstream (sustainable) credit pro-gramme. Two-thirds of IGVDG clients graduate to BRAC's mainstream microfinance programmes (Sultan, 2002).

These three cases demonstrate contextually appropriate but different institutional responses to poverty. In Bosnia-Herzegovinia, poverty is largely a consequence of recent war. This means there are high levels of education and physical client assets and that PRIZMA is able to increase its depth of poverty outreach without compromising financial perform-ance. In South Africa, the economic conditions are such that even clients with no previous business experience are able to productively use credit. SEF is consequently able to work with some of the poorest people in the country and also maintain good if not 'best practice' financial performance. SEF has thus made a deliberate choice to place greater emphasis on its social objectives even though this may be to the detri-ment of its financial performance. Finally, BRAC's pursuit of its poverty reduction mission has led it to try to address the needs of people in chronic poverty who are excluded from the mainstream microfinance programme. In this case BRAC has determined that grants are needed to reach these people, only some of whom are likely to become clients of its mainstream credit programme.

MFIs that target poor households may inadvertently exclude their target clients. Exclusion of very poor people, for example, may occur because of systematic programme exclusion, self-exclusion, or, especially in group-based models, exclusion effectively determined by other bor-rowers (Simanowitz with Walter, 2002). The focus of MFI performance management systems on financial objectives demonstrates how this process of exclusion may occur. Staff incentive schemes that emphasize portfolio outstanding or numbers of loans disbursed provide incentives for loan officers to target experienced clients who need little support and who will require relatively large loans or make large savings deposits. Poorer clients with little business experience and the need for relatively small loans are likely to be excluded. In addition, targets such as achieving high rates of repayment may create conflict amongst group members, or force clients into debt with moneylenders to repay the MFI.

Since many MFIs do not collect basic social performance data, such as the poverty level of their clients, MFIs are often unaware of the impact of these incentives and cannot correct the 'mission drift'.

Through analysis and programme design, greater depth of outreach can be achieved. This can, but must not always affect financial performance.

4.3 Managing trade-offs

MFIs can manage their social and financial performance, extend the frontiers and adjust the balance of social and financial objectives by adjusting products, services, organizational culture, staff incentives and management systems. This requires information. For financial performance this is available, but measures of social performance are at an early stage of development.[12] Given a lack of social performance data, MFIs often have to make operational decisions based on financial performance alone. Consequently they are much more likely to respond to financial pressures and signals in their management information systems, and to make decisions that tend to prioritize financial over social objectives.

MFI managers need information for day-to-day and strategic decisions on social and financial performance. Table 4.2 presents a possible decision-making tool, which combines social and financial information, in this

Table 4.2 Framework for comparing financial and social performance

	Product A					Product B				
	− −	−	0	+	+ +	− −	−	0	+	+ +
Financial										
Portfolio outstanding										
Average loan size										
Staff productivity										
Arrears										
Savings (amounts and regularity)										
Social										
Reaching target market										
Client loyalty (drop-out)										
Client satisfaction										
Benefits										
Individual and household										
Wider community										

case comparing the results of the piloting of two new loan products, A and B. Information is given on the nature and the relative magnitude (neutral, small, large) of any trade-off between financial performance and social impacts. Such information would allow managers to make more informed decisions in their day-to-day performance management. It would also allow for decisions to be made where trade-offs exist between social and financial objectives, for example allowing for donor investment in activities that yield high social and low financial returns.

SEF in South Africa uses a framework similar to the model in Table 4.2 (Roper, 2003). Based on a client monitoring system which produces regular reports on a range of poverty and impact indicators, it is used by clients, field staff and management as part of its strategic and operational decision-making. SEF tracks social and poverty-related indicators from all clients on each loan cycle. These are entered into a computerized management information system (MIS) and allow for specific patterns of impact to be analysed.

This analysis can help shed light on differences in performance between branches or between loan officers; differences in performance depending on the time of year a loan is given, or based on the total amount of money disbursed or the loan size given, or for combinations of loans; differences in performance for clients at different poverty levels or depending on age or marital status; patterns of client drop-out; characteristics of clients who are performing well in terms of financial performance and/or in terms of impact; and on characteristics of branches or staff that are performing well, as illustrated in Table 4.3.

PRIZMA undertakes a similar process of management of its social performance, focusing on two key social objectives – outreach to very

Table 4.3   Client information collected by SEF

Operational performance	Operational input variables	Client status variable	Client performance variables
• Client drop-out • Growth in average loan size • Arrears	• Area • Branch • Loan officer • Loan cycle • Loan size (cumulative loan amounts; increase in loan size) • Loan use • Combinations of loans	• Poverty score • Age of clients • Household size • Marital status • Sex • Number/age/sex of dependents	• Change in poverty score • Impact indicators (housing, food, education, business value) • Savings (amount, regularity) • Attendance at centre meetings

poor people, and ensuring low client exit rates. These are translated into performance objectives, which form part of organizational and branch performance appraisal, and are included in the annual auditor's management letter. In addition PRIZMA uses its MIS to segment its portfolio in relation to poverty outreach, and is thus able to identify patterns, trends and issues to investigate. This performance management system enables PRIZMA to maintain a strong poverty focus in its work, and provides detailed and timely information for decision-making.

BRAC's approach to managing its social performance has been more incremental. BRAC's focus has been to understand how certain client groups use its services, and why others are excluded or fail to benefit from using the services. In response to this, BRAC has developed new products and services, and has designed new and appropriate delivery mechanisms for different target client groups. A clear understanding of the needs of different people and the costs for delivering appropriate services has allowed BRAC to differentiate three programmes, each with a different mandate and cost structure. Clear information allows for appropriate design and delivery.

4.4 Conclusions

The notion of 'best practices', may well mask the complexity of microfinance and its trade-offs. Standardized assessments do not always fully take of account the operating environment or the social benefits that may result from investment in an MFI with strong social objectives. A common framework could provide benchmarks and standards for social performance. The work of *Imp-Act* suggests that it is possible and cost-effective for MFIs to design systems for monitoring and assessing their outreach performance, 'social performance rating criteria and benchmarks'.[13] Such systems should clearly state the social objectives in relation to its target group, and outline how the specific strategy of the MFI is likely to achieve the stated objectives. They should also assess the profile of the clients actually reached by the programme and how clients use the services provided by the MFI. The latter should include disaggregation of patterns of use by different client groups as well as an assessment of whether the services meet client needs, of client satisfaction, and of the reasons why some clients leave the programme or become inactive. In addition, monitoring systems should cover changes in client status in relation to social objectives, such as changes in poverty status, increased empowerment or enterprise growth. Given the interest in understanding the contribution of microfinance towards the fulfilment of the Millennium Development Goals, there is an opportunity to create a standardized framework of social indicators to which MFIs can report.[14] Finally, any such system should also describe how social performance information is used to improve the services of the MFI and show how the quality of information is ensured and the system improved.

Notes

1 Didier Thys, former director of the MIX, quoted in Daley-Harris, 2003, p. 8. It is important to note that the MIX is not a representative sample of MFIs, but represents the more financially successful organizations that voluntarily report detailed financial data to the MIX.

2 At the time of writing, the *MicroBanking Bulletin* received data from 231 MFIs that report to the MIX. Of these, 139 are financially self-sufficient, 18 of whom reach very poor clients, and 78 of whom serve poor clients (as defined by average loan balances below 20 per cent of GNI per capita and between 20 and 150 per cent of GNI per capita, respectively (for more information, see www.themix.org); Hulme and Mosley, 1996; Sebstad and Cohen, 2001.

3 See discussions around the US Microenterprise Self Reliance Act, which says that 50 per cent of all US funding for microenterprises be targeted to the very poor. www.microfinancegateway.org

4 According to the Microcredit Summit of 2002, 79 per cent of microfinance clients worldwide are women.

5 Cheston and Kuhn (2002) provide a detailed discussion about the theories, assumptions and reality behind the targeting of women in microfinance. These fall into five categories: greater poverty of women; women spend more of their income on their families; efficiency and sustainability of microfinance institutions; women's equal access to financial resources as a human rights issue; and as a means or entry point in the empowerment of women.

6 However, just 'working with women' does not necessarily maximize the potential of microfinance to achieve social impacts such as gender equity. A simple focus on providing financial services to women may or may not lead to positive gender changes such as women's empowerment (Cheston and Kuhn, 2002; Mayoux, 2000).

7 This section draws on a similar analysis presented by Greeley (2003a and 2003b), which discusses the nature of the poverty reduction approaches adopted by members of the *Imp-Act* Thematic Group, Microfinance for the Very Poor. The ideas in this section owe much to the work of this group.

8 Figures for 2002 show that CYSD was reaching over 10,500 clients in 373 villages and seven urban slums.

9 The nature of BRAC's structure, which includes a range of development, technical and marketing services, means that the costs of these non-financial services are not fully covered by the microfinance programme.

10 For further information, see CGAP Focus Note 21, 'Linking Microfinance and Safety Net Programs to the Poorest: The Case of IGVGD in Bangladesh', at: www.cgap.org

11 Households consuming less than 1800kcal per person.
12 For information about the International Social Performance Taskforce and initiatives taking place to monitor, assess and manage social performance refer to www.microfinancegateway.org/resource_centers/socialperformance and www.Imp-Act.org
13 See *Imp-Act* Guidelines for Social Performance Management in Microfinance.
14 This framework is currently being developed by CGAP and the MIX.

5
Smart Subsidies*

Jonathan Morduch
New York University

5.1 Introduction

'Smart subsidy' might seem like a contradiction in terms to many microfinance experts. Worries about the dangers of excessive subsidization have been central to microfinance conversations since the movement first gained steam in the 1980s. From then on, the goal of serving the poor has been twinned with the goal of long-term financial self-sufficiency on the part of microbanks: aiming for profitability became part of what it means to practise good microfinance. The influential 'Pink Book', a newly reformulated set of 'donor guidelines on good practice in microfinance', for example, includes the idea that 'microfinance can pay for itself, and must do so if it is to reach very large numbers of people. Unless microfinance providers charge enough to cover their costs, they will always be limited by the scarce and uncertain supply of subsidies from donors and governments.'[1]

The appropriate role of subsidies, it has been argued repeatedly, is thus minimal: for the most part, subsidies are to be limited to start-up funding of new institutions, after which they should be withdrawn.[2] As the Pink Book puts it: 'Donor subsidies should be temporary start-up support designed to get an institution to the point where it can tap private funding sources, such as deposits' (CGAP, 2004a, p. 1).

Anti-subsidy lines are starting to soften, though, and practitioners argue that if continuing subsidies are available, they would be foolish not to take advantage of them.[3] Even well-established commercial banks happily accept subsidies when offered. How should such subsidies be designed then? And when can they be used most effectively?

The idea of 'smart subsidy' springs from the premise that subsidies are neither inherently useful nor inherently flawed. Rather, their effectiveness depends on design and implementation. Smart subsidies are interventions designed to maximize social benefits while minimizing distortions and mistargeting. A beginning point is recognition that the same forces driving efficient outcomes in free markets – that is, hard budget constraints, clear bottom lines and competitive pressure – can also be deployed in contexts with subsidies. If deployed well, subsidies can increase the scale of microfinance outreach, increase access to commercial finance, and increase depth of outreach to the poor. By the same token, over-reliance on subsidies and poorly designed subsidies can limit scale and undermine incentives critical to building strong institutions.

The discussion in this chapter first puts the issue of subsidies and microfinance into historical perspective (Section 5.2). The following section raises issues around valuing subsidies with an emphasis on accounting for opportunity costs and risk. The potential to 'crowd in' other donor funds provides one way a subsidy can be 'smart' (Section 5.3). Additional elements of smart subsidy – that avoid dependence on donors – are then described. Particular emphasis is put on subsidies that are transparent, rule-bound and time-limited. Section 5.4 draws conclusions.

5.2   Subsidies and microfinance

Arguments against subsidizing banking are not new. In 1973, for example, the United States Agency for International Development (USAID) rolled out a 20-volume study of efforts to improve rural credit markets abroad, the USAID *Spring Review of Small Farmer Credit*. The *Spring Review* was a mammoth effort involving over 50 consultants and USAID staff, oriented around case studies of subsidy-dependent state banks. John Hatch, founder of FINCA, described the *Spring Review* as 'a multi-volume anthology of lending disasters. From one country paper to another one finds mention of exceptionally high levels of uncollectible loans, negligent loan supervision, preferential attention to larger farmers, minimal coverage of the potentially eligible farm population, and many other common problems.'[4] Most of the problems were traced back to a lack of the kinds of incentives that competition forces onto commercial banks.

The *Spring Review* was followed by a series of books published by the World Bank in the 1980s, again pointing to the abuse of subsidies and the lack of incentives in state-supported banks (see, for example, Adams, Graham and Von Pischke, 1984). Subsidies were depicted as an impediment to serving the poor, despite the high-minded rhetoric that defended their use. The poor would do better, it was argued, by allowing capitalism to work without intervention. In the 1990s anti-subsidy ideas provided the context for early discussions around microfinance policy, and they were contemporaneous with a view on microfinance that was coalescing at USAID and heavily influenced by the Ohio State University (e.g., Adams, Graham and Von Pischke, 1984; Adams and Von Pischke, 1992). One line draws on the logic of the *Spring Review* and its follow-ons: dependence on subsidies subverts incentives for efficiency and professionalism in financial institutions.

The evidence abounds. China, for example, heavily subsidizes its rural banks in the name of poverty reduction and development. Cheng Enjiang (2003) estimates that, largely as a result, the delinquent loan rate of small loans delivered through the state Rural Credit Cooperatives was about 35–40 per cent and that the on-time repayment rate for government 'poverty loans' was about 50 per cent. Similar examples have been played out in Latin America, Africa, and elsewhere in Asia.

An independent second line reinforced the first. It bows to the reality that aid budgets are limited, so dependence on subsidies means severely limiting the scale of microfinance. Only tapping purely commercial funding sources, it is argued, will permit massive scale. If one does not fully accept the first argument, it seems hard to deny the second. The donor consortium CGAP, the Consultative Group to Assist the Poorest, has long argued that scale is equated directly with poverty reduction – that is, that reducing subsidies should be supported on pure *equity* grounds. Based on a non-random sample of 11 programmes (and using the unreliable but easy-to-calculate metric of average loan size to gauge depth of outreach) CGAP's *Focus Note* 2 of 1995 argued that 'among high-performing programmes there is no clear trade-off between reaching the very poor and reaching large numbers of people. It is scale, not exclusive focus, that determines whether significant outreach to the poorest will occur.'[5]

The syllogism proceeds thus: large programmes can reach the very poor. Being financially self-sufficient is the route to assure a large scale. Thus, being financially self-sufficient is the best way to reach the very poor. This is a complicated argument built on a series of assumptions for which there was little solid evidence at the time (for an analysis, see Morduch, 2000). All the same, it helped to tie notions of pro-poor microfinance tightly to a vision of 'financial sustainability'.

Twenty years later, the anti-subsidy position has softened at the World Bank in general, and in microfinance circles specifically. Partly, the softening is driven by a growing concern with global poverty reduction by policy-makers, prodded by the quest to reach the UN Millennium

Development Goals. Recent studies show that microfinance serves poor and low-income households, but has weak outreach to the 'very poor'. Studies completed as part of legislation mandated by the US Congress show that in Peru, Kazakhstan and Uganda, roughly 15 per cent of microfinance customers were among the 'poorest half' of the poor, as defined by the official poverty lines in their countries. In Bangladesh, 44 per cent were found to be among the 'poorest', a figure lower than expected. Not everyone is equally concerned about the plight of the poorest (or agrees that microfinance is the best tool to reach the poorest), but the failure to achieve deeper outreach has been a growing policy concern, especially within the UN system.[6] The question is raised as to when (smart) subsidies can help.

The shifting view on subsidies is also driven by the fact that subsidies, for good or bad, are in fact an ongoing part of microfinance. The reality is that much of the microfinance movement continues to take advantage of subsidies – some from donors, some from governments, and some from charities and concerned individuals. The *MicroBanking Bulletin* of July 2003, for example, shows that 66 out of 124 microlenders surveyed were financially sustainable, a rate just over half. For microlenders focusing on the 'low-end', just 18 of 49 were financially sustainable as of the July 2003 accounting, a 37 per cent rate. On one hand, the data show that even programmes reaching poorer clients can do so while covering the full costs of transactions. But, on the other hand, the norm remains subsidization.[7]

A third reason for a softening of the anti-subsidy position arises from analytical concerns. The propositions put forward against subsidies were best seen as rules of thumb, and as time has passed, the need for analytical nuance became clearer. With greater analytical clarity, possibilities for effective and efficient subsidization have emerged. In particular, five claims have been re-examined:

- Subsidized credit does not equal 'cheap credit' (meaning credit at interest rates well below rates available elsewhere in the local credit market) and the poor incentives that ensue. The early attacks on subsidized state banks centred (justifiably) on their 'cheap credit' policies – interest rates on loans that were sometimes negative in inflation-adjusted terms and small if positive (e.g., Adams, Graham and Von Pischke, 1984). But the jump from criticizing 'cheap credit' to criticizing other kinds of subsidies has been recognized as being too great a leap. Today, cheap credit is a well-understood problem, and a first principle of smart subsidies is to avoid cheap credit.

- Profitability does not equal efficiency. New data show that efficiency (lean management structures, low unit loan costs, high numbers of loans per staff member) depends largely on giving staff the right incentives and using information well. *The MicroBanking Bulletin*, for example, shows highly efficient institutions that are subsidized, as well as some that are profit-making. It also shows profit-making institutions that are not particularly efficient.
- Profitability does not equal sustainability (as judged by the ability to survive over time). Consider a programme that enjoys a temporary monopoly, charges high rates, and posts profits. It will be 'financially sustainable' according to the standard measures. But the bank is vulnerable to new entrants who may skim off good clients and undermine the long-term viability of the business. In comparison, a well-run but subsidized microbank may well be more viable over the long term.[8] A realistic long-term strategy is what matters most, and this is not reflected in snapshot measures of current profitability. Profitability does not guarantee large scale, nor does subsidization necessarily limit it.
- Profitability does not guarantee access to commercial finance, nor does lack of profitability necessarily foreclose such access. In the United States, for example, most universities and hospitals operate on a not-for-profit basis, but many obtain commercial financing for parts of their operations.[9] Similarly, microfinance institutions routinely mix funding sources – some subsidized, some at commercial rates.
- 'Subsidizing the microfinance institution' is not distinct from subsidizing customers. All subsidies ultimately aid customers, so often-repeated directives to 'subsidize the institution, not the customers' only have meaning in narrowly prescribed circumstances. Donor guidelines include: 'Donors should focus their support on building capacity' (CGAP, 2004). But, holding all else the same, where funds are fungible, the ultimate consequence is the reduction of costs that must be passed on to customers.

While these arguments point to the possibility for the constructive use of subsidy, how and when should it be done?

5.3   Valuing subsidies

Subsidies have financial costs to donors. In the case of a grant, the cost is simply the value of the grant. In the case of a soft loan, the 'opportunity cost' must be factored in. The true cost of a soft loan is the size of the loan multiplied by the difference between the expected return from the recipient organization (assuming that there is a return) and the return in the next-best use of the funds (i.e., the opportunity cost). Soft loans also carry risk, and costs should account for risk of non-payment or delayed payment as well as the risk of currency fluctuations. Loan guarantees are becoming more common, and they also carry costs – for example, from the necessity of setting aside reserves and from expected losses. These costs are not always explicit, but should be counted.[10]

The value of the subsidy for the donor and for the recipient need not be the same. Consider a donor whose funds can earn 10 per cent per year if invested in the stock market. Instead, the donor makes a 'soft' investment in a microfinance institution with a return of 2 per cent per year. The implicit cost for the donor (ignoring risk and inflation) is the difference between the two returns – that is, 8 per cent per year. For the recipient, though, the value depends on the cost of *their* next-best source of funds. If that cost is, say, 20 per cent per year, then the net value of the loan is the difference between 20 and 2 – that is, a saving of 18 per cent of the loan size per year.

But if the next-best source of funds is, say, mobilizing deposits from customers, and if doing so comes at a unit cost of 8 per cent per year, the net financial gain to the recipient of getting a soft loan at 2 per cent is far smaller: just 6 per cent per year. In this latter case, the soft loan has two strikes against it. First, the donor gives disincentives to mobilize savings. Second, the donor would be able to transfer more net resources by giving a grant (in an amount equal to 8 per cent multiplied by the size of the loan) rather than by actually making the loan. In getting a grant, the recipient institution would still have incentives to mobilize savings, but would also get extra help from the donor. If the donor was particularly keen on seeing savings volumes rise, he could go further and design the grant as an explicit match against new savings mobilized.

The examples show that the design of smart subsidies hinges on taking into account the multiple sources of funds available to recipients (other loans, savings, equity) – and the multiple alternative uses of funds available to donors. Smart subsidies thus begin with a reckoning of 'opportunity costs' for all participants.

The idea translates to the social dimension as well. Calculating implicit financial costs is only one part of valuing subsidies. The other part is to calculate the broader social costs and benefits. Here, the relevant notion is the 'social opportunity cost'. Social benefits include the jobs created, income raised, school attended, and so on, that the social investment generates directly. Social opportunity costs are the foregone social benefits from making the social investment under consideration rather than using the funds in a different way. It's the social value of the next-best project. The net social value of a given investment is the difference between the direct social benefits expected and the social opportunity cost. Donors thus should have a reckoning both of the expected social benefits of investing in the given project and the social benefits generated by alternative investments. A full-blown cost-benefit analysis is unnecessary, but cost-effectiveness analysis (where a given objective – like poverty reduction – is maximized per dollar invested) provides a natural frame.

5.4 'Crowding in' and 'crowding out'

Implicit in the above is the notion that donor funds typically constitute just one part of overall financing for a development finance institution. Given this context, donors use their resources more effectively when they act as catalysts for additional resources. The idea is to 'crowd in' funding, rather than to crowd it out.

Providing guarantees is a good example (or offering subordinated debt in which the donor is willing to be repaid after other lenders are repaid). Consider the case of a recent securitization deal between India's largest private bank, ICICI, and the microlender SHARE Microfin Ltd.[11] In order for ICICI to agree to pay for a portfolio of 42,500 loans served by SHARE (SHARE continues to service the loans, but interest and principal go to ICICI), ICICI required protection against unexpected loan losses. ICICI demanded an 8 per cent first loss guarantee. If customers refused to repay SHARE, ICICI did not want to be left vulnerable. The eventual deal emerged when the Grameen Foundation funded most of the required guarantee by giving SHARE US$325,000 in capital. SHARE, for its part, contributed approximately US$25,000. The loan portfolio was valued at US$4.3 million, so the guarantee amounted to 8 per cent of that (i.e., US$344,000).

The Grameen Foundation's US$325,000 was thus used to 'crowd in' an additional US$4.3 million from ICICI. While ICICI receives the profit from its shares, SHARE gains by spreading its risk and getting an immediate capital infusion. In this case, subsidy helped to attract commercial capital – not only that, it was pivotal in finalizing the deal. The experience undercuts the simple idea that subsidization and commercial capital are at odds. Here, in fact, they are complementary.

Guarantees are powerful not just because they reduce risk for other potential investors. They can also be powerful when they signal information about the recipient's strength and efficiency. Presumably, the Grameen Foundation went into the deal with SHARE and ICICI after reckoning that the risks were not excessive. By putting their money behind that belief, the Grameen Foundation could signal to outsiders that SHARE was an institution in which it is worth investing.

Similarly, simply making a substantial loan to an organization can signal a belief in the strength of the institution, and being willing to accept subordinated debt status goes even further. In the decision to make a grant versus a loan or guarantee, the latter two options mean bearing risk. Rather than avoiding risk, the donor can signal their belief in the strength of the institution by deliberately accepting risk. This is 'smart' as long as the donor's perceptions are indeed right.[12]

The other way that donors crowd in other investors is by providing broad oversight (and perhaps even joining the board) of the recipient institution. If the donor has a strong reputation for prudent leadership and oversight, their involvement is likely to provide additional incentives for other investors to participate, even commercial investors.[13] Again, the donor not only brings subsidies but also the ability to crowd in other investors.

Reducing dependence

So far, the discussion has considered the broad picture of investment strategies. Here, a few examples are given of the potentially 'smart' design of specific subsidies. One fear, touched on above, is that subsidization can create dependence on donors. In this case, incentives for recipient institutions to cut costs would be undermined. Dependence, though, is largely a problem of design. A well-designed subsidy can provide incentives to cut costs.

Consider the case of a voucher programme in Chile.[14] The government would, say, auction US$1 million-worth of vouchers. One voucher would be worth US$1,000 if the holder could show that they had made a successful loan to a poor household. The vouchers were auctioned and sold to the development finance institution that bid highest. Say that an institution successfully bid US$900,000 for the vouchers. This means that the bank paid US$900 of its own money to make a US$1,000 loan.

How does this affect the institution's returns? If the bank charges an interest rate of 20 per cent interest on a US$1000 loan, the bank nets US$1200 – $900, taking into account the US $900 cost of the voucher. The return on the loan is (US$1200 – US$900)/US$900 = 33 per cent. The advantage of the auction is that it ensures that the institution with the lowest costs is the one that gets the vouchers.

Another important mechanism to reduce the risk of dependence is to make sure that subsidies are time-limited. A common example is start-up subsidies, and that notion is extended below.

Start-up subsidies for institutions

The Pink Book privileges start-up subsidies for institutions, limited to the first five to ten years of operation. Start-up subsidies have the advantage of being time-limited and relatively transparent. By restricting the subsidies to a limited period, the fear of dependency is diminished. This rule-based aspect of the subsidy reduces the weak incentives created by soft budget constraints – that is, that recipients will not face the consequence of failing to achieve financial targets. Here, instead, the donor makes clear that the subsidies are only available for a short time, after which the institution is expected to become self-sufficient.

The common goal is to allow institutions to immediately charge customers fees and interest rates at levels that would only be feasible once the institution reaches a larger scale. In the start-up stage, the subsidies make up shortfalls – and thus are, in fact, subsidies of the customer, not the institution.

The logic is clear. It's fair to ask, though, what 'start-up' really means. If 'start-up' subsidies are appropriate when an institution is just building its first branches, why would they be less appropriate when the institution chooses to expand to a wholly new area where it has to build up, essentially, from scratch? In the very beginning, when building the first branch, there is, of course, much learning-by-doing that must be done, and the subsidies are particularly helpful. Later expansion should be easier, and a prudent institution will put aside a part of current earnings to fund future expansion. All the same, a donor may be able to hasten the expansion process by broadening the notion of 'start-up' subsidy to cover major expansions – without creating important incentive problems.

Start-up subsidies for customers

One of the reasons that start-up subsidies are justified is that it takes time for an institution to achieve scale economies. To a degree this is true when working with new clients too – at any stage in the life of an institution. New clients generally start with the smallest loans, and such loans tend to have high transaction costs per unit.

At BRAC in Bangladesh, for example, initial loans to new customers are so small (just 2500 taka) that BRAC loses money servicing them at the given interest rate (15 per cent charged on a flat basis, roughly equivalent to a 30 per cent per year effective interest rate). At loan sizes of 4000 taka and more, BRAC can recover costs with interest earnings, but not at 2500 taka. BRAC calculates that it cross-subsidizes at a rate of 225 taka on a 2500 taka loan, suggesting that BRAC would need to raise effective interest rates by about 9 percentage points for small loans. BRAC's management, though, fears that effective interest rates of 40 per cent would be unaffordable for the poorest borrowers and could undermine social goals.

The subsidies (actually 'cross-subsidies' in this case) are not associated with 'cheap credit' and all of the negative trappings that entails. Instead, they are strategically deployed and targeted to aid the poorest customers. While it may be possible to use cross-subsidization to cover the extra costs of small loans (using profits from larger loans to offset losses on smaller loans), cross-subsidization runs into trouble when competitors swoop in and steal away top customers with the lure of cheaper interest rates, a problem that happened most dramatically in Bolivia in the late 1990s. A 'smart subsidy' could be designed that is restricted to new customers with small loans only; to be smart, it would have to be time-delimited, rule-bound and transparent. It should also be verified that the subsidy does not give the recipient institution an unfair competitive advantage over others in the market – a highly unlikely prospect in this context.

BRAC used a version of this approach in designing their Income Generation for Vulnerable Group Development (IGVGD) programme, which subsidized potential clients who were not yet ready to borrow from microlenders at 'market' interest rates. First, BRAC argued, they needed training and time to build businesses to a minimum scale. This initiative was built around a food aid scheme sponsored by the World Food Programme. The resources of the food aid programme were integrated into a programme that provided both 18 months of food subsidies and half a year of skills training, with the aim of developing new livelihoods for the chronically poor. Participants were also expected to start saving regularly in order to build discipline and an initial capital base. When the training programme was completed, households were expected to be able to 'graduate' into BRAC's regular programmes.

The programme focused on households headed by women who own less than a half-acre of land and earn less than 300 taka ($6) per month. The training included skills like livestock raising, vegetable cultivation and fishery management. After an 80 per cent success rate in a pilot programme with 750 households, BRAC rolled out the programme throughout Bangladesh, and IGVGD had served 1.2 million households by 2000.[15] A follow-up study by Imran Matin and David Hulme (2003) showed that the programme was associated with a dramatic increase in income for households just after completing the programme. But within another three years, average income had fallen by nearly 60 per cent from its peak. Part of the cause was that when the food subsidy was removed, households sold business assets and used BRAC loans to purchase food rather than invest in businesses, leaving households not much better off than they had been in the beginning. Matin and Hulme thus argue for additional measures that help households from slipping back and that account for the different speeds at which households progress.

Syed Hashemi, though, stresses that we should not lose sight of the fact that two-thirds of IGVGD participants graduate successfully to regular microfinance programmes, although it is not clear how to best support the remaining third (and the 10 per cent of applicants rejected for being old, disabled or otherwise unpromising in microbusiness).

The subsidies at BRAC are not large in the scheme of things. Taken together, Hashemi (2001) estimates that IGVGD subsidies amount to about 6725 taka (about $135 in 2001). The largest component is 6000 taka for the food subsidy (provided by the World Food Programme), and the remainder is about 500 taka for training costs and 225 taka to support small initial loans to participants (the first loans are typically about $50). For $135 per participant, BRAC aims to forever remove the need for participants to require future hand-outs. To achieve that aim, efforts to ensure sustainable impacts must be implemented and success rates improved, but, even as it stands, the IGVGD is an important model for other programmes. BRAC itself has launched a new initiative, Targeting the Ultrapoor, that builds on the IGVGD and also combines training and subsidies for the very poor.

5.5   Conclusions

The arguments against subsidies spring from fears that they would undermine the long-term viability of microfinance and limit its scale. There is plenty of evidence to suggest why: badly designed subsidies have too often led to inefficiency, dependence, and a failure to effectively meet the needs of the poor. But economic analysis also shows that in principle, subsidies in modern microfinance can be well designed. And, if so, they can be part of efforts to achieve meaningful transformations in the lives of clients, without sacrificing the integrity of the institution. Doing it well in practice remains the ongoing challenge. The great number of subsidized programmes that can boast impressive efficiency benchmarks and high repayment rates gives cause for optimism, though.

But even if the case for strategic subsidies is stronger than microfinance advocates have let on, arguments for financially sustainable microfinance continue to have power. One concern is with incentives. While subsidies can help outreach to poor clients, there is always a fear that subsidies make institutions flabby. By subsidizing costs, pressure is removed that would have otherwise pushed management to seek efficiency gains and to experiment with new procedures. 'Dynamic efficiency' may thus be sacrificed in the cause of reducing inequality in the short term. Donors should be prepared to tackle the problem head on and condition receipt of future funds on the achievement of realistic efficiency goals. The objective, in principle, is to maintain 'hard budget constraints' rather than allowing constraints to soften, but this is easier to say than to do.

Another concern is that relying on subsidies can inherently limit the scale of operations. There are times when this is certainly so, and it would be advantageous to serve more people with less subsidy. But, by the same token, there will be times when advantages flow from serving fewer people, but are reaching out to the poorest and most underserved. In practice, the trade-offs may not in fact be so stark. BRAC's collaboration with the World Food Programme, for example, shows that using subsidies can actually *expand* the scale of outreach (and not just help with depth of outreach).

A third concern is with innovation: the donors' strong push for financial sustainability has forced some microlenders to devise innovations to slash subsidies – a feat thought to be impossible before. Such 'induced innovation' (Esther Boserup, 1990) suggests that the static framework of cost-benefit analyses may overstate the benefits of subsidies: when push comes to shove, some programmes have shown that the subsidies are less vital than once thought.

A final concern emerges from a world in which donors (and the tax-payers who fund them) tend to grow restless and eager to move on to the next project and a new set of concerns. In the 'rational' analytical world where decisions are made according to cost-benefit analyses, there is no space for 'donor fatigue'. Instead, if a programme is shown to be worthy of support year after year (and this is not yet nailed down with respect to microfinance), it should get support year after year. But donors and practitioners are well aware that the actual world looks different, and their warning is that microlenders need to prepare for the day when subsidies disappear as donors choose to move on. If there is no source of subsidy, then there can be no meaningful debate on their use. One hope of smart subsidy is that not only will better design of subsidy enhance the effectiveness of donor investments, but, in doing so, smart subsidy may also encourage greater levels of overall donor support.

Notes

* A revised version of an early version of this chapter, titled 'Subsidy and sustainability', was published as Chapter 9 of *The Economics of Microfinance*, ed. Beatriz Armendáriz de Aghion and Jonathan Morduch (Cambridge, MA: The MIT Press, 2005). Parts of the present chapter have been distilled as 'Smart subsidy for sustainable microfinance', published by the Asian Development Bank's *Finance for the Poor* newsletter. The paper was initially prepared for the conference on Microfinance and Public Policy at Cambridge University on November 20, 2003. The ideas have developed through conversations with a wide range of people, but especially Frank DeGiovanni, Diana Barrowclough, Richard Rosenberg and Christopher Dunford. The present version contains some of the earlier material but develops arguments in quite different ways. I have been fortunate for comments on this version from Bernd Balkenhol and Jonathan Conning. The Ford Foundation provided financial support for which I am grateful. The ideas, though, are mine and do not necessarily reflect those of foundation staff or other individuals.

1   The idea is part of 11 'principles of microfinance' that were formulated as part of the revision of the Pink Book. The guidelines were endorsed by leaders of the G8 countries on 10 June 2004 at their summit on Sea Island, off the coast of Georgia. The Pink Book was produced by the Consultative Group to Assist the Poor (CGAP, 2004, p. 1).

2   See, for example, the original 'Pink Book' of 1995. 'International experience shows that successful intermediaries have achieved operational efficiency in three to seven years, and full self-sufficiency, that is, covering all financing costs at non-subsidized rates within five to ten years.' See: http://www.gdrc.org/icm/inspire/donor-guidelines.html.

3   For example, the revised version of the 'Pink Book' allows that subsidies in the form of soft loans can be justified 'to assist financial institutions to serve sparsely populated regions or otherwise difficult-to-reach populations ...' (CGAP, 2004a).

4   The observation is by John Hatch (1974, p. 3), who at the time was a graduate student in Wisconsin. Hatch would later become the founder of FINCA, the village banking network.

5   The *Focus Note* was written by Mohini Malhotra, former Operations Manager, CGAP Secretariat, from a summary of USAID Program and Operations Assessment Report No. 10 (Christen et al., 1995).

6   Data are from Morduch (2005a). Some current microfinance customers likely started out among the very poor and have since grown less poor. Data on incoming microfinance customers (rather than current customers in aggregate) would show higher levels of poverty if that is true. Also note that these data are from just four countries and pertain to relatively small samples.

7   Definitions of 'low-end' vary. As the Microcredit Summit Report 2003 (Daley-Harris, 2003, fn. 5) notes in the present context, 'It must be noted that the *MicroBanking Bulletin*'s definition of institutions reaching the low-end of the population is "measured by an average loan size of less than 20 percent of GNP per capita or less than US$150." These measurements are clearly inferior to [participatory poverty assessments and related tools]. For example, the Bulletin includes Compartamos of Mexico in the group as reaching the low

end of the population, but [Consultative Group to Assist the Poor's] more rigorous Poverty Assessment Tool found that 50 percent of Compartamos' entering clients were in the upper third of the community and 75 percent of entering clients were in the upper two-thirds of the community.' It should be noted that these 124 microlenders in the *MicroBanking Bulletin* data are already a special bunch, sustainability-wise. The *Bulletin* database include only programmes that have indicated particularly strong commitments to achieving financial sustainability and have allowed their financial accounts to be reworked by *Bulletin* staff to bring numbers into closer conformity with international accounting principles. The Grameen Bank, for example, is not included. In terms of financial management, the programmes are thus skimmed from the cream of the global crop. We lack comparable data on the 2572 programmes counted by the Microcredit Summit at the end of 2002, but the bulk presumably perform less strongly that the select 124 in the *MicroBanking Bulletin* in terms of financial performance.

8   Or consider a microlender that ties its fortunes to the ability to raise commercial capital. Without recourse to donated funds, even small business downturns can destroy the operation as risk-adjusted returns fall below that of alternative investments available to profit-maximizing investors.

9   This example was provided by Jonathan Conning.

10   One helpful resource (on government-sponsored guarantees) is Mody and Patro (1996).

11   Details are taken from Chowdhry et al. (2005).

12   A donor with a reputation for having a strong social commitment may, paradoxically, have a more difficult time signalling others about the creditworthiness of a given recipient since the outsiders are apt to be unsure whether the signal pertains mostly to riskiness or to the general social worth of the institution.

13   Frank Abate of Women's World Banking suggested that this was a powerful phenomenon in investments in South Africa, where the presence of (prudent) donors providing subsidized funds also helped to mobilize commercial funds (presentation at Columbia University, 11 October 2005).

14   This example was suggested by (and developed by) Jonathan Conning, and I am grateful to him, drawing on a discussion by Elisabeth Rhyne of ways to downscale commercial banks.

15   The data and follow-up study reported here are from research in Matin and Hulme (2003).

Part III
Empirical Analysis

6
Efficiency in Microfinance Institutions: An Application of Data Envelopment Analysis to MFIs in Peru

Yves Flückiger and Anatoli Vassiliev
University of Geneva

6.1 Introduction

Efficiency in social and financial performance is increasingly being acknowledged as a key condition for possible public sector support. In this chapter, MFIs are considered as production units transforming inputs, or resources, into outputs. Inputs may include labour, financial resources, office space, computer terminals and so on. The number of clients reached, MFI's operating income, loan portfolio volume, portfolio of small loans targeted at the poorest clients and several other variables of interest may be considered as outputs. Efficiency of a production unit, be it an MFI, a commercial bank or a cement plant, depends on how well this unit utilizes inputs or available resources to maximize outputs. Banks, which are close to MFIs by their type of activity, often measure efficiency by the ratio of total expenses to earned income. However, the specific characteristics of MFIs, such as their social mission or not-for-profit structure, mean that many commonly used performance measures – profitability, cost efficiency, and the like – are inappropriate for evaluating overall MFIs' performance.[1] Clearly, a performance evaluation methodology simultaneously taking into account *multiple* efficiency criteria is needed to assess the degree to which the MFIs are both socially and financially efficient.

The objective of this chapter is to propose such a methodology and to illustrate its use in the context of the microfinance industry. To achieve this objective, we analyse a small set of recent data collected from the balance sheets and profit-and-loss accounts of 40 microfinance institutions active in Peru in 2003. The efficiency measurement method known as DEA is used for measuring the financial and social performance of microfinance institutions.

The chapter is organized as follows: the first section briefly summarizes research on the performance measurement of microfinance institutions; it also explains the reasons for using the DEA technique. The following sections introduce the method and describe the data set used for performance measurement. The results are reported in the concluding section, together with some particular specifications of the DEA model.

6.2 Previous research on MFIs' performance evaluation

The social and financial performance of microfinance institutions is frequently measured using accounting ratios. The *MicroBanking Bulletin* (2000) reports a number of such studies. The *Bulletin* uses several indicators of 'outreach' to measure the degree to which the MFIs succeed in attaining the poorest borrowers (i.e., their social goal), and it also employs several indicators to evaluate the MFIs' overall financial performance, or 'sustainability' (i.e., their financial goal).

To measure the MFIs' outreach, such indicators as number of borrowers, total loan portfolio (these are said to be the measures of the 'breadth' of outreach), average loan balance (ratio of total loan portfolio to the number of borrowers) and the ratio of average loan balance to GNP per capita (these are said to be the measures of the 'depth' of outreach) are used. The idea behind the outreach indicators is the following: as the small borrowers are presumed to be the poorest ones, the MFIs should service the largest possible number of small borrowers. Indeed, their social mission gets closer to its accomplishment when the number of small borrowers increases.

To measure the MFIs' overall financial performance, such indicators as adjusted returns on assets (ratio of adjusted net operating income to average total assets), operational self-sufficiency (operating income/ operating expense) and financial self-sufficiency (adjusted operating income/adjusted operating expense) are used. Well documented case studies using both outreach and financial performance ratios may be found in the *MicroBanking Bulletin* (2000, pp. 29–37). Typically, diverse accounting ratios reported for one particular MFI are compared to the average values of these ratios calculated over a peer group of similar MFIs (e.g., MFIs of similar size and/or operating in the same region).

Although accounting ratios furnish useful information about the MFIs' performance as compared to a peer group, they provide only a limited picture of how well the microfinance institutions' management is reaching the objective of serving the poorest borrowers and that of profitability and/or cost minimization. There are several reasons for this.

First, as the *Bulletin* reports, not one, but several accounting ratios are used to measure the MFIs' achievements. Hence, an institution may perform better than the industry's average with respect to one indicator, or a group of indicators (e.g., indicators measuring the outreach), and at the same time underperform with respect to some other indicators (e.g., sustainability). Therefore, it is unclear whether the analysed institution shows an overall performance which is better or worse than its peer group average. Hence, a problem of aggregation of several performance indicators into one single efficiency measure appears.

One may overcome the above-mentioned problem by weighting several performance indicators and computing their weighted sum in order to establish a clear efficiency ranking of MFIs. The weights may be fixed by the industry's experts. However, this approach is somewhat arbitrary – indeed, the weighting scheme may be subjective. Moreover, some institutions may be such good performers with respect to one goal (e.g., outreach) that it may be reasonable to 'forgive' them less satisfactory achievements with respect to another goal (e.g., sustainability). A rigid weighting scheme unduly penalizes such institutions. Therefore, it is desirable to establish a single (or scalar) efficiency measure (called efficiency score hereafter) allowing for a clear ranking of MFIs. This measure should also 'automatically' weight all the performance indicators so that institutions showing very good results in attaining some objectives, but less impressive results in attaining some other objectives, are credited for their good performance.

Second, in the *Bulletin*'s case studies, the accounting ratios measuring the efficiency of analysed MFIs are compared to the *average* values of their peer groups. This is obviously a useful exercise: it allows us to understand whether the analysed MFI performs better or worse than the industry's average institution. This comparison may help to understand the reasons for the over- or underperformance. Yet, we argue that the peer group constituted of all the MFIs active in a given country or region is not the best (or at least not the only possible) reference.

Indeed, the peer groups reported in the *Bulletin*'s case studies are constituted of more or less efficient institutions. Computing the average values of the efficiency indicators over a peer group leads to a comparison of an existing MFI to a non-existent, 'average' MFI. However, we may also want to compare an MFI to an existing institution, and, moreover, to an efficient one. Indeed, comparison leads to the exchange of best managerial practices, knowledge, business tools, corporate culture, and so on, from one institution to another. Obviously, no knowledge transmission is possible from an average, that is, virtual MFI. Moreover, if we want to transmit managerial practices among institutions, we also want the practices transmitted to be the best ones, not the 'average' ones in its Case Studies section.

To conclude, when comparing a particular institution to a peer group, it makes sense to choose a peer group constituted not of all (even comparable in size and located in the same region) MFIs, but of efficient MFIs only. These efficient MFIs (one or several), which are our new peers, should of course be comparable (e.g., in size, input usage, output production) to the analysed institution. It appears useful to us to compare the performance of each inefficient institution to that of its comparable efficient peer. The inefficient institution is offered the opportunity to learn the best management practices from its efficient peers. This may be done by comparing the management practices and finding out what the best performers are doing differently from the least efficient MFIs. This possibility of identifying the best managerial practices does not exist when a single MFI is compared to the average MFI active in a region.

There are also other reasons to complement the usual accounting ratio analysis by using another approach, presented below. These include, among others, the issue of returns to scale and that of identifying the efficiency drivers. These reasons will be better presented after an alternative efficiency measurement model is introduced. This is the objective of the next section.

6.3   Performance analysis methodology

Currently, the measurement of productive efficiency is a well-established field in economics so that many methods are available (Fried, Knox Lovell and Schmidt, 1993). All these methods rely on the same idea: performance of an institution is evaluated either on the basis of the ability of this institution to provide as many services as possible with resources at its disposal, or alternatively, on the basis of its ability to use the smallest possible amount of resources to produce a given amount of services.

To implement an efficiency measurement model in the spirit of those presented by Fried and colleagues (1993), it is necessary to specify the services the microfinance institutions provide (these services may be measured by the size of the small loans portfolio, large loans portfolio, interest rates charged, etc.), the resources they employ (these may include salary costs, other operating expense, etc.), and the characteristics of their operating environment. Once that is accomplished, a performance measure can be developed that compares observed and optimal service/resource data for each MFI.

To compute efficiency scores for the microfinance institutions, we propose to take the route initiated by Charnes, Cooper and Rhodes (1978) and to use the technique named Data Envelopment Analysis (DEA; see Seiford and Thrall, 1990, for a review of literature). The idea of the DEA may be summarized as follows: a best practice piece-wise linear production frontier is estimated, and the distance from each MFI to the frontier is computed. If the MFI is situated on the frontier, it is considered to be efficient; if the MFI is distant from the frontier (the meaning of the word 'distant' will be explained in what follows), it is considered to be inefficient. The more distant an MFI is from the frontier, the more important its inefficiency.

Figure 6.1 presents a simplified view of the efficiency comparison of microfinance institutions. The three MFIs depicted (A, B and C) use only one resource (denoted by x) to provide only one service (denoted by y). It is assumed that if a particular resource/service combination is observed, all resource/service combinations involving no less resource use and no more service provision are feasible. The logic behind this assumption is that it is always possible to offer fewer services that are currently provided with given resources (e.g., the MFI A can produce in whatever point of the segment AA'), and it is similarly possible to use additional resources to provide the current level of services (e.g., the MFI B can produce in whatever point of the segment BB'). It is also assumed that all linear combinations of the observed resource/service observations are feasible, so that all the combinations situated on the segment AB are feasible.

In the input–output space of Figure 6.1 the line A'ABB' represents the estimated best practice frontier, that is, all the feasible resource/service combinations such that no MFI situated on the frontier may increase the service production without increasing the resource usage, nor decrease the resource usage without decreasing the service production. The MFIs A and B are situated on the frontier – hence, they are fully efficient. The MFI C is distant from the frontier – hence, it is inefficient. Indeed, C can increase its service production while keeping the resource usage the same – this results in a vertical move towards the frontier. The inefficient MFI C can alternatively decrease its resource usage keeping the service production constant – this results in a horizontal move to the

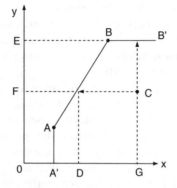

Figure 6.1 Best practice frontier in one input, one output space

frontier. Hence, the distance to the frontier may be measured in two alternative directions. One speaks about input-oriented efficiency measure when the distance is measured horizontally and one speaks about output-oriented efficiency measure when the distance is measured vertically. Whatever direction is chosen, the larger the distance to the frontier, the larger the inefficiency.

To obtain a quantitative measure of inefficiency of MFI C, the efficiency score may be computed in the input orientation: $E_{in} = 0D/0G$ (Farrell, 1957). This score is smaller than 1; it measures the feasible resource reduction that the MFI C could attain if the services (amounting to 0F) were produced efficiently. For Example, if $E_{in} = 0.7$, then the institution can produce the same amount of services by using only 70 per cent of its current resources. Alternatively, the efficiency score may be computed in the output orientation: $E_{out} = 0E/0F$ (Farrell, 1957). This score is larger than 1; it measures the feasible increase in service provision that the MFI C could attain keeping its resource usage constant (amounting to 0G) if the services were produced efficiently. For example, if $E_{out} = 1.3$, then the institution can increase its service provision by 30 per cent, using the same resources.

A similar simplified example is depicted in Figure 6.2, where the three observed MFIs A, B and C use the same amount of resources to produce two services, say the total portfolio of 'small' loans targeted at the poorest clients (y_1) and that of 'large' loans (y_2). Using a similar argument as the previous one, the efficient frontier may be described by the line A'ABB'. MFIs A and B are fully efficient; C could produce more of either y_1, or y_2, or both, given its resource usage. Hence, institution C is inefficient. In this two-services case, the output-oriented efficiency score E_{out} may be

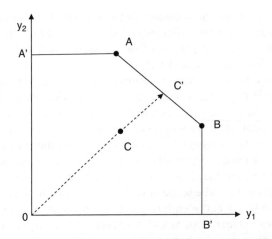

Figure 6.2 Best practice frontier in two output coordinates

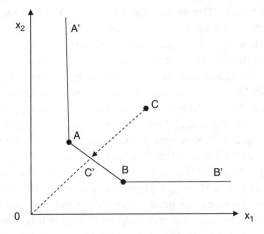

Figure 6.3 Best practice frontier in two input coordinates

computed as the ratio OC'/OC; it measures the feasible *equiproportionate* increase in the provision of *both* services y_1 and y_2.

Finally, the construction of input oriented efficiency score may be illustrated in the case of the usage of multiple resources as depicted in Figure 6.3. The institutions A, B and C all produce the same amount of services and use two resources, say salary costs (x_1) and other operating expenses (x_2). The efficient frontier is given by the line A'ABB'; MFIs A and B are fully efficient whereas C is inefficient, because it could use less resources to produce the same amount of services. In this two-resources case, the input oriented efficiency score E_{in} may be computed as the ratio $0C'/0C$; it measures the feasible *equiproportionate* reduction in the usage of *both* resources x_1 and x_2.[2]

To sum up, DEA allows us to evaluate the efficiency of microfinance institutions that pursue several social and financial objectives and use multiple resources. The brief description of DEA presented above shows that meaningful efficiency scores may be obtained when comparing each institution to the industry's best practice frontier. Efficient peers may be identified for each inefficient MFI (this issue is left apart for the moment). The inefficient MFIs may learn the best management practices from these efficient institutions. The scope of DEA is not limited to the computation of efficiency scores and identification of efficient peers. Productivity (or returns to scale characteristics) and effects on efficiency of exogenous operating conditions may also be analysed. These issues are of great importance to the microfinance industry, as outlined in numerous articles.

For example, referring to the inefficiency of MFIs in Latin America, Brand (2000) says: 'The reason for this inefficiency is twofold. First, many MFIs have not fully exploited the economies of scale required to maximize efficiency. There are many small MFIs serving too few clients to operate efficiently.' The nature of scale economies may be analysed by means of DEA, and a clear distinction between productivity and efficiency may be done. The analysis of scale economies is an especially interesting subject. According to some authors, economies of scale produce significant cost savings for young MFIs as they build their client base. After reaching a certain size, however, the cost reductions related to the increasing size of MFIs are drastically reduced (Brand, 2000).

According to Brand (2000), 'many programs operate in non-competitive environments where there is little pressure to improve efficiency.' The efficiency measurement techniques implemented through the estimation of production frontiers may help to distinguish between efficient and inefficient MFIs. If the efficiency is systematically compared between the MFIs operating in the same country or region, the total efficiency may be increased even in the absence of competition, for example through the implementation of a quasi-market incentive mechanisms.

6.4   Data sources and variable construction

The data set

In order to measure the performance of microfinance institutions, the data on MFIs should be classified into two groups; inputs (referring to the resources used) and outputs (referring to the services provided). Instead of accounting ratios often used in performance evaluation, Data Envelopment Analysis requires the use of the raw data used to compute these ratios. For example, one of the ratios often used to measure the MFIs' overall financial performance is the adjusted return on assets (*MicroBanking Bulletin*, 2000). The DEA requires the knowledge of variables composing this ratio, that is, adjusted net operation income in nominator (which may be considered as an output), and average total assets in denominator (which may be considered as an input).

The next requirement concerns the volume of data. DEA is a statistical technique, so that a quite large number of observations (MFIs) is necessary. Small data sets may plague the analysis, especially with respect to the construction of the efficient peer groups. Consider, for example, an analysis conducted on a pooled data set of MFIs active in different countries. This may lead to a comparison of an inefficient African MFI to an efficient Latin American MFI. However, the usefulness of such a comparison is questionable, as these institutions operate in very different environments.

In this chapter we analyse the efficiency of 40 microfinance institutions active in Peru in 2003. Our data set is small, and more data would be desirable. The Peruvian microfinance industry comprises several types of institutions such as MFIs, credit unions, and even financial companies and commercial banks which specifically target micro-entrepreneurs and grant micro-loans (Didoni, 2003). The sample analysed in this chapter comprises only microfinance institutions, excluding banks and financial companies. The sample includes: 13 municipal institutions active in Peruvian cities other than Lima, called Cajas Municipales (CMAC); one municipal institution active in Lima; 12 MFIs active in rural areas, called Cajas Rurales (CRAC); and finally, 14 MFIs called Edpymes which are primarily designed to channel funds from donated sources or multilateral institutions to small and micro-entrepreneurs. According to Didoni (2003), Peruvian microfinance is more developed in urban areas than in rural ones.[3] Balance sheet figures, profit-and-loss accounts and the number of staff are available as of September 2003. The first step of our analysis is to choose the variables to be entered as inputs and outputs into the DEA model.

The output variables

The performance evaluation of MFIs should take into account two objectives of these institutions. The choice of output variables depends on these objectives. The first objective of MFIs consists in increasing the economic welfare of the poorest people. Democratizing credit is the social mission of MFIs. The second objective is financial performance and sustainability. To attain financial self-sufficiency, MFIs should control operating costs and improve profitability.

Inputs and outputs should take into account both objectives of MFIs: social and financial. Traditional microfinance indicators of outreach (i.e., the number of the poorest clients attained – the social mission) include the number of borrowers, total loan portfolio, average loan balance per borrower, and ratio of average loan balance to GNP per capita, and so on. The number of borrowers or the number of small loans is not available in our data. Instead, we use the total loan portfolio, an asset reported in the MFI's balance sheet (loans, hereafter), as indicator of outreach. The use of total loan portfolio as an indicator of outreach is based on the idea that the larger the loan portfolio, the higher the number of small loans granted and the number of the poorest borrowers served. Obviously, this hypothesis might be too strong; therefore, more data on loan portfolio would be necessary for better performance evaluation. Since the main purpose of our chapter is to illustrate the use of DEA in the microfinance industry, we perform our analysis with this not fully satisfactory indicator of outreach. The issue of the best indicator of outreach is left for further research. Loans will appear in the output side of our DEA model.

The second output should account for the financial performance. The data available in the profit-and-loss accounts are quite rich, so that several options for choosing financial performance indicator are available. These data include, among others, operating income, net operating income, profit (or loss) realized, and the like. All these financial indicators are potentially interesting, and we could include all of them into the DEA model. However, as these variables are strongly correlated (i.e., they provide very similar information), we chose the net operating income (NOI, hereafter) as an indicator of MFIs' financial performance.

The input variables

The inputs of microfinance institutions are the resources used to produce their services. We chose to include in our model the number of staff working at the MFI (staff comprises managers, officers, employees and other personnel), the MFI's total assets, and its operating expense (defined as the sum of interests paid, financial operating costs and administrative expense). A personnel variable is traditionally included in the list of inputs in the efficiency measurement literature. Including total assets and operating expense is more specific to the literature on

Table 6.1 Descriptive statistics and coefficients of correlation for MFI inputs and outputs

Variable	Mean	Standard deviation	Minimum	Maximum
Inputs				
Staff	107.88	106.44	13	487
Assets	74,127.67	102,839.70	1,978.15	446,380.00
Operating expense	7,968.88	9,460.65	424.78	43,428.98
Outputs				
Loans	48,844.90	67,726.81	1,045.10	274,530.80
Net operating income	3,759.25	7,219.88	−7,838.06	30,836.77

Coefficients of correlation	Staff	Assets	Operating expense	Loans
Inputs				
Staff	1			
Assets	0.8985*	1		
Operating expense	0.9531*	0.9772*	1	
Outputs				
Loans	0.9052*	0.9930*	0.9715*	1
Net operating income	0.7916*	0.9394*	0.9046*	0.9434*

Notes: * Statistically significant at the 5% level.

banks and microfinance institutions. Note that inputs are measured in different units: total staff is measured in number of persons, and total assets and operating expense are measured in monetary units.

Table 6.1 summarizes the descriptive statistics for three inputs and two outputs. Since the mean values of all variables are equal to or larger than their standard deviations, the Peruvian microfinance institutions differ substantially with respect to their input usage and output production. This reflects a diversity of situations, management practices, and possibly technical efficiency.

6.5 Efficiency analysis with the DEA model

Different specifications of the Data Envelopment Analysis technique may be used to estimate technical efficiency. Depending on the choice of specification, we may answer different questions as to the possibilities of improving the MFIs' technical efficiency. Below we report two possible DEA specifications.

Radial output-oriented DEA model

The output-oriented Data Envelopment Analysis model answers the question 'by how much may the MFI's outputs be equiproportionally expanded, keeping its inputs constant'. Microfinance institutions are evaluated on the basis of their ability to utilize inputs (or resources) at their disposal to provide the maximum amount of loans and to realize the maximum net operating income. We assume that production technology of microfinance institutions is characterized by variable (i.e., locally increasing, constant and/or decreasing) returns to scale (VRS), which is the least restrictive hypothesis (scale economies are discussed later).

The estimation of the DEA model shows that the average output efficiency score E_{out} in the sample of 39 microfinance institutions[4] equals 1.17, with standard deviation of 0.1616. This implies that on average, Peruvian microfinance institutions are capable of providing 117 per cent of their current output level, both with respect to loans and to the net operating income. Twelve out of the 39 MFIs analysed (30.77 per cent) are fully efficient and cannot increase their loan portfolio and net operating income. The maximum score corresponding to the lowest efficiency equals 1.55, implying that the corresponding MFI can grant 55 per cent more loans and simultaneously realize a net operating income 55 per cent larger than its current values. The potential increases in the levels of outputs are feasible keeping constant the current MFIs' inputs usage, that is, without increasing the staff, operating expense and total assets.

Output efficiency score E_{out} measures the feasible increase in output production that an MFI could, *ceteris paribus*, attain. The knowledge of this score and of current output levels allows us to compute the potential output levels that the MFI should attain in order to be fully efficient. These levels are computed by multiplying the observed output levels by efficiency score: $y_T = E_{out} \cdot y_{observed}$, where y denotes the outputs. We refer to the output levels y_T as to targets. Table 6.2 reports the efficiency scores and efficient output levels (targets) for 39 microfinance institutions from our sample.

Efficiency scores allow us to rank the MFIs from the least to the most efficient, and inefficient MFIs might be identified. However, such a simple ranking does not help in understanding why inefficiencies arise, or how the efficiency may be improved. DEA methodology has the advantage of proposing some specific guidance for such an analysis. For each inefficient unit, an efficient benchmark might be identified. This benchmark may be a unique fully efficient MFI, which is the most desirable case, or a set of several efficient MFIs. In the latter case, a weighted average of these MFIs is aggregated into a virtual MFI, which is the efficient benchmark. Identifying efficient benchmarks for each inefficient institution may be a useful exercise. Indeed, the performance of inefficient microfinance institutions could be improved by discovering what their efficient peers are doing differently.

For all efficient MFIs, the number of dominated inefficient institutions is also reported in Table 6.2. This is the number of times the efficient MFI appears as a benchmark for the inefficient ones. If this number is zero, the MFI is efficient 'by default'. Efficiency 'by default' occurs when an MFI is very different from the others as to its output mix or resource usage.[5] This MFI is not comparable to the rest of sample, and the estimated efficiency score is not robust: the institution may be inefficient even if it is identified as efficient. Microfinance institutions efficient 'by default' should be analysed on the case study basis (and not by means of DEA).

How is the analysis of efficiency by DEA related to the traditional analysis of accounting ratios? Including the net operating income as an output and the total assets as an input leads to an efficiency measurement model that attributes a high efficiency value to microfinance institutions that have a high return on assets (ROA, the ratio of net operating income to total assets).

In a similar way, if we include in the model total loan portfolio as an output and the MFI staff as an input, then those MFIs will appear as highly efficient whose employees succeed in disbursing large amounts of loans: a measure of employee productivity. Finally, microfinance institutions that succeed in disbursing the largest amount of loans and realizing the largest net operating income per unit of operating expense are considered to be the most efficient, according to DEA. Hence, our choice of inputs and outputs is economically meaningful and corresponds to the social and financial objectives of MFIs. The resulting efficiency measure is related to the traditional ratio analysis.

Non-radial input-oriented DEA model

The alternative input-oriented specification of DEA addresses the question of how much the use of inputs (resources) can be reduced, keeping outputs constant. Otherwise stated, the efficiency of microfinance institutions is evaluated on the basis of their ability to disburse their current volume and number of loans and to gain their current net operating income by using the smallest possible amount of resources.

As in the previous section, we can assess the extent, *ceteris paribus*, of the possible equiproportional reduction in the usage of all three MFIs'

Table 6.2 Results of estimation of output-oriented DEA model with variable returns to scale

Number	MFI	Score	Efficient benchmarks [Number of dominated units]	Observed		Target		Local returns to scale
				Loans	Net operating income	Loans	Net operating income	
1	Alternativa	1	[7]	2,753.5	271.9	2,753.5	271.9	IRS
2	Camco Piura	1	[0]	1,045.1	105.4	1,045.1	105.4	IRS
3	Confianza	1.14	1 (0.20) 8 (0.71) 39 (0.10)	22,720.4	1,230.3	25,828.6	1,398.7	IRS
4	Crear Arequipa	1.05	6 (0.94) 9 (0.05) 39 (0.01)	18,667.7	1,429.9	19,554.4	1,497.9	DRS
5	Crear Cusco	1	[1]	4,382.9	391	4,382.9	391	IRS
6	Crear Tacna	1	[10]	13,723.7	1,085	13,723.7	1,085	CRS
7	Crear Trujillo	1.08	8 (0.99) 9 (0.01)	4,979	93.8	5,395.3	101.7	DRS
8	Credivisión	1	[18]	4,656.8	439.5	4,656.8	439.5	CRS
9	Edyficar	1	[12]	87,149.8	5,262	87,149.8	5,262	DRS
10	Nueva Visión	1.02	1(0.75) 8 (0.22) 39 (0.03)	8,631.2	623.3	8,791.7	634.9	IRS
11	Proempresa	1.06	6 (0.33) 8 (0.46) 9 (0.21)	23,441.6	1,155.2	24,885.6	1,226.3	DRS
12	Pro Negocios	1.27	6 (0.16) 8 (0.84) 39 (0.00)	5,483.6	262.2	6,964.7	333	IRS

#			[1] [0]					
13	Raiz	–	–	2,916.7	261.5	2,916.7	261.5	–
14	Solidaridad	1	[1]	11,215.5	654.3	11,215.5	654.3	IRS
15	CRAC Cajamarca	1	[0]					IRS
16	CRAC Cajasur	1.22	8 (0.69) 29 (0.24) 39 (0.06)	39,302.5	1,451.2	47,839	1,766.4	IRS
17	CRAC Chavín	1.21	6 (0.05) 8 (0.94) 39 (0.01)	6,815.7	258.1	8,268.1	313.1	IRS
18	CRAC Cruz de Chalpón	1.36	1 (0.26) 8 (0.67) 39 (0.07)	14,298	450.8	19,386.7	611.2	IRS
19	CRAC Libertadores de Ayacucho	1.55	8 (0.93) 9 (0.01) 39 (0.06)	11,665.6	164.4	18,040.8	254.2	DRS
20	CRAC Los Andes	1.24	1 (0.60) 5 (0.12) 14 (0.27) 27 (0.01)	4,102.4	418.2	5,074.6	517.3	IRS
21	CRAC Nor Perú	1.24	1 (0.70) 27 (0.00) 29 (0.09) 39 (0.21)	48,606.6	2,991.2	60,077.7	3,697.2	IRS
22	CRAC Profinanzas	1.46	8 (0.91) 9 (0.03) 39 (0.06)	13,382.8	471.2	19,565.7	688.8	DRS
23	CRAC Prymera	1.3	8 (0.95) 29 (0.02) 39 (0.03)	10,964.8	356.8	14,230.1	463	IRS

Continued

Table 6.2 Continued

Number	MFI	Score	Efficient benchmarks [Number of dominated units]	Observed Loans	Observed Net operating income	Target Loans	Target Net operating income	Local returns to scale
24	CRAC Quillabamba	1.41	8 (0.87) 9 (0.05) 39 (0.07)	17,484.4	230.8	24,693.2	325.9	DRS
25	CRAC San Martín	1.46	6 (0.67) 9 (0.01) 39 (0.31)	54,470.7	833.7	79,750.5	1,220.6	DRS
26	CRAC Señor de Luren	1.27	1 (0.71) 27 (0.00) 29 (0.14) 39 (0.15)	41,525.8	958.8	52,559.2	1,213.6	IRS
27	CMAC Arequipa	1	[4]	274,531	30,836.8	274,531	30,836.8	CRS
28	CMAC Chincha	1.14	1 (0.70) 8 (0.26) 39 (0.04)	10,736.6	410.9	12,247.3	468.8	IRS
29	CMAC Cusco	1	[5]	124,893	13,756.2	124,893	13,756.2	CRS
30	CMAC Del Santa	1.11	6 (0.68) 9 (0.24) 39 (0.08)	42,572.5	3,025.4	47,464.1	3,373	DRS
31	CMAC Huancayo	1.26	8 (0.38) 29 (0.04) 39 (0.47) 40 (0.11)	94,174.2	9,202.4	118,923	11,620.8	CRS

32	CMAC Ica	1.14	8 (0.60) 39 (0.15) 40 (0.26)	46,646.6	4,925.3	53,359.1	5,634	DRS
33	CMAC Maynas	1.38	6 (0.56) 8 (0.10) 9 (0.18) 39 (0.16)	42,534.1	2,701.1	58,701.4	3,727.8	DRS
34	CMAC Paita	1.36	6 (0.77) 9 (0.10) 39 (0.13)	35,020.5	2,216	47,470.3	3,003.8	DRS
35	CMAC Pisco	1.23	6 (0.20) 8 (0.77) 39 (0.03)	10,480.7	571.4	12,894.4	702.9	IRS
36	CMAC Piura	1.01	27 (1.00)	271,974	24,135.2	274,531	24,362	DRS
37	CMAC Sullana	1.22	6 (0.25) 9 (0.26) 39 (0.49)	110,339	8,838.9	134,812	10,799.3	DRS
38	CMAC Tacna	1.27	8 (0.59) 9 (0.02) 39 (0.39)	71,133.9	5,829.1	90,204.9	7,391.9	DRS
39	CMAC Trujillo	1	[23]	222,014	21,089.1	222,014	21,089.1	CRS
40	Caja Municipal de Crédito Popular Lima	1	[2]	69,559.7	8,820.1	69,559.7	8,820.1	CRS

Notes: CRS = constant returns to scale; IRS = increasing returns to scale; DRS = decreasing returns to scale.

inputs: staff, total assets and operating expense. However, it does not seem reasonable to reduce staff and total assets. The assets of Peruvian microfinance institutions comprise such elements as loan portfolio, provisions and cash. Reducing these items may compromise the institutions' viability.

We propose to evaluate the extent to which only one input – the operating expense – may be reduced, keeping all other inputs and outputs constant. Since the model evaluates the extent of possible reduction of only one input instead of the equiproportionate reduction of all inputs, the efficiency measure is called non-radial instead of radial (Banker and Moorey, 1986).

The idea of non-radial efficiency measure is illustrated in Figure 6.4. The radial efficiency measure evaluates the distance from the MFI C to the point C′ on the efficient frontier. The non-radial efficiency measure evaluates the distance from C to C″: only input x_1 is reduced, while input x_2 is kept constant.

The results of efficiency estimation for selected Peruvian MFIs are reported in Table 6.3 for illustrative purposes. The mean efficiency score for 39 institutions equals 0.7368 (with standard deviation 0.1972). Thus, the MFIs could operate with 73.69 per cent of their current operating expenses, on average, if all of them were fully efficient.

Productivity drivers: returns to scale

Brand (2000) emphasizes that productivity of microfinance institutions may depend on their size. It could be that some MFIs are too small, or alternatively, too large to operate in the most productive way, that is, to

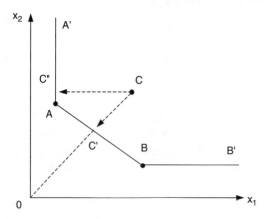

Figure 6.4   Measuring the non-radial efficiency

Table 6.3 Results of estimation of input-oriented DEA model with variable returns to scale

Number	MFI	Score	Efficient benchmarks [Number of dominated units]	Observed operating expense	Target operating expense
1	Alternativa	1.00	[1]	724.7	724.7
2	Camco Piura	1.00	[10]	424.8	424.8
3	Confianza	0.63	2 (0.63) 8 (0.20) 29 (0.17)	4,294.9	2,684.8
4	Crear Arequipa	0.65	8 (0.93) 29 (0.02) 39 (0.05)	4,039.1	2,609.2
5	Crear Cusco	1.00	[0]	995.8	995.8
6	Crear Tacna	1.00	[0]	2,674.3	2,674.3
7	Crear Trujillo	0.57	2 (0.21) 8 (0.78) 29 (0.01)	1,706.3	974.5
8	Credivisión	1.00	[9]	983.1	983.1
9	Edyficar	1.00	[0]	17,979.1	17,979.1
10	Nueva Visión	0.89	1 (0.49) 2 (0.28) 8 (0.20) 39 (0.03)	1,577.8	1,404.0

maximize output to input ratios. DEA allows the joint estimation of efficiency and of returns to scale properties.

Let us first introduce the difference between the concept of technical efficiency and that of scale economies. Technical efficiency refers to the distance from the observed MFI to the efficient production frontier. Scale economies refer to changes in the output to input ratio that occur when the size of an MFI increases or decreases.

Returns to scale may be illustrated in the simple one-input, one-output case as depicted in Figure 6.5. Productivity refers to the slopes of the dashed lines, which are equal to the output to input ratios. Efficiency refers to the distance from a point, say A, to the efficient frontier. Two production frontiers are depicted: one characterized by constant returns to scale (CRS), and the other characterized by variable returns to scale (VRS).

The VRS production frontier is composed of increasing, constant and decreasing returns to scale parts (points on the left of C, between C and D, and to the right of D, respectively). Returns to scale are increasing (decreasing) if an increase in input use is followed by an increase (decrease) in productivity. One may easily see that the highest productivity corresponds to the constant returns to scale part (segment CD) of the VRS frontier. Hence, the MFIs that are situated on the increasing (decreasing) returns to scale part of the production frontier can improve their productivity by increasing (decreasing) their size. The concept of returns to scale may be easily generalized to multi-input, multi-output production processes.

An inefficient microfinance institution may improve its productivity without changing its size (which is measured by input usage in Figure 6.5). This may be done by eliminating technical inefficiency. The inefficient MFI A in Figure 6.5 may first move vertically by eliminating inefficiency and place itself on the production frontier. If one is willing to improve the productivity further, then MFI A can increase its size until the CRS part of efficient frontier is attained (this occurs at point C).

The concepts of efficiency and productivity do not necessarily coincide. The socially preferred situation is that of constant returns to scale (which corresponds to maximum average productivity). However, MFIs situated on this part of the production frontier may be revealed as inefficient. Also, the MFIs situated on the increasing returns to scale part of the frontier (e.g., A) may be inefficient, or MFIs situated on the decreasing returns to scale part of the frontier (e.g., B) may be efficient.

For each microfinance institution, we may infer the type of local returns to scale (Kerstens and Vanden Eeckaut, 1999). The inference of returns to scale is based on the radial output-oriented DEA model of

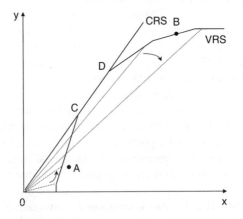

Figure 6.5 DEA production frontier under constant (CRS) and variable (VRS) returns to scale

Section 6.1 above. The type of local returns to scale is reported in the last column of Table 6.2. Among 39 microfinance institutions analysed, 7 exhibit constant returns to scale, 17 are situated on the increasing returns to scale part of the production frontier, and 15 are characterized by decreasing returns to scale. The MFIs that are characterized by increasing (decreasing) returns to scale may benefit from centralization, for example, through mergers (decentralization, e.g. from splitting), after having eliminated the technical inefficiency. The institutions characterized by constant returns to scale should not change their size.

6.6 Conclusions

The social mission of microfinance institutions is to reach the poorest segments of population and to offer them lending and saving services. At the same time, MFIs should tend towards financial self-sufficiency. Nowadays, financial sustainability is more important than it was in the past: currently, the donors are more likely to invest in financially or operationally sustainable institutions. Efficiency now represents a crucial consideration in the microfinance industry.

Therefore, a performance evaluation methodology is needed to assess the degree to which the microfinance institutions are both socially and financially efficient. In this chapter we decided to use data envelopment analysis, a statistical performance measurement methodology, to evaluate the efficiency of 40 Peruvian microfinance institutions. The use of DEA in the microfinance literature is relatively new,[6] but we believe that this method is well suited to take into account the multiple objectives of MFIs.

The levels of inefficiency reported in this sample are quite high for two reasons: first, this study mainly aimed at illustrating how data envelopment analysis may be used in microfinance. Thus, the specification of inputs and outputs used for the performance estimation may not be precise enough to capture all country-specific features of microfinance in Peru. Second, the chapter does not address the important issue of the dependence between efficiency and the MFIs' operating environment (e.g., rural or urban), funding structure or management practices (e.g., whether loan officers are specialized or not). *MicroBanking Bulletin*'s Case Studies (2000) and Farrington (2000) report evidence of such dependence. Hence, this illustrative study represents a necessary first step in the use of data envelopment analysis in microfinance, and calls for further research.

Notes

1   See Evers (2000) for a comparison between microfinance institutions and banks.
2   In practice, efficiency scores are computed by using mathematical programming techniques. For the technical details, the reader may refer to numerous text-books (e.g., Fried, Knox, Lovell and Schmidt, 1993) or articles (e.g., Seiford and Thrall, 1990).
3   The data on Peruvian microfinance institutions are published by the Superintendecia de Banca y Seguros (SBS) of Peru and may be obtained from the web site http://www.sbs.gob.pe.
4   The MFI Riaz is excluded from estimations as an outlier.
5   For example, an institution of much larger size than the others will typically appear efficient 'by default'.
6   A similar application can be found in Nieto, Cinca and Molinero, 2004.

7
Efficiency in Financial Intermediation: Theory and Empirical Measurement

Thorsten Beck
World Bank

7.1 Introduction

There is a large variation in financial intermediary development across countries: Private Credit to GDP was 173 per cent in the United States in 2003, but only 2 per cent in Mozambique.[1] This variation is critical to countries' socio-economic performance: countries with higher levels of credit to the private sector as a share of GDP experience higher GDP per capita growth and faster rates of reduction in the headcount, that is, the share of population living on less than a dollar a day (Beck, Levine and Loayza, 2000; Beck, Demirguc-Kunt and Levine, 2007). However, economists and policy-makers are not just interested in the amount of society's savings that is channelled by intermediaries to the most deserving borrowers, but also in the efficiency with which this happens. The interest spread – the difference between lending rate and deposit rate – has been one of the most prominent measures of efficiency. While interest rate spreads vary typically between 2 and 4 per cent in developed financial systems, they often reach 10 per cent and more in developing countries and are over 30 per cent in Brazil (Laeven and Majnoni, 2005).

This chapter first discusses the theoretical background of interest rate spreads as a measure of efficiency in financial intermediation in general, by contrasting a world with perfect information, no agency problems and zero transaction costs with the real world where quite different conditions prevail. We then show the empirical relationship between efficiency and depth and breadth of financial systems across countries. Next, we take a closer empirical look at the components of the interest rate spread, which will lead us to the driving factors behind efficiency of financial intermediation. We will distinguish between factors at the bank-, sector- and country-level. A section on policy lessons concludes.

7.2   Interest spreads and credit rationing: theory

Interest rate spreads, or imperfect channelling of financial resources from savers to investors, do not exist in a purely theoretical world characterized by the absence of transaction costs and asymmetric information. In such a world, financial institutions would not be needed to mobilize savings and allocate loans, as savers would assign their savings directly to borrowers based on perfect knowledge of investment possibilities. Access to external finance would be frictionless, limited only by the inter-temporal wealth constraint of the borrower, which would be known equally well and with certainty by both the lender (saver) and the borrower (investor). Investment decisions would thus be independent of financing and consumption decisions, and based purely on the expected return of the investment project.

Financial intermediaries and organized financial markets arise to alleviate market frictions, such as transaction costs, uncertainty about project outcomes, and information asymmetries.[2] These market frictions make it difficult to decouple investment from financing decisions. The same market frictions not only lead to a wedge between the interest rates that borrowers have to pay on their loans and the interest rate that savers receive on their deposits, but they also might result in credit rationing, as we will discuss below. We will focus on three major sources of market frictions and their effects on spreads and credit rationing.[3]

Let us take first fixed intermediation costs. Transaction costs associated with screening and monitoring borrowers and processing savings and payment services drive a wedge between the interest rate paid to depositors and the interest charged to borrowers. However, these costs are not necessarily proportional to the transaction size. Fixed costs exist at the transaction, client, institution, and even system level: processing a loan application, screening borrowers *ex ante* and monitoring them *ex post* entail costs that are, at least in part, independent of the size of the loan. Similarly, at the level of a financial institution, operating costs range from the brick-and-mortar branch network to legal services and to accounting systems, and are largely independent of the number of clients or the size of their transactions. Fixed costs even arise at the level of the financial system, including in terms of regulatory costs and the costs of payment clearing and settlement infrastructure, which are again, and up to a point, independent of the number of regulated institutions.

Intermediation costs do not only drive a wedge between savings and lending rate, in a world with uncertain revenue streams they can also lead to credit rationing of borrowers with demand for small loans, as shown – among others – by Williamson (1987). Increasing transaction costs with smaller loan sizes drive up the loan interest rate the lender has to charge in order to recover her costs and thus increases the probability of non-payment.

We consider next constraints on the ability to reduce lending risk through diversification. Idiosyncratic, that is, borrower-specific risk, would in principle be diversifiable or insurable in a world with complete markets. The limits to idiosyncratic risk diversification observed in the real world are, at least in part, a reflection of some form of market incompleteness, including the lack of sufficient markets for hedges and other insurance products. If they are unable to diversify risks in a competitive market, risk-adverse creditors include a risk premium in the lending interest rate, increasing the lending interest rate beyond the level necessary to cover the creditor's marginal cost of funds plus the transaction costs discussed above.

Finally, we consider agency problems due to information asymmetries. The inability of the lender to perfectly ascertain the credit worthiness of the borrower and her project ex-ante and monitor the implementation ex-post gives rise to the classical principal-agent problem and can be separated into adverse selection and moral hazard.[4] The inability to ascertain the riskiness of a borrower results in the interest rate serving as a screening device, with higher interest rates rationing lower risk borrowers out of the market (Stiglitz and Weiss, 1981). While higher risk can be compensated for by charging a risk premium, the usefulness of the interest rate as a screening device decreases with higher premiums, as the degree of riskiness in the pool of interested borrowers increases. The absence of verifiable information thus can lead to the rationing of high-risk borrowers at a level below the equilibrium interest rate. Second, high costs of monitoring over the life of the loan and of enforcing the loan contract in case of default result in moral hazard risk, the risk that the borrowed resources are not used for the original purpose, but rather for consumption or for riskier investments. Again, while increasing the risk premium serves as a screening tool, the interest rate's usefulness decreases in the premium as the incentive to divert resources for riskier projects increases; and this can effectively result in credit rationing.

Figure 7.1 illustrates the non-linear relationship between the lending interest rate and the expected return for the bank. The horizontal axis denotes the nominal loan interest rate i, while the vertical axis denotes

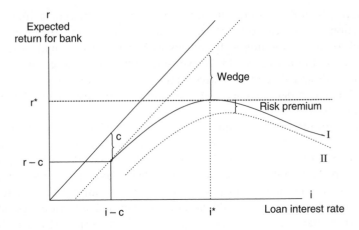

Figure 7.1   Market frictions and the interest rate spread

the expected return to the bank r. The 45 degree line denotes the linear relationship between nominal interest rate and expected return for the bank in a world without any market frictions. In the real world of market frictions, however, the expected return is not only lower than the nominal interest rate but also increases less than the nominal interest rate. Abstracting from the fixed component, transaction costs result in a first wedge illustrated by a parallel line to the 45 degree line, that is, for a given interest rate i, the return for the lender is i – c, and where c is transaction or operating costs. The non-linearities due to scale (fixed component of transaction costs) and agency problems are illustrated by curve I. The non-linear wedge between the 45 degree line and curve not only implies that the default probability increases with the lending interest rate, causing r to rise less than i; it also implies that, as the lending rate increases beyond a given threshold, denoted in Figure 7.1 by i*, the expected return begins to decrease.

Thus, at (i*, r*), the marginal revenue to the creditor due to a contractual increase in the lending interest rate is fully offset by the marginal expected loss due to a higher probability of default. Curve I, however, is drawn after subtracting from the interest rate any idiosyncratic risk premium. Curve II, on the other hand, takes into account the risk premium and, hence, is always to the right of curve I, with the vertical distance between the two curves measuring the premium charged by creditors for non-diversifiable risk. To the extent that the risk premium increases with the level of the lending rate (reflecting the increase in the ex-ante

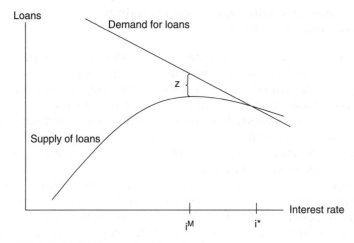

Figure 7.2   Market frictions and credit rationing

probability of default), curve II would be flatter than curve I and would have a lower flexion point, as drawn in Figure 7.1. Note that the widening of the wedge between i and r as i increases is common to both curves. This is because the probability of default rises with the lending interest rate, independently of the reasons (costs, risk-adjusted profits or risk premium) that push that rate up. Both curves have a flexion point and a downward-bending part; as interest rates rise beyond a threshold, the return to the lender decreases.

The non-linear relationship between nominal interest rate and return to lender can result in a backward-bending supply curve and credit rationing, as shown by Stiglitz and Weiss (1981) and in Figure 7.2. If the market-clearing interest rate i^M is on the backward-bending part of the supply schedule, that is, demand and supply schedules intersect at $i^M < i^*$, there will be credit rationing, illustrated by z in Figure 7.2. Rather than increasing the interest rate up to the point where demand is satisfied, lenders supply only up to the nominal interest rate i^* and ration out borrowers who would have been offered loans in a traditional, price-clearing market. Together, Figures 7.1 and 7.2 illustrate that inefficiencies in financial intermediation lead not only to a higher spread between the return depositors receive on their savings and the rate borrowers have to pay for their loans, but also to lower depth and breadth of the financial system, as the riskiest and costliest borrowers are rationed out.

7.3   Interest spreads and credit rationing: cross-country evidence

The previous section showed that a large wedge between deposit and lending interest rates is associated with credit rationing and thus a lower level of credit channelled to borrowers. Can we confirm this theoretical prediction with data? Since there are no good comparable cross-country data on interest rate spreads, we turn to data on net interest margins and consider the empirical association of net interest margin as a share of total earning assets, averaged over all banks in a country, with measures of depth and breadth of the financial system.[5]

Figure 7.3 shows the negative association of net interest margins with Private Credit to GDP for a sample of over 100 countries, with data averaged over the period 1999–2003.[6] This suggest that countries with lower net interest margins, thus less inefficiency and less deadweight loss for savers and borrowers, experience higher levels of financial intermediary development, a higher levels of saving intermediated to the country's private sector.

Figure 7.4 shows that countries with lower interest rate margins experience higher use of loan services, as measured by loan accounts per capita. Here, we use data from a recent data compilation effort on the access to and use of banking services, by Beck, Demirguc-Kunt and

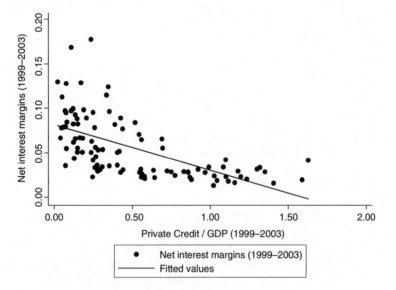

Figure 7.3   Development and efficiency of financial intermediaries

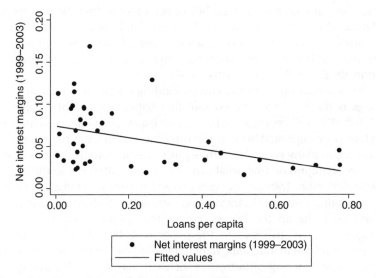

Figure 7.4 Outreach and efficiency of financial intermediaries

Martinez Peria (2007). While certainly a crude and imperfect proxy for the share of the population with access to lending services, it is the most consistent currently available indicator of lending services use across countries. Figure 7.4 shows that banking systems with higher interest margins are also characterized by lower outreach, that is, by a lower penetration of the use of credit services in the economy.

The negative association between the efficiency and the depth and breadth of financial intermediation as shown in Figures 7.3 and 7.4 is a correlation rather than a causal relationship. The same inefficiencies impact the shape and flexion points of the interest-return curve in Figure 7.1 and of the loan-supply curve in Figure 7.2. As the theoretical analysis has already suggested, we have to look for common causes of both low levels and low efficiency of financial intermediation. Before we do, however, we will take a closer look into the component of interest rate spreads, that is, we undertake a statistical decomposition of the preferred measure of bank inefficiency.

7.4 Decomposing spreads

The decomposition of interest rate spreads can be a useful exercise in examining the factors that drive inefficiency and thus high intermediation costs in a banking market.[7] However, it should be stressed that such an exercise is not an end in itself, but rather a tool to find the underlying deficiencies in the environment in which banks operate and identify policies to remedy these deficiencies. In the following, we will use the example of interest rate spreads in Kenya to illustrate this process; for more detail, see Beck and Fuchs (2004).

We will start out with the cost of funding for banks, which in most cases is the weighted interest rate that banks pay on their deposits. However, not all deposits can be used for loans, a certain share has to be retained or deposited with the central bank as reserve requirements. Further, in many countries with deposit insurance systems, banks have to pay premiums on their total deposits, which further add to the cost of intermediation. Transaction taxes also add to the intermediation costs.

Operating costs, that is, transaction costs related to deposit and lending services, make up the largest part of the spread in most countries (Figure 7.5). As discussed in the previous section, these costs entail expenses related to individual transactions and customers, such as screening and monitoring of borrowers, or costs associated with savings or payment services, and general operating expenses related to branches, computer systems, security arrangements and so on. In practical terms, these are wage costs, equipment costs (computers, vehicles, etc.) and

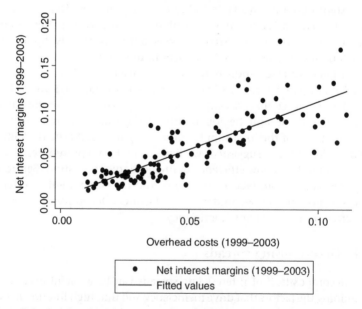

Figure 7.5   Overhead cost drive interest margins

building costs (explicit or implicit rents). It is here that the productivity of financial institutions can make a big difference: how many clients are being served by one employee? What is the deposit and loan volume per employee? How many clients are being catered to by one branch? Or in more technical terms: how well does a bank use its inputs (labour, equipment, buildings) to produce output (loan, deposit and payment services).[8] Overhead costs relative to total assets vary between 1 or 2 per cent in many developed countries, to over 5 per cent in many developing countries (Beck, Demirguc-Kunt and Levine, 2000). In the case of Kenya, average operating costs are 5.6 per cent, although there is a large variation across banks, discussed below (Table 7.1).

Provisions for loan losses are part of the interest rate spread as banks have to take into account historic losses when contracting new loans. Historic and projected loan losses relate directly to the agency problems and the lack of diversification possibilities discussed above. Non-performing loans add to the cost of intermediation, because they represent opportunity costs in terms of interest revenue foregone and because they tie up resources that could otherwise be lent. It is here that sound credit policies and banks' risk management come into play, as well as the contractual and information framework in which financial institutions operate and which we will discuss below.

The residual between the sum of deposit rate (i.e. the marginal cost of funding, reserve requirements and other indirect taxes, overhead costs and loan loss provisions) and the lending rate are before-tax profits, out of which profit taxes have to be paid. While textbook models suggest that perfect competition should do away with any profits, one has to remember that growing banks need a certain minimum amount of profits

Table 7.1 Spread decomposition for Kenyan banks

	All banks	State-owned banks	Domestic private	Foreign banks
Average lending rate	18.1	19.8	17.2	17.7
Average deposit rate	3.2	2.9	4.7	2.2
Overhead cost	5.6	4.4	5.3	6.6
Loan loss provisions	2.5	4.9	1.5	1.8
Reserve requirements	0.3	0.3	0.4	0.2
Tax	1.9	2.2	1.6	2.1
Profit margin	4.5	5.2	3.7	4.9
Total spread	14.9	16.9	12.5	15.5

Source: Beck and Fuchs (2004) and author's calculations using data from the CBK. All data are for 2002.

to maintain their capital adequacy ratio, that is, they need some profit to keep capital in line with a growing loan book. However, there are large differences across countries in the profitability of financial institutions, which can indicate either large variation in competitiveness of banking systems or variation in country risk; in particular, foreign banks might insist on large returns in small developing countries to compensate for a high degree of country-level economic and political uncertainty. In the case of Kenya, we note a relatively high profit margin, but again with variation across different banks (Table 7.1).

7.5   Explaining spreads

While the decomposition of spreads allows us to identify the items in the banks' balance sheets that make up the spread, this rather mechanical exercise is only the first step towards analysing the driving factors behind high intermediation costs. For the purpose of the following discussion, we will distinguish between factors at three different levels: the level of individual institutions, the level of the banking system and the country-level. While such a division might seem somewhat artificial when it comes to certain factors, it is helpful in discussing policy options that help reduce intermediation costs.

Take first the level of the individual institutions. The composition of both deposit and loan portfolio can be an important driver. Lending to certain sectors, such as agriculture, is riskier and might imply higher costs. The absence of risk diversification possibilities can also lead to prohibitively high risk premiums and credit rationing. Ownership is an important determinant of efficiency. While government-owned banks are consistently found to have higher margins and spreads (Demirguc-Kunt, Laeven and Levine, 2004; Micco, Panizza and Yañez, 2007) there is mixed evidence in the case of foreign-owned banks: while foreign-owned banks in developed economies are typically less efficient, foreign-owned banks in developing countries are often more efficient, that is, have lower overhead costs and net interest margins.[9] Interestingly, the lower overhead costs and net interest margins are often in spite of higher wage costs due to expatriate salaries; this seems to be more than offset by higher productivity. This is illustrated in the case of Kenya. While foreign-owned banks have higher overhead costs than domestic banks, they have lower interest spreads than government-owned banks and only somewhat higher spreads than private domestic banks. The difference is explained by the much higher loan loss provisions of government-owned banks compared to privately owned banks, both domestic and foreign (Table 7.1).

Bank size can also be a driving factor for intermediation efficiency. Larger banks can enjoy scale economies by spreading the fixed component of transaction costs over more clients and over more volume of deposit and loans (Demirguc-Kunt, Laeven and Levine, 2004). Larger banks might also be able to better diversify risk stemming from different sources, that is, both from agency problems, as well as from borrower-specific production risk.

Consider next the level of the banking system. Both ownership structure and size structure can have important repercussions here, too. A large share of government-owned banks does not only drive up the average spread faced by depositors and borrowers, but through their dominating role, inefficient government banks can provide rents to privately owned, more efficient banks that charge the same spread while enjoying higher profits. This does not seem to be the case in Kenya, where government-owned banks actually have the highest profit margins of all banks (Table 7.1); however, it can be argued that the rents provided by government-owned banks allow foreign-owned banks to be less efficient and less innovative in their quest to lower overhead costs. Strong entry by foreign banks, on the other hand, can put competitive pressure on domestic banks (Claessens, Demirguc-Kunt and Huizinga, 2001). Scale economies on the individual bank level also have repercussions on the level of the banking system. On the one hand, small banking systems with a few large banks might be able to overcome disadvantages of small size. On the other hand, relying only on a few large banks might have negative repercussions for the competitiveness of the financial systems. It should be noted, however, that market structure indicators such as the number of banks, concentration ratios or Herfindahl indices are not very good indicators of competitiveness (Demirguc-Kunt, Laeven and Levine, 2004; Claessens and Laven, 2004). More important than the market structure is the contestability of the market, that is, the ease with which new banks can enter the market. This puts the focus on regulatory policies that critically influence the contestability of the banking system. However, it also emphasizes the importance of supervisory practices; allowing undercapitalized and fragile banks to compete with healthy ones can again result in rents for the healthy institutions, as is the case in Kenya, where a history of small bank failures in recent history has created mistrust by the public in small private banks, which in turn gives large foreign-owned banks a stronger market position than their market share and structural market indicators would suggest (Beck and Fuchs, 2004).

On the country level, the contractual and informational frameworks and the macroeconomic environment are critical in determining intermediation efficiency. Financial contracts depend on the certainty of legal rights and predictability, and the speed of their fair and impartial enforcement and a more efficient contractual framework can have a dampening effect on several components of the intermediation spread (Demirguc-Kunt, Laeven and Levine, 2004; Laeven and Majnoni, 2005): it helps reduce overhead costs as the cost of creating, perfecting and enforcing collateral decreases, and reduces loan loss provision as better contract enforcement reduces incentives for borrowers to willingly default; at the same time it increases the share that creditors can recover in case of default.[10] And it can reduce the profit margin by affecting competition: lower costs of creating and perfecting collateral can lower the costs of switching creditors and reduce hold-up of borrowers by the main creditor.

Similarly, improvements in the informational framework can reduce information costs. More transparent financial statements and credit information sharing lower the cost of screening and monitoring borrowers and reduce adverse selection by making it more likely that lenders choose plums rather than lemons, thus reducing future loan losses.[11] Sharing negative information on borrowers through credit registries also reduces the perverse incentive to default deliberately on one's commitments. By allowing borrowers to build up 'reputation collateral' in the form of a credit history, credit information sharing can have a positive impact on competition, as borrowers are able to offer their positive credit history to other creditors. Finally, macroeconomic instability, can drive up spreads as it exacerbates the information asymmetries discussed in Section 7.1 (Demirguc-Kunt, Laeven and Levine, 2004; Huybens and Smith, 1999).

Country characteristics beyond the institutional framework, such as size and the general costs of doing business, can be an important factor of the efficiency with which financial institutions operate. Many developing countries suffer from the triple problems of smallness: small clients, small institutions and small markets. These diseconomies of scale and lower possibilities of diversifying risk lead to higher intermediation costs and can, as discussed in Section 7.2 result in rationing of clients. Figure 7.6 illustrates this by plotting net interest margins against the absolute size of financial systems in US dollars – countries with smaller financial systems experience higher margins. Small countries should therefore put a premium on policies encouraging entry of foreign banks that are able to reap benefits of scale economies across subsidiaries in different countries, on integration of financial markets across countries, and on allowing their citizens access to financial services across borders.

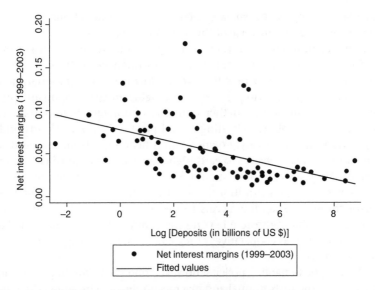

Figure 7.6 Small financial system have higher net interest margin

General costs of doing business constitute another country-level constraint and include high costs due to deficiencies in the transportation and communication networks and electricity provision.[12] Inefficiencies in input markets, such as labour markets or telecommunication markets, might drive up costs and impede innovation.[13]

7.6 Conclusions and policy lessons

Market frictions give rise to financial intermediaries and organized financial markets, but it is the efficiency with which financial institutions can reduce these market frictions that determines the depth, breadth and efficiency of the financial system. While the efficiency of financial institutions is reflected in interest spreads and margins, one has to consider the underlying causes in order to formulate sensible policy lessons. Profit-maximizing financial institutions aim to provide financial services in a cost-effective manner, but subject to two important constraints: the competitive environment and the general institutional framework. Over the past years, financial institutions around the globe have developed new products (simple transaction account), new delivery channels and methods (correspondent banking, mobile branches, phone and e-finance), new lending techniques (group lending, non-traditional collateral) and new screening methodologies (credit scoring), with direct repercussions for overhead costs and spreads. Many of these innovations have also helped expand the universe of the bankable population.

While technology has certainly played an important role, it is competitive pressure which in the end pushes financial institutions to be more efficient, and it is here that we can identify a first important role for government. Allowing or even encouraging entry by sound and prudent new institutions, whether domestic or foreign, is important to maintain contestability. Creating a level playing field also means finding ways to avoid privately owned banks benefiting from the need of government-owned banks to earn higher spreads. Beyond the commercial banking system there should also be a lively competition with non-bank financial institutions. Avoiding segmentation in the financial sector through expanding access to the payment system or the credit information sharing system beyond the commercial banks to bank-like institutions such as cooperatives or regulating MFIs can help the financial system stay competitive.

These market-enabling policies, however, find their limit in constraints imposed by the institutional and macroeconomic environment. Market-developing policies, that is, policies addressing deficiencies in the contractual and informational frameworks and policies maintaining macroeconomic stability, can have important medium- to long-term repercussions for the efficiency with which financial institutions operate. Beyond the financial system, the cost of doing business can impose important constraints.

A proper and careful analysis of a country's financial system can not only help identify deficiencies, but can also help policy-makers prioritize. What is the binding constraint on financial institutions to become more efficient and thus to help deepen and broaden the financial system? If it is lack of competition, market-enabling policies fostering contestability are called for. If it deficiencies in the contractual and informational frameworks, reforms in these areas are at a premium. If the problem is part of wider problems of high costs of doing business, then they should be addressed.

Notes

1 Private Credit to GDP is a standard measure of financial intermediary development and is the ratio of claims by deposit money banks and other financial institutions on the private, domestic non-financial sector relative to GDP.
2 See Levine (1997, 2005) for an overview of this literature.

3 This is a shortened version of the discussion in Beck and de la Torre (2007) who also distinguish between payment-/savings and loan services and between idiosyncratic and systemic risk elements.

4 Empirically it is very difficult to distinguish between adverse selection and moral hazard, as discussed by Karlan and Zinman (2006).

5 While spreads are the difference between *ex ante* contracted loan and deposit interest rates, margins are the actually received interest revenue on loan minus the interest costs on deposits. The main difference between spreads and margins are lost interest revenue on non-performing loans.

6 All data are from the Financial Structure Database, as described in Beck, Demirguc-Kunt and Levine (2000), unless otherwise noted.

7 Throughout the chapter, we abstract from non-interest revenue of banks, both directly related to savings and loan services and related to non-lending business.

8 See Berger and Humphrey (1997) for an overview of this literature.

9 See Clarke et al. (2003) for an overview.

10 There is a recent, but large literature on the relationship between legal system efficiency and financial development, following the seminal work by La Porta et al. (1997). For an overview, see Beck and Levine (2005).

11 See among others, La Porta et al. (1997), Jappelli and Pagano (2002), Miller (2003), Love and Mylenko (2003).

12 Beck, Demiguc-Kunt and Martinez Peria (2007) find a positive cross-country association of geographic branch and ATM penetration with rail and communication infrastructure.

13 See, for example, discussion on South Africa (World Bank, 2004), and the discussion in Claessens, Dobos, Klingebiel and Laeven (2003).

8
Efficiency Drivers and Constraints: Empirical Findings

Yousra Hamed
International Labour Office

8.1 Introduction

This chapter shows the effect of several key variables on the financial and social performance of 45 MFIs. The purpose is to determine the exogenous or endogenous nature of those variables. Financial performance is measured by financial self-sufficiency and operational self-sufficiency, and social performance is measured by a set of indicators commonly used in the *MicroBanking Bulletin* (*MBB*) and the MIX (Microfinance Information eXchange).

The chapter is divided in six sections. The following section explains the methodology used, Section 8.3 looks into the sample features. Section 8.4 classifies MFIs by their poverty outreach and financial performance using a multiple correspondence analysis. The last section examines factors that are expected to determine how well an MFI does in terms of financial and social performance: location, legal form, staff costs, scope for externalizing transaction costs and subsidies.

8.2 Methodology

Institutional performance has three dimensions. The first two, in line with the dual objective of microfinance, are social and financial. The third dimension, efficiency, is about the optimality of input combinations and output pricing. Factor analysis is a useful method to apply to this kind of issue, as it describes multidimensional performance (or under-performance). The appropriate method for survey analysis is the multiple correspondence method. This technique examines the links between qualitative variables so as to yield a typology of institutions based on similarities. The more two MFIs have common modalities, the closer they are. The distance between two modalities determines their likeness. Clustering simplifies the identification of mutual associations between modalities, that is, the connection between two variables, and the link between observations (MFIs), as well as the examination of the average characteristic of a cluster.

The first step is to transform the numerical variables into qualitative variables to make the data more homogenous and adapted to a multiple correspondence analysis. Cluster analysis allows the partitioning of an original population into subsets (clusters), so that the data in each cluster share some common features identified by proximity according to pre-determined distance measures. The agglomerative hierarchical clustering that we will use starts by considering each MFI as a distinct group. Through a similarity index computed for all potential pairs of individuals, the two closest institutions are grouped, and so forth. The iteration is repeated until all observations belong to the same cluster.

To obtain the hierarchical tree, the Ward method will be used. The optimal partition in groups is determined in such a way that the variation is low within a group but high among two different groups. The last step consists in introducing as illustrative variables groups of variables concerning the location, the legal form and so on to characterize the different clusters. When the results of the method are not significant we shall turn to a crossed table of two variables.

8.3   The data

The data on the social and financial performance of MFIs were generated in 2004 and 2005 by way of a questionnaire-based field survey. These 45 MFIs operate in Africa, Asia, Latin America, Eastern Europe and MENA and in 21 countries. Twenty-six MFI are listed on the MIX (Microfinance Information eXchange).[1] The survey carried out in the framework of this Geneva International Academic Network (GIAN) research project covers microfinance institutions that had at least 3000 clients, operated continuously between 1999 and 2003 and were able to produce audited financial statements for the entire period (see Annex I for details).

The survey questionnaire was designed through several rounds of discussions amongst the four institutions participating in the research project: the University of Geneva; the ILO; the Geneva Institute of Development Studies (IUED) and Cambridge University. The individual surveys were carried out by postgraduate students and consultants under the respective supervision of the four institutions.

Table 8.1   Sample MFIs by region

Region	Number of MFIs
Africa	12
Asia	10
Europe	3
Latin America	9
MENA	11
Total	45

Source: GIAN survey.

The construction of a random sample was constrained for a number of reasons: of the 21 countries in which the 45 sample MFIs operate, a third are not subject to a regulation, others do not have representative professional associations that could produce a complete list of operational MFIs. The 45 institutions were selected using three selection criteria: the MFI had to be willing to share information and had to have at least 3000 clients and dispose of audited financial statements for the five consecutive years 1999–2003. The description of the sample features follows the definitions used in the *MBB* to construct peer groups, namely region, age, portfolio size, legal form, range of financial services, delivery techniques, target market and financial self sufficiency (*MBB*, 2005).

Over half of the sample MFIs had more than eight years of operations. Two MFIs had fewer than four years, namely CACTRI in Bolivia which was established in 1963 as a social NGO with a microcredit component; in 2000, it transformed into a regulated institution and changed its activities and procedures; and Banque du Caire, a downscaling Egyptian bank. Forty per cent of the sample are small MFIs, with a portfolio of less than US$4 million if in Latin America and US$2 million if located in the other regions. The MFIs with large portfolios make up a quarter of our sample. The same size distribution applies when looking at the number of clients: 47 per cent of MFIs have less than 10,000 clients.

NGOs are the most common legal form in our sample, followed by cooperatives (Africa and Latin America) and non-banking financial institutions (NBFI) which have a company legal form. Nearly half of the MFIs of our sample provide only microcredit, but several MFIs also take deposits and offer micro-insurance or money transfers. The delivery technique commonly used combines individual and group lending. Often, MFIs begin with one delivery technique before they broaden their approach to satisfy client demand (the Moroccan case for the individual loans introduction) or to adapt strategy (the case of Egyptian institutions that introduced group loans to deepen their outreach after having reached financial self-sufficiency with individual loans). In terms of target market, the largest share of the MFIs of our sample (42 per cent) targets the very poor with an average loan amount of less than 20 per cent of GDP per capita. MFIs that serve the better off make up 20 per cent of the sample.

The financial self-sufficiency ratio measures the capacity of an MFI to cover its costs on market terms and conditions. This ratio is thus adjusted for subsidies received. However, we were not always able to calculate the ratio rigorously,[2] and had to use rating reports, wherever available.

8.4 MFI clusters

Combining the variables for financial and social performance, we seek to distinguish exogenous and endogenous variables. The selection of indicators, the determination of thresholds and interpretation are in line with *MBB* methods, based on the literature and consider the means and standard deviations.

To capture information on the financial performance of MFIs the questionnaire was designed to generate data for the two most relevant indicators of financial performance, namely operational and financial self-sufficiency. Operational self-sufficiency is defined as operational revenues / (financial expenses + loan loss provision expenses + operational expenses). This ratio measures the capacity of an MFI to cover its operational costs with its revenues (regardless of the source). Besides being a financial indicator, the operational self-sufficiency ratio can also be considered as an indicator of allocative efficiency. The financial self-sufficiency adjusts the operational self-sufficiency for inflation, subsidies and accounting norms.[3] Practically speaking, financial self-sufficiency measures the capacity of an MFI to cover its expenses with revenues priced at market rates and conditions. Positive financial self-sufficiency is the mark of a healthy MFI, but it does not necessarily mean that it stops receiving subsidies: in fact, an MFI can be financially self-sufficient while still receiving subsidies, provided it generates enough income to pay for all the expenses that would result from contracting these resources at market rates.

In addition to the classic financial performance indicators, operational self-sufficiency and financial self-sufficiency, the questionnaire data should permit the generation of data for supplementary indicators for financial performance used in the *MBB* and MIX:

- return on assets;
- loan loss provisions per outstanding loan portfolio;

- portfolio at risk at 90 days past due;
- loan loss rate; and
- provisions for past due loans of 30 days and more.[4]

For social performance the indicators included:

- average loan amount as per cent of GNP per capita;
- share of loans covered by joint liability only;
- deposits collected as a percentage of total liabilities;
- average deposit amount as per cent of GNP per head;
- percentage of women clients;
- literacy and numeracy amongst clients;
- existence of poverty targets etc.

Applying multivariate analysis to the data, following the above 2 groups of variables, generated four major types of MFIs ('clusters'),[5] as shown in Table 8.2.

The first type of MFIs is poverty focused and financially self-sufficient. The group consists of 21 MFIs with an explicit poverty focus in the mission statement, use of poverty criteria to target clients, a group-based lending methodology, a 100 per cent female clientele, and downmarket targeting reflected in the average loan ratio of less than 20 per cent of the GDP per capita. On the other hand, they have a very low write-off ratio (less than 0.5 per cent) that expresses a clean portfolio, and thus good financial performance regarding this very indicator.

The second group of 22 MFIs is not poverty focused. Most of them require fixed asset as collateral and do not use solidarity groups for all clients. Both features discourage the poorest from applying for a loan. They also target the high end of the market with an average loan amount between 150 and 250 per cent of GDP per capita. Financial performance is not significant: none of its indicators appear in this cluster.

Table 8.2　MFI types – 3 clusters (social and financial performance)

Types		Number
1	Poverty focused and financially self-sufficient	21
2	Not poverty focused	22
3	Missing data	2
	Total	45

Note: A summary of the multivariate analysis followed by the clustering result.

This might suggest that this cluster has many financial performance features and none is more significant than any other. To establish whether this is the case, we break down the sample into more than the two initial clusters in order to obtain a finer differentiation.

The first group in Table 8.2 now appears subdivided into two clusters in accordance with the previous features. From the social performance point of view, the two have the same characteristics as the initial cluster, but they differ in terms of financial performance. Cluster 2 maintained and achieved a rise in its financial performance indicators: the majority of the MFIs in this cluster provision the at risk portfolio at 30 days, have a low loan loss provision share (less than 5 per cent of the total portfolio), a good write-off ratio (less than 0.5 per cent only of the portfolio is not reimbursed) and a matching at risk portfolio after 90 days overdue (almost 70 per cent of the MFIs have an at risk portfolio of less than 0.5 per cent).[6]

The second original cluster in Table 8.2 is now broken down into three clusters (types 3, 4, 5 in Table 8.3) that shed more light on its financial performance characteristics. Four MFIs are not financially self-sufficient with a loan loss provision share that exceeds 10 per cent of the total expenses (good performance is below 5 per cent and is applied by almost 50 per cent of the sample); eight MFIs still remain without a financial feature, and nine MFIs are rather financially self-sufficient: a percentage between 0.5 and 2 per cent of the portfolio is at risk (almost 50 per cent of the MFIs who answered this question have an at risk portfolio of less than 0.5 per cent), a medium loan loss provision share (between 5 and 10 per cent while the loan loss provision share consistent with a good financial performance is less than 5 per cent), and average performance in the write-off ratio.

Table 8.3 MFI types – 6 clusters (social and financial performance)

Types		Number
1	Poverty focused	9
2	Poverty focused and financially self-sufficient	13
3	Not financially self-sufficient	4
4	Not poverty focused	8
5	Not poverty focused and moderately financially self-sufficient	9
	Missing data	2
	Total	45

Note: A summary of the multivariate analysis followed by the clustering.

Box 8.1   MECREF, Niger

MECREF (Mutuelle d'Epargne et de Crédit des Femmes) is a cooperatively organized MFI, set up in 1998 and located in the greater Niamey area in Niger. As its name indicates, it sees its role in providing appropriate financial services to women, thus enhancing their empowerment. In June 2004 it had 7261 members, including 405 groups and 64 associations. At the end of 2003 the gross loan portfolio stood at over €815,000. Group loans are required for all transaction below FCFA 100,000, unless the client has sufficient collateral. Only 9 per cent of clients obtained a loan below this amount in 2003. At the other end of the scale, 8 per cent of clients received 32 per cent of loans in 2003, in the form of individual loans exceeding FCFA 2.5 million. The bulk of loans went to more middle-class women entrepreneurs. The closeness of the Niamey market explains its solid financial performance, with positive operational self-sufficiency and financial self-sufficiency values. It should be noted, however, that this MFI continues to receive substantial subsidies from Développement international Desjardins (DID), ADF (African Development Foundation), SNV (Netherlands Development Organization), Oxfam and World Vision, representing 9 per cent of operating income if one considers the cash subsidy and nearly 30 per cent of total operating income and if one also takes into account in-kind subsidies (e.g., equipment, vehicles).

Boxes 8.1, 8.2 and 8.3[7] give examples of three MFIs, two of which are financially self-sufficient MFIs, with different social aims and results. Considered in their local context, external factors (such as legal form, location, size, lending methodologies) would appear to influence both the social and financial performance of an MFI.

Roughly speaking the five clusters categorized in Table 8.3 can be grouped in three, consisting of a group that on the whole scores high on both poverty outreach and financial return (22 MFIs), a second that scores low on both accounts (12 MFIs), and a last group that scores medium on financial performance but low on the social one (9 MFIs). It is obviously of interest to verify whether low or high performance is the result of poor or good (technical) efficiency.

Comparing now the three clusters from the point of technical efficiency and using the following yardsticks, we see that the efficiency levels differ and combine in many ways, sometimes not the expected ones, with social and financial performance.

The selected indicators for efficiency are:

- administrative expenses per loan outstanding;
- cost per borrower;
- number of clients per loan officer, per staff member;

- share loan officers on total staff;
- loan officer salary compared to the minimum wage;
- average processing time per loan.

The first two indicators are used by the *MBB*; the third one belongs to the list of efficiency indicators referred to in the microfinance guidelines (SEEP, 2002; *MBB*, 2002); the fourth ratio is used by many rating agencies, for instance PlaNet rating; the fifth is inspired by the *MBB*, but here instead of dividing the loan officers' salary by the GNP per capita, we divide it by the minimum wage.[8] The last ratio is our own.

The effect of a single efficiency indicator (workload), introduced as an active variable to the multivariate analysis, is insufficiently significant and does not change much of the cluster's composition (the answers to

---

Box 8.2   CAME, Mexico

CAME (Centro de Apoyo al Microempresario) is an MFI of the NGO variety created in 1990. At the end of 2003 it had close to 40,000 members and thus represents a medium-sized MFI in the Mexican context. Its gross loan portfolio at the same date was $5.9 million. It operates on the outskirts of the greater Mexico City area. Within its cluster it is a relatively sound performer financially, catering to the moderately poor. Its mission is to reach the financially excluded. CAME offers two loan products, group loans for income generation and individual loans, 87 per cent and 13 per cent of the gross loan portfolio respectively in 2003. The group loan is collateral-free, but requires prior deposits between 10 and 50 per cent of the loan amount which is deposited in an individual account with BANSEFI, a public bank. A substantial proportion of group members appear to drop out of their group (27.5 per cent in 2003) reflecting a different perception of the costs and benefits of this delivery technique between the MFI and its clients. Many group members, 80 per cent female, seem to feel constrained by the loan ceiling of Pesos 20,000, whilst the ceiling on individual loans is Pesos 50,000. These individual loan products are targeted at micro-entrepreneurs, and require a guarantee at 200 per cent of the loan amount plus a personal guarantee from a third party. Here again there is a relatively high percentage of clients who do not come back after their first individual loan cycle, namely 30 to 40 per cent, which is attributed to the repayment modality requiring debtors to make weekly cash payments at a branch of BANSEFI. CAME's mission is to help the population that is financially excluded; because of its choice of geographical zone, it caters primarily to the moderately poor, operating in the informal economy, but having access to social and physical infrastructure, with a large share of men migrating for the week to the Mexico City urban area. This is not a zone of extreme poverty such as one can still find in some backward rural areas in Mexico. CAME's operational self-sufficiency and financial self-sufficiency are positive since 2001.

Box 8.3   SEF, South Africa

The Small Enterprise Foundation is a South African MFI created in 1991 and having NGO legal status. It is focused on the poor and the very poor (average loan less than 5 per cent of GNP per capita) with the aim of eliminating poverty, using a group loan methodology addressed to a majority of rural female clients. At the end of 2004 it had reached 22,100 clients, almost equally divided between poor and very poor clients. At the end of 2004, the gross loan portfolio stood at over $2 million. After more than 12 years of operations, SEF was almost operationally, but not yet financially self-sufficient. The environment, or more precisely the labour market, in South Africa is quite unique. Income inequality problems make MFIs recover high salary costs from revenues based on clients who can only afford small loans. This creates a salary burden for the MFI (the highest in the world) that drives the ratio of total expenses/gross loan portfolio to more than 100 per cent in 2001 and impedes financial performance. The managers face significant obstacles in improving productivity to compensate for the divergence between staff and client living standards. They face the option of moving up-market or closing.

---

this single question do not change the shape of the scattered plot). We find similar results if we introduce it as an illustrative variable. In order to determine the behaviour of the predetermined clusters from the efficiency point of view, we fixed the clusters as a variable by an 'archivage' procedure. This new variable (with as many modalities as the clusters) can be crossed with the efficiency indicators one by one in case the multivariate analysis does not give satisfactory results.

Table 8.4 shows that the majority of the MFIs in the cluster characterized by simultaneous good financial and social performance also score high on the efficiency criteria 'work load'. This is one of the reasons that allow them to be financially self-sufficient despite catering for the poor. Following this, one would expect that MFIs performing badly on both social and financial dimension (cluster 2) to also have poor scores in terms of work load and the ones performing rather badly (cluster 3) to also have a weak workload. However, Table 8.4 shows that it is not the case. So there must be other efficiency variables that better explain the differences in social and financial performance.

We therefore introduced the different efficiency variables one by one for the multivariate analysis, with the following results:[9]

- The ratio 'loan officers per total staff' is only significant within the clusters composed by MFIs that target up-market and have mediocre or no financial performance. Their efficiency, expressed by this particular ratio, is limited (the ratio loan officers / total staff is below 50 per cent).

- The analysis shows that the efficiency indicator 'average outstanding loans per client' shows low values in poverty-oriented MFIs whose financial performance is modest.[10]
- The efficiency ratio 'operational expenses/gross loan portfolio' is significant in two clusters. It is low (less than 15 per cent, hence expressing efficiency) in poverty-oriented MFIs and medium (between 15 and 30 per cent, expressing a limited efficiency) in financially self-sufficient MFIs.
- The cost per borrower ratio is low (less than $50) for the cluster of MFIs catering to the poor and high (more than $200) for the ones reaching the high end.
- The loan officer's salary compared to the minimum wage is an efficiency indicator with low values in poverty-focused MFIs (loan officer's wage = minimum wage), in a medium range in financially self-sufficient ones (a loan officer is paid two to four times the minimum wage), and very high values signalling low efficiency in factor use (ten times and more of the minimum wage) in rather financially well-performing, but not poverty-focused MFIs.

As a summary, the analysis of the efficiency indicators taken one by one shows that the MFIs with limited efficiency are mostly up-market and with no or weak financial performance. The financially self-sufficient institutions are fairly efficient or not at all, while the poverty-focused

Table 8.4 Clusters and workload

	Client/loan officer (37–150)	Client/loan officer (150–300)	Client/loan officer (300 +)	Total
Poverty focused + financially self-sufficient	6	6	10	22
Not poverty focused + not financially self-sufficient	2	7	3	12
Not poverty focused + moderately financially self-sufficient	2	0	7	9
Missing data	0	2	0	2
Total	10	15	20	45

Table 8.5   MFI types – 4 clusters (social and financial performance and efficiency)

Types	Number
Poverty focused, not fully financially sustainable and efficient	8
Not poverty focused, not fully financially sustainable and not efficient	8
Poverty focused, financially sustainable and partly efficient	14
Not poverty focused, partly financially sustainable and not efficient	12
Missing data	3
Total	45

ones are on average more efficient. The poverty-oriented ones can be either efficient or inefficient, according to the chosen efficiency variable. However the clusters' affiliation and weight were practically stable with the use of different efficiency indicators.

As a last step of the analysis, we introduce all the efficiency variables at once. We observe the changes in the scattered plot and the new clustering division according to the three dimensions: efficiency, and social and financial performances.

By applying multivariate analysis to the data, following the three groups of variables, four major types of MFIs ('clusters') emerge (Table 8.5).

The first type of MFI is poverty focused, efficient but not fully financially sustainable. This group consists of eight efficient MFIs with low cost per borrower (less than $50) and a low administrative expenses ratio (below 15 per cent of the total expenses are dedicated to operational expenses). The yield on gross loan portfolio is between 0 and 25 per cent,[11] a modest financial performance.[12] The MFIs of this group cater to the predominantly very poor with average loan amounts of less than 20 per cent of GDP per capita.

The second group consists of eight MFIs that are less focused on the poor as shown by relatively large average client deposits (20 to 150 per cent of GDP per capita), they have a low level of financial sustainability (reflected by a high ratio of portfolio at risk after 90 days overdue, loan loss provisions exceeding 10 per cent plus no operational self-sufficiency reached) and an insufficient level of efficiency.

The variables used to compute the clusters do not all appear in the final clustering. It depends on their significance vis-à-vis the answers for the MFIs composing the cluster over the whole set of variables. For some of the cases, the three dimensions indicators are not significant and do not appear in the clusters.

The third type of MFI comprises 14 institutions that are modestly efficient. The loan officers are paid two to four times the minimum wage (the most efficient MFIs pay the minimum wage. The less efficient pay even more than 10 times the minimum wage). They also got reasonable staff productivity figures (each loan officer handles between 100 and 200 clients). The MFIs of this cluster perform reasonably well financially, with provisions for bad debt of less than 5 per cent and a loan loss ratio of less than 0.5 per cent. The operational self-sufficiency and financial self-sufficiency do not appear in the current clustering. They are poverty focused because about 80 per cent of them have average loan amounts of less than 20 per cent of GNP per capita and do not ask for real collateral while granting loans.

The fourth category consists of 12 MFIs that are not very efficient, perform modestly in terms of financial sustainability, and are not very much focused on the poor. The average transaction sizes of $500 and more shows both an up-market targeting and a limited efficiency. The later is confirmed by high administrative costs per clients ($200 and more) and a low work load. But at the same time they have a good efficiency indicator: the processing time for the first loan is quite short (1–4 days). We can conclude that their efficiency is mixed. This type of MFI tends to charge relatively high interest rates of 25 per cent and more, concealing a mediocre level of efficiency. The underlying fragility is likely to be exposed as soon as the local financial market gets more competitive (see the case study of Mali in Chapter 10).

This shows that it is perfectly possible that MFIs – notably those grouped in cluster 1 – can be both efficient in comparison to the entire sample and at the same time not break even. This is an interesting outcome by itself, confirming anecdotal evidence and intuition, but it is only part of the argument. Worse, it could even lead donors and government to jump to the conclusion that they just need to pick a type of MFI and drop the other groups, for example, only support MFIs that maximize financial returns, or alternatively only the highly poverty focused MFIs. What really matters for a rationalization of policy support is to unpack performance within each group of MFIs. Our point is that donors should accept and welcome the variety in missions and statements of MFIs that is unfolding over all regions and focus their attention on the relative efficiency within each group or cluster of MFIs.

The combination of features in these clusters is in many respects counter-intuitive: what is it that brings about the combination of poverty focus and good financial performance in some MFIs, whilst in others everything that can go wrong seems to converge: no poverty focus, poor financial results and low technical efficiency?

8.5   Performance drivers and constraints

In order to understand the factors that determine whether a given MFI is more positioned towards poverty outreach or more inclined to reach full financial sustainability quickly, we selected five determinants, namely location, legal form, staff costs, scope for cost externalization and access to subsidies. The dependent variables are thus, on the one hand, poverty outreach (measured by the above mentioned indicators) and, on the other hand, financial performance, measured by operational and financial self-sufficiency.

The age of an MFI, its market, size, ownership, the range of services provided and so on make a difference to the efficiency frontier in financial and social performance. Given that MFIs operate in disparate local markets, with very different degrees of accessibility, competitiveness and organizational maturity, it is crucial to shed some light on the exogenous determinants for performance, such as differences in delivery methodology and institutional maturity.

In rural areas transaction costs are higher, because of lower population density, remoteness of clients, limited economies of scale, high-risk activities and rigid production cycles. Location also has implications for social performance as the poverty rate in rural areas tends to exceed that in urban areas.[13] Our survey confirms that MFIs that cater to the very poor are located in rural areas, whilst MFIs that cater to the high end of clients operate in urban areas.

The results of multivariate analysis on a set of variables of the three dimensions plus localization indicators are shown in Table 8.6. The 20 MFIs with a predominantly rural outreach cater to the poor (75 per cent of them are in the *low end* segment); their efficiency is average (low cost per borrower but loan officers paid two to four times the minimum wage), and their overall financial performance in several respects is good (a write-off ratio below 5 per cent of the portfolio and a loan loss provision

Table 8.6   Location and poverty level

	Low end (<20%)	Broad (20–149%)	High end (150–249%)	Small business	All
Majority/all rural	10	5	0	1	16
Minority/not rural	8	10	6	2	26
Missing data	1	1	0	0	2
All	19	16	6	3	44

share below 0.5 per cent of the total expenses). The 24 MFIs that are urban-oriented cater to a more *up-market* clientele and are not efficient (the credit officers are less than half the total staff which leads to a bigger fixed 'unproductive' expenses, a weak work load per loan officer, a high cost per borrower exceeding $200 and loan officers paid up to ten times the minimum wage).

Crossing the financial variables with location gives results on these specific measures: the rural MFIs are equally divided between having reached operational self-sufficiency and not yet, whilst the urban MFIs are clearly more operationally self-sufficient; this applies also to financial self-sufficiency. As Table 8.7 illustrates, location seems, then, to be a strong determinant of financial performance.

Our sample contains 21 NGOs, 16 cooperatives, seven non-banking financial institutions and one bank. One could assume that the legal form pre-disposes the poverty orientation of an MFI or its market orientation. Non-banking financial institutions, for example, presumably will seek a different trade-off of profitability and social mission than NGOs. Cooperatives being member service organizations cater to people with a common bond, not necessarily the poor. The survey results, through multivariate analysis on the three dimensions and legal form variables, show that a cluster composed of 15 MFIs with NGO status are efficient in terms of low cost per borrower and high work load, whilst at the same time keeping a pronounced focus on the poor (Table 8.8). NGOs come out as most committed to their social mission with consistent targeting practice. Most of them are operationally self-sufficient (somewhat surprisingly, but probably hiding substantial subsidy elements, since very few of them have reached financial self-sufficiency).

Non-banking financial institutions, by contrast, do not have such very poor clients, but do not on the whole outperform the other legal forms in terms of operational self-sufficiency results (see Table 8.9). Cooperatives are not strictly poverty focused relative to the other legal types, and their financial results are mediocre. Looking at financial sustainability (financial self-sufficiency), NBFIs slightly outperform the other legal types of MFIs: 43 per cent are financially sustainable, compared to 38 per cent of NGOs and 31 per cent of cooperatives.

Local labour market conditions and the ease of finding suitably qualified and honest staff members are factors that determine whether an MFI can afford to position itself as more focused on the poor or whether, to the contrary, it is obliged to go up-market precisely because of relatively high levels of staff costs that can only be accommodated in larger average transactions (see Box 8.3). Staff costs are a substantial cost item.

Table 8.7 Location and operational and financial self-sufficiency

	Operational self-sufficiency			Financial self-sufficiency			All
	Not operationally self-sufficient	Operationally self-sufficient	Missing data	Not financially self-sufficient	Financially self-sufficient	Missing data	
Majority/all rural	8	9	0	10	3	4	17
Minority/not rural	3	22	1	10	12	4	26
Missing data	0	2	0	1	1	0	2
All	11	33	1	21	16	8	45

Table 8.8 Legal form and poverty level

	Low end (<20%)	Broad (20–149%)	High end (150–249%)	Small business	All
NGO	11	8	2	0	21
Cooperative	4	5	4	3	16
NBFI	4	2	0	0	6
Bank	0	1	0	0	1
All	19	16	6	3	44

They make up the largest part of operating costs: in our sample, an average 45 per cent. To some extent an MFI can influence staff costs, for example through a performance-based salary system. On the other hand, staff costs cannot infinitely be compressed: for example, if the MFI operates in rural areas, or goes for labour-intensive small-scale transactions: a portfolio with very poor clients implies usually high staff costs because of the need for follow up and monitoring.

Looking at staff-related indicators through a multivariate analysis combining different efficiency indicators like staff costs as a proportion of total costs, staff costs as a proportion of the loan portfolio, wages paid in relation to bank wages, and wages paid in relation to the minimum wage with the three dimensions indicators (efficiency, social and financial performance), one finds a unique group of MFIs that can be characterized by the majority of staff costs indicators. It is a group of poverty focused, partly efficient and financially self-sufficient MFIs. They pay their staff fairly high (staff costs range from 11 to 20 per cent of the total portfolio and loan officers are paid 2 to 4 times the minimum wage). The performance-based wage share is less than 50 per cent; the majority of the MFIs of the sample that apply this strategy have a performance-based wage composed of over 50 per cent. Their inefficiency must have a link with their staff costs management strategy.

Crossing staff costs and poverty level, we find a group of MFIs catering to the relatively well-to-do that pays their staff well (Table 8.10); in fact, 67 per cent of MFIs that pay well – sometimes ten times the minimum wage – operate in the *high end* market segment. The other group of MFIs that caters to the poor tends to be characterized by lower wages: 12.5 per cent of those that work with the very poor have efficiency ratios of staff cost/loan portfolio ratios of more than 20 per cent against 33 per cent in more up-market MFIs. Poorly paying MFIs are all poverty focused.

This could be explained by a relative abundance of labour force (loan officers and administrative staff), or it can reflect the MFI policy to

Table 8.9 Legal form and operational and financial self-sufficiency

	Operational self-sufficiency			Financial self-sufficiency			All
	Not operationally self-sufficient	Operationally self-sufficient	Missing data	Not financially self-sufficient	Financially self-sufficient	Missing data	
NGO	(14.3%) 3	(85.7%) 18	(0.0%) 0	(52.4%) 11	(38.1%) 8	(9.5%) 2	(100.0%) 1
Cooperative	(31.3%) 5	(68.8%) 11	(0.0%) 0	(43.8%) 7	(31.3%) 5	(25.0%) 4	(100.0%) 16
NBFI	(42.9%) 3	(57.1%) 4	(0.0%) 0	(42.9%) 3	(42.9%) 3	(14.3%) 1	(100.0%) 7
Bank	(0.0%) 0	(0.0%) 0	(100.0%) 1	(0.0%) 0	(0.0%) 0	(100.0%) 1	(100.0%) 1
All	11	33	1	21	16	8	45

compress costs. The drawback of such a policy is that low wages seem to attract the less qualified and, as a result, the portfolio quality and the MFI performance may deteriorate (Morduch, Demirguc-Kunt and Cull, 2005[14]).

This is confirmed by our results (Table 8.11) where MFIs that pay their loan officers (LO) the minimum wage have the worst financial performance. Only 33 per cent of them reached operational self-sufficiency, while 80 per cent of those paying two to four times the minimum wage and 100 per cent of those paying more than ten times the minimum wage have reached it.

To get a better grip on staff costs some MFIs resort to an incentive system of performance-based salaries, linked, for example, to the number of loans handled by a staff member, or the overall loan volume, or a combination of both plus the past due ratio. This pay system is more

Table 8.10 Staff costs as a percentage of loan portfolio and poverty level

Staff/portfolio (%)	Low end (<20%)		Broad (20–149%)		High end (150–249%)		Small business		All	
0–10	(56.3%)	9	(58.3%)	7	(66.7%)	2	(100.0%)	3	(61.8%)	21
11–20	(31.3%)	5	(25.0%)	3	(0.0%)	0	(0.0%)	0	(23.5%)	8
20%	(12.5%)	2	(16.7%)	2	(33.3%)	1	(0.0%)	0	(14.7%)	5
All	(100.0%)	16	(100.0%)	12	(100.0%)	3	(100.0%)	3	(100.0%)	34

Table 8.11 Loan officer salaries (LO) and operational self-sufficiency

	Not operationally self-sufficient		Operationally self-sufficient		Missing data		All	
LO = 1 x minimum wage	(66.7%)	2	(33.3%)	1	(0.0%)	0	(100.0%)	3
LO = 2–4 x minimum wage	(20.8%)	5	(79.2%)	19	(0.0%)	0	(100.0%)	24
LO = 5–10 x minimum wage	(15.4%)	2	(76.9%)	10	(7.7%)	1	(100.0%)	13
LO = 10+ x minimum wage	(0.0%)	0	(100.0%)	3	(0.0%)	0	(100.0%)	3
Missing data	(100.0%)	2	(0.0%)	0	(0.0%)	0	(100.0%)	2
All		11		33		1		45

Table 8.12 Variable pay systems and operational and financial self-sufficiency

	Operational self-sufficiency			Financial self-sufficiency			All
	Not operationally self-sufficient	Operationally self-sufficient	Missing data	Not financially self-sufficient	Financially self-sufficient	Missing data	
0%: not applicable	4	3	0	6	1	0	7
< 50%	1	7	0	2	4	2	8
>= 50%	1	10	1	4	7	1	12
All	6	20	1	12	12	3	27

prevalent amongst MFIs with high operational or financial self-sufficiency scores (Table 8.12).

In principle all MFIs seek to externalize transaction costs either by delegating specific functions to clients or third parties. Al Majmoua and many other Lebanese MFIs, for example, subcontract the front office operations with clients to a partnering bank. The fact that it is a common arrangement in the whole country and even for small microfinance projects like ADR shows that the regulatory and institutional framework are of great importance to externalize transaction costs.

Another solution to cost control is to substitute real by social collateral and to transfer the costly processes of selection, monitoring, pressure and enforcement to peers in the same group.

Group loans methodology is always correlated with poor clients: 75 per cent of the MFIs using only group methodology cater to the low end, even though only 18 per cent of those lending to individuals and 44 per cent of those mixing the two methodologies serve this same category of poor client (Table 8.13).

However, the financial performance is better for those MFIs diversifying their lending methodology: 80 per cent of these MFIs have reached operational self-sufficiency and more than 50 per cent to have reached financial self-sufficiency (Table 8.14). It seems that even if the poverty focused MFIs transfer some of their costs to clients through the solidarity group methodology, lending to the poorest remains costly.

Another way to externalize transaction costs is to use voluntary workers. But not all MFIs operate in an environment with a supply of volunteer labour.

The use of volunteers is the hallmark of cooperatives, but it is not a guarantee of a poverty focus (more than 50 per cent of the MFIs resorting to the use of volunteers serve the broad market; see Table 8.15) nor of a

Table 8.13 Lending methodology and poverty level

	Low end (<20%)	Broad (20–149%)	High end (150–249%)	Small business	All
Individual loans	2	6	3	0	11
Group loans	6	2	0	0	8
Individual + group loans	11	8	3	3	25
All	19	16	6	3	44

Table 8.14 Lending methodology and operational and financial self-sufficiency

	Operational self-sufficiency			Financial self-sufficiency			All
	Not operationally self-sufficient	Operationally self-sufficient	Missing data	Not financially self-sufficient	Financially self-sufficient	Missing data	
Individual loans	3	7	1	8	2	1	11
Group loans	3	5	0	5	0	3	8
Individual + group loans	5	21	0	8	14	4	26
All	11	33	1	21	16	8	45

Table 8.15 Volunteer labour and poverty level

	Low end (<20%)	Broad (20–149%)	High end (150–249%)	Small business	All
No use of voluntary workers	17	9	4	1	31
Use of voluntary workers	2	7	2	2	13
All	19	16	6	3	44

high level of financial performance (MFIs that do not use volunteer work are more sustainable operationally and financially; see Table 8.16).

Subsidies allow an MFI to position itself on the continuum between poverty outreach and financial self-sufficiency. They give more freedom in setting mission and vision. At the same time, subsidies are also widely seen as causes of market distortions combined with a negative effect on management in an MFI.

For reasons of data availability we measured subsidies as a stock, relating them to assets at a given point in time. This makes MFIs of different age and maturity comparable, as the dynamics of subsidies suggest that they are most important when an MFI is first getting off the ground. However, even for a static-comparative analysis, not enough data on subsidies was available, which limits the significance of the observations below and calls for further data collection and analysis.

As might be expected, the degree of subsidization and poverty focus seem to go hand in hand: 70 per cent of MFIs with over 50 per cent of resources on a grant basis operate at the *low end* of the market compared to 30 per cent of MFIs that have less than 50 per cent of their resources as grants (Table 8.17).

Over a quarter of MFIs with positive operational self-sufficiency receive subsidies representing between 50 and 100 per cent of their balance sheet. Without subsidies these MFIs would go out of business immediately. In our sample those MFIs with a substantial degree of subsidization do even better in terms of operational self-sufficiency than other MFIs receiving proportionately fewer subsidies; to a lesser extent this also applies to the link between subsidies and financial self-sufficiency (Table 8.18). This seeming paradox can be explained by the fact that some MFI continue to receive grants and transfers although, according to their books, they are already fully financially

Table 8.16 Volunteer labour and operational and financial self-sufficiency

	Operational self-sufficiency			Financial self-sufficiency			All
	Not operationally self-sufficient	Operationally self-sufficient	Missing data	Not financially self-sufficient	Financially self-sufficient	Missing data	
No use of voluntary workers	7	24	1	14	14	4	32
Use of voluntary workers	4	9	0	7	2	4	13
All	11	33	1	21	16	8	45

Table 8.17 Subsidies and target market

	Low end (<20%)	Broad (20–149%)	High end (150–249%)	Small business	All
0–50%	6	8	4	2	20
50–100%	7	3	0	0	10
Missing data	6	5	2	1	14
All	19	16	6	3	44

sustainable and would be perfectly capable of doing without any grant; 43 per cent of MFIs that are moderately subsidized have positive financial self-sufficiency values, and 60 per cent of heavily subsidized MFIs (i.e., more than 50 per cent of assets) have positive financial self-sufficiency values.

8.6 Conclusions

In contrast to other development strategies, microfinance is a cost-effective intervention. That is at least its promise. Usually the performance of MFIs is measured with regard to this self-financing capacity, the financial self-sufficiency ratio (financial self-sufficiency), assuming always that poverty outreach actually happens.

The question is to what extent financial performance depends on management choices and decisions, and to what extent it is constrained by the local market and environment. The answer determines not just the accountability of an MFI's management, but constitutes the basis on which government and donor support can be justified. Given the diversity of operating environments and the rich variety of institutional types both influencing the position of a given MFI on the trade-off between financial and social performance, it would appear timely to ground donor support on a more general, fair and neutral criterion. We believe that this criterion is efficiency.

This chapter briefly presents the results of the 2004–05 GIAN survey. It shows the effect of several key variables on the financial and social performance of 45 MFIs. We determined the exogenous and endogenous nature of these variables and their effect on the financial performance – measured by both financial and operational self-sufficency – as well as the social performance, to arrive at a set of efficiency indicators; the statistical and multivariate analysis suggests that MFIs can be

Table 8.18 Subsidies and operational and financial self-sufficiency

Subsidies as % of total assets	Operational self-sufficiency			Financial self-sufficiency			All
	Not operationally self-sufficient	Operationally self-sufficient	Missing data	Not financially self-sufficient	Financially self-sufficient	Missing data	
0–50	(28.6%) 6	(71.4%) 15	(0.0%) 0	(52.4%) 11	(42.9%) 9	(4.8%) 1	(100.0%) 21
50–100	(10.0%) 1	(90.0%) 9	(0.0%) 0	(30.0%) 3	(60.0%) 6	(10.0%) 1	(100.0%) 10
Missing data	4	9	1	7	1	6	14
All	11	33	1	21	16	8	45

classified in three clusters, combining social and financial performance in different ways. We have, secondly, seen that the efficiency scope is distinct from financial performance, confirming the possibility of establishing efficiency as a neutral criterion for performance measurement and monitoring. In a third step, we examined the influence of five factors that determine where an MFI positions itself on the continuum between a very pronounced poverty focus and a very strong market approach. Lastly, the data allowed us to distinguish between technical efficiency across all types and clusters of MFIs, and technical efficiency as a relative measurement tool, namely in relation to MFIs within the same cluster.

Distinguishing efficiency from the financial outcome in this way, in our view provides a more rational framework on which government and donor agencies can base their decision to continue, expand or terminate their support to individual MFIs.

Notes

1   www.themix.org
2   The data related to hidden subsidies was incomplete or unusable. Moreover, the understanding of what a subsidy includes is different. For example, some institutions do not consider operational subsidies as subsidies and fail to declare them.
3   The adjustment for inflation aims to cancel the inflation effects on equity and fixed assets. The main adjustments take into account of in-kind and cash subsidies, bringing the calculation of loan loss reserves and provision expenses in line with accepted and established international practices.
4   For further analysis, we will create two different groups (risk and portfolio quality, and financial performance) and use more financial indicators such us ROA and ROE.
5   With this method we can establish classes of MFIs without having a predetermined hypothesis. However, according to the variables' level of significance, they may or may not appear as features of the class. Then, they do not affect the different types.
6   The main financial performances of operational and financial self-sufficiency do not appear much in the composition of the four clusters. They do not seem to be a strong feature of the clusters: financial self-sufficiency only appeared in the second cluster. The presence of a feature or not depends on its significance in the cluster: did many MFIs of the same cluster answer this question in the same way?
7   Boxes 8.1 and 8.2 benefited from the contribution of Amadou Diop of the IUED.
8   We wanted also to divide it by the average wage in the banking sector, but the information was not available in all countries.
9   For some of the cases the efficiency indicator is not significant and does not appear in the clusters. The details of the multivariate analysis are available upon request.

10   This ratio can also be interpreted as a poverty outreach indicator.

11   When the yield on portfolio is high, it suggests a good financial performance but in the mean time it can indicate a weak efficiency and an up-market target (since an MFI is supposed to transfer its financial gains to the clients by lowering the interest rate thus the yield).

12   It can also be considered as a sign of caring for the poorest clients by applying a lower interest rate.

13   In Morocco for example, two-thirds of the poor live in rural areas (World Bank, 2001).

14   The authors found that investing more on staff costs, for individual-based lenders, is one key means of achieving profitability. This finding is contrary to the general wisdom that profitability is largely a function of reducing costs.

9
Measuring the Performance of MFIs: An Application of Factor Analysis

Giovanni Ferro Luzzi and Sylvain Weber
University of Geneva

9.1 Introduction

MFIs face a double challenge: not only do they have to provide financial services to the poor (outreach), but they also have to cover their costs in order to avoid bankruptcy (sustainability). Both dimensions must therefore be taken into account in order to assess their performance.

There is currently no widely accepted measure for assessing the social performance of MFIs, outreach always being defined in terms of several indicators, like the percentages of female and rural clients or the average loan size (Schreiner, 2002). Very few attempts have been made to aggregate those numerous indicators into one single measure, although it would be useful since it would give a straight and accurate view of the outreach. Zeller, Lapenu and Greeley (2003) provide some hints for building such a measure, either by assigning arbitrary weights to each of the indicators, or by deriving the weights through principal components analysis. In this chapter, we generalize their second method: we apply factor analysis[1] to a set of indicators not only related to social performance but also to financial performance. Each of the factors created will represent one dimension of performance, according to the indicators they are composed of.

The factors determining MFIs' performance are not clearly known either. To the best of our knowledge, Hartarska (2005) was the first to present evidence on the determinants of MFIs' performance in a multi-dimensional context. However, she estimates different equations for each of the indicators. The methodology we propose here goes two steps further. First, using factor analysis, we create a synthetic index for each

153

of the two dimensions. We calculate thereafter how each MFI scores for each of these indices and use the values obtained as the dependent variables of a regression. In so doing, we need only estimate one equation for outreach and one for sustainability. Second, instead of estimating single equations, we will make use of a simultaneous-equations model, to take account of a possible dependence between outreach and sustainability. Even if the relationship between outreach and sustainability is still not clearly determined yet (Conning, 1999; Zeller and Meyer, 2002), one can assume there exist some links and must allow the equations to be connected.

The rest of the chapter is organized as follows. Section 9.2 briefly describes the data set used for our empirical estimations. Section 9.3 presents the principles of factor analysis as well as the results obtained with this technique on our sample. In order to have a better understanding of the factor analysis results, we use cluster analysis to create groups of MFIs in Section 9.4. The second step of the analysis is explained in Section 9.5, where we look for the determinants of MFIs' performance. Section 9.6 summarizes the main results and concludes.

9.2 The data

The sample used is composed of 45 microfinance institutions surveyed in the framework of the GIAN research project. This covers the period 1999–2003. Since the previous chapter and annexes at the end of the book provide a complete description of the data set, we focus here only on the variables selected for our analysis.

We retained six variables among the huge quantity that were collected to perform the factor analysis. We were, in fact, constrained by the relatively small number of MFIs surveyed. Indeed, factor analysis is data consuming and it would not have made any sense to include too many variables on such a small sample of observations. The six variables retained are described in Table 9.1.

The majority of these variables are indicators of outreach. The loan size is usually taken as a proxy for the *depth* of outreach, which can be defined as the value that society attaches to the net gain of a given client, following the terms of Schreiner (2002). It is only when the average loan size is very small that the MFI touches the really poor. The percentage of female borrowers is a proxy for the depth of outreach as well, since loans to women are more highly valued by society. One can also expect that an MFI will serve poorer individuals if it lends to groups. Hence, the higher the share of borrowers organized in groups, the deeper

Table 9.1 Description of variables

Variable	Description	Values
FEMALE##	Percentage of female borrowers	Continuous variable (%)
GROUPLOAN##	Lending methodology: percentage of active clients organized in groups	Continuous variable (%)
POVCRIT	Use of poverty criteria to target clients	0 = no 1 = yes
COLLATERAL	Assets required as collateral	0 = no 1 = yes
LOANSIZE##	Average loan / GNP per capita	Continuous variable (%)
OSS##	Operational self-sufficiency (Total revenues / Total expenses)	Continuous variable

the outreach. The use of poverty criteria indicates the MFI is more oriented toward poorer people, so that when *POVCRIT* equals 1, the outreach should be enhanced. As a lender who does not impose physical collateral to its clients could serve poorer users and thus reach deeper outreach (Navajas et al., 2000), a deeper outreach will be attained if *COLLATERAL* is 0.

In fact, only the last variable, operational self-sufficiency (*OSS*), represents a financial measure. It would have been interesting and desirable to include other variables related to sustainability, such as the return on assets (*ROA*) or the return on equity (*ROE*). Unfortunately, they had far too many missing values in our data set, which made them unusable for our present purposes.

9.3 Factor analysis: theory and practice

Theoretical view

The main idea behind using factor analysis in the context of MFIs' performance is to exploit the fact that there are several components of performance (sustainability and outreach), each of which translates into many observable variables. From these many variables, factor analysis will enable us to create one synthetic indicator for each dimension considered: one for outreach and one for sustainability. Each dimension will be composed of a combination of the observed variables described in Table 9.1. With the data we have at hand, we expect *OSS* to capture the sustainability dimension in itself, since it is the only financial variable available. We also expect all other variables to be combined in another factor to create the outreach dimension of performance.

Formally, factor analysis assumes that each measured variable x_j is due to some unobserved common factors f_k and an idiosyncratic effect s_j:

$$x_j = \sum_k a_{jk} f_k + s_j$$

or, in matrix notation:

$$\mathbf{x} = \mathbf{A} \cdot \mathbf{f} + \mathbf{s},$$

where the $\mathbf{x}$ vector includes all observed (standardized) variables, $\mathbf{A}$ is the matrix of factor loadings, $\mathbf{f}$ is the vector of (latent) common factors, and $\mathbf{s}$ is similar to a residual, and includes what is known as the variables' unique factors.

One problem we must address is the fact that some of our variables are dichotomous. In such instances, it is known that the Pearson's correlation matrix is biased and will unavoidably lead to biased estimates of the factor loadings if used as the basis for a factor analysis (Olsson, 1979). We will thus need to calculate different types of correlation coefficients, according to the nature of each pair of variables:

- *tetrachoric* between two dichotomous variables;
- *polyserial* between one dichotomous variable and one continuous variable;
- *Pearson's* between two continuous variables.

The resulting matrix will then be used as the starting point of the factor analysis.

The first step in factor analysis is to decide how many factors are relevant to the model. As we shall see in the empirical part, this choice is guided by some simple rules.

The next problem encountered is that the factor loadings matrix $\mathbf{A}$ defined above is not uniquely determined. To ensure a solution, one has to introduce constraints on the parameters in the original model. In general, one requires the first factor to have maximal contribution to the common variance of the observed variables, the second to have maximal contribution to this variance subject to being uncorrelated with the first, and so on. However, it is possible that a more interpretable solution can be achieved using a transformed model, obtained by a process known as *factor rotation*. Various methods for the rotation of factors are available and we will make use of an oblique one (*promax* with power 3), which allows the factors to be correlated, rather than independent. In our case, this is indeed what we want, as we expect the different dimensions of performance to be linked: MFIs can be performant on both dimensions at the same time, even if it is likely that MFIs trying to be the most socially performant will encounter some difficulty in being financially effective. Trade-offs are sometimes inevitable, but synergies among the different dimensions are also possible (Zeller and Meyer, 2002).

Once a representation of the data in this form is considered adequate, every MFI can be ascribed a *score* on each derived factor that will inform us on how it behaves on the corresponding dimension of performance.

Empirical results

Now that factor analysis has been briefly exposed from a theoretical point of view, we turn to the empirical results. Even if the same analysis has been made for each available year (1999–2003), some figures will only be displayed for 2003, since they are comparable across years.

As stated before, the correlation matrix is the departure point of the factor analysis. It is therefore interesting to have a look at correlations, which are shown here for 2003 (Table 9.2).

Table 9.2 immediately confirms that the first five variables pertain to a similar group, since their correlation is quite high in absolute value. By contrast, the correlation between the operational self-sufficiency and the other variables is very weak. We therefore expect that the latter will

Table 9.2 Correlation matrix for 2003

	FEMALE03	GROUP-LOAN03	POVCRIT	COLLA-TERAL	LOANSIZE03	OSS03
FEMALE03	1.000					
GROUPLOAN03	0.417	1.000				
POVCRIT	0.554	0.504	1.000			
COLLATERAL	− 0.600	− 0.631	− 0.885	1.000		
LOANSIZE03	− 0.450	− 0.314	− 0.792	0.810	1.000	
OSS03	0.263	0.017	0.098	− 0.115	0.042	1.000

constitute a dimension by itself in the factor analysis. This matrix of correlations is then used to extract the factors via principal component factors.

The next step involves choosing the appropriate number of latent factors. To this end, we rely on some standard statistical and visual tools, commonly used in factor analysis, although one should be aware that most of these rules are somehow ad hoc and cannot avoid value judgments. One method which has been put forth is to exclude factors with eigenvalues smaller than one, since the factors retained in this way account for more variance than the average for the variables. Another method is to keep just enough factors so that the cumulated variance explained is no less than 70 per cent. Eventually, an examination of the plot of the eigenvalues against the corresponding factor numbers, the so-called Scree diagram, can help the choice. The rate of decline tends to be fast for the first few factors, but then levels off. The 'elbow', or the point at which the curve bends, is considered to indicate the maximum number of factors to extract. Another way to use the Scree plot is to draw a straight line connecting the lowest eigenvalues, the threshold being where this line separates from the eigenvalues' line.

Table 9.3 contains the eigenvalues, as well as the associated proportion of variance explained by each latent factor for the years 1999–2003. Based on this information, it is quite easy to choose two factors. Indeed,

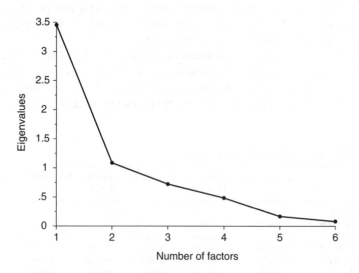

Figure 9.1 Scree plot for 2003

all of the criteria given above indicate that the two-factor solution is the best for every year. First of all, we get two eigenvalues higher than one for every year. Secondly, if we want to keep enough factors to have a cumulated variance of 70 per cent, we should keep two factors. Finally, as can be seen from Figure 9.1 (only drawn for 2003), the second and following eigenvalues are located on a straight line, indicating a two-factor solution as well.

Next, we apply a rotation of the factors to provide a more meaningful and easily interpretable solution loading matrix. As previously stated, it makes sense to allow the different dimensions of performance to be correlated. We therefore apply an oblique rotation that involves the

Table 9.3 Eigenvalues and proportion of variance explained

Year	Factor	Eigenvalue	Proportion	Cumulative
1999	1	3.274	0.546	0.546
	2	1.050	0.175	0.721
	3	0.684	0.114	0.835
	4	0.599	0.100	0.934
	5	0.286	0.048	0.982
	6	0.106	0.018	1.000
2000	1	3.286	0.548	0.548
	2	1.044	0.174	0.722
	3	0.864	0.144	0.866
	4	0.655	0.109	0.975
	5	0.138	0.023	0.998
	6	0.012	0.002	1.000
2001	1	3.366	0.561	0.561
	2	1.081	0.180	0.741
	3	0.604	0.101	0.842
	4	0.537	0.090	0.931
	5	0.313	0.052	0.984
	6	0.099	0.017	1.000
2002	1	3.523	0.587	0.587
	2	1.017	0.170	0.757
	3	0.712	0.119	0.875
	4	0.503	0.084	0.959
	5	0.167	0.028	0.987
	6	0.076	0.013	1.000
2003	1	3.454	0.576	0.576
	2	1.087	0.181	0.757
	3	0.724	0.121	0.878
	4	0.486	0.081	0.959
	5	0.167	0.028	0.987
	6	0.081	0.014	1.000

introduction of correlations between factors. The resulting loadings are presented in Table 9.3. Once again, very similar results are found for each year.

A glance at Table 9.4 reveals that *FEMALE, GROUPLOAN* and *POVCRIT* load positively and quite highly on the first factor, indicating that a higher value of these variables leads to a higher score on the factor 1. On the contrary, *COLLATERAL* and *LOANSIZE* load strongly and negatively, meaning that the MFI which has a smaller value for one of these two variables will have a higher score on factor 1, everything else being equal. Since a deeper outreach is associated with a higher value of *FEMALE, GROUPLOAN* and *POVCRIT* and a smaller value of *COLLATERAL*

Table 9.4   Rotated factor loadings (oblique rotation) and unique variances

Year	Variable	Factor 1	Factor 2	Uniqueness
1999	*FEMALE99*	0.7060	0.1508	0.4861
	GROUPLOAN99	0.6583	0.1616	0.5479
	POVCRIT	0.9092	0.0147	0.1740
	COLLATERAL	− 0.8793	0.2766	0.1336
	LOANSIZE99	− 0.8421	0.0308	0.2881
	OSS99	− 0.0964	0.9686	0.0460
2000	*FEMALE00*	0.5788	0.2385	0.5898
	GROUPLOAN00	0.6339	0.0885	0.5829
	POVCRIT	0.9539	0.0735	0.0754
	COLLATERAL	− 0.9465	0.0608	0.1080
	LOANSIZE00	− 0.8627	0.2565	0.2194
	OSS00	− 0.0862	0.9536	0.0941
2001	*FEMALE01*	0.7605	0.1180	0.4323
	GROUPLOAN01	0.6365	− 0.2834	0.4652
	POVCRIT	0.9264	0.0837	0.1560
	COLLATERAL	− 0.9475	− 0.1249	0.1189
	LOANSIZE01	− 0.7842	0.1586	0.3259
	OSS01	0.1006	0.9806	0.0553
2002	*FEMALE02*	0.5956	0.3862	0.3708
	GROUPLOAN02	0.6799	− 0.0558	0.5553
	POVCRIT	0.9606	− 0.0497	0.1009
	COLLATERAL	− 0.9403	− 0.0507	0.0872
	LOANSIZE02	− 0.8779	0.1343	0.2754
	OSS02	− 0.0716	0.9812	0.0704
2003	*FEMALE03*	0.6307	0.3899	0.3636
	GROUPLOAN03	0.6708	− 0.0093	0.5522
	POVCRIT	0.9276	− 0.0172	0.1448
	COLLATERAL	− 0.9623	− 0.0069	0.0716
	LOANSIZE03	− 0.8810	0.1988	0.2461
	OSS03	− 0.0882	0.9707	0.0802

Table 9.5 Correlation between factors

Year	Correlation factor 1/factor 2
1999	− 0.0102
2000	0.2168
2001	− 0.1282
2002	0.2581
2003	0.1733

and *LOANSIZE*, factor 1 clearly reflects the social dimension of performance and can be termed 'social performance'. The second factor is clearly
related to financial efficiency, since *OSS* is the only variable that exhibits
a loading of considerable size. We therefore label this factor 'financial
performance'.

As shown in Table 9.5, the correlation between the two factors is low
and its sign is not consistent across the five years. Consequently, our
results do not confirm nor contradict the existence of a trade-off
between the two dimensions of performance.

9.4   Cluster analysis

In order to facilitate the understanding of the results obtained in the
previous section, we will now make use of a statistical procedure that
allows to group objects based on the characteristics they possess, namely
cluster analysis. This technique allows the partitioning of an original
population into subsets (clusters), so that the data in each subset (ideally)
share some common trait – proximity according to some defined distance measure. The goal is thus to bring together individuals having relatively similar characteristics, while individuals belonging to different
groups are as disparate as possible. With the agglomerative hierarchical
clustering method, the main steps of the groups' identification procedure are as follows. Let there be n observations (the 45 MFIs) with m
characteristics (the two scores of performance). At the beginning, every
observation is considered as a separate group. A similarity index – the
Euclidean distance between the average scores of two clusters – is computed for all $n \cdot (n\text{-}1)/2$ potential pairs of observations and the two closest
are grouped. In the next step, the same procedure is applied to the n-1
remaining clusters, which implies $(n\text{-}1) \cdot (n\text{-}2)/2$ distances. This process
goes on until all observations belong to the same group, and hence cre-
ate a hierarchy of clusters.

This method leaves open the choice of the final number of clusters. Many stopping rules can help this decision and we will make use of two criteria, which are described as the best out of the 30 investigated by Milligan and Cooper (1985): the pseudo-t^2 and the pseudo-F.

Large values of the pseudo-F index indicate distinct clustering and one must therefore maximize this statistic. The opposite is true for the pseudo-t^2, and one should choose the number of clusters so that this index is low and has much larger values next to it. It is advisable to look for a consensus among the two statistics, that is, local peak of the pseudo-F combined with a small value of the pseudo-t^2 and a larger value of the latter for the next cluster fusion.

We applied this procedure to group the MFIs of our data set on the basis of the two scores ascribed to them through factor analysis and for each year. The results are displayed in Table 9.6, where the first 15 cluster groupings can be examined. Taking 1999 as an example, we see that the pseudo-F is maximized for 10 clusters, whereas the pseudo-t^2 is maximal for three groups, indicating the presence of four clusters. The solution of five clusters seems to be the best compromise, since the pseudo-F is quite low for four clusters but noticeably higher for five clusters.

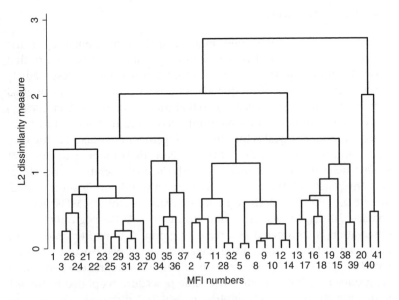

Figure 9.2 Dendrogram for 2003 cluster analysis

Note: Fewer than 45 MFIs appear in the graph because of missing values in the variables included in factor analysis.

Table 9.6 Statistics for determining the number of clusters

Number of clusters	1999		2000		2001		2002		2003	
	Pseudo-F	Pseudo-t^2	Pseudo-F	Pseudo-t^2	Pseudo-F	Pseudo-t^2	Pseudo-F	Pseudo-t^2	Pseudo-F	Pseudo-t^2
1	–	14.19	–	13.03	–	4.63	–	6.23	–	10.69
2	14.19	6.03	13.03	6.84	4.63	5.27	6.23	12.82	10.69	38.49
3	9.06	25.29	11.24	26.54	5.23	27.57	10.50	47.22	28.68	24.44
4	19.84	15.93	23.26	15.62	15.69	19.82	32.63	20.89	21.65	16.95
5	28.34	11.42	25.29	10.06	22.44	12.83	33.86	17.12	23.15	17.66
6	29.09	9.63	30.16	9.17	24.99	11.28	44.91	20.23	31.64	5.72
7	29.27	3.66	33.55	58.57	29.25	5.58	51.43	3.82	29.36	5.78
8	29.52	4.10	30.60	11.06	27.62	16.55	48.60	4.39	27.03	27.51
9	28.30	5.59	35.97	15.41	31.09	8.17	47.87	3.92	35.66	6.59
10	31.70	.	45.09	1.83	36.39	5.54	46.67	14.30	39.54	3.17
11	30.17	4.64	42.88	7.00	36.40	5.18	54.96	1.54	38.60	8.83
12	30.53	.	44.82	6.99	36.13	11.48	51.90	121.93	45.01	4.94
13	29.43	5.61	53.76	2.40	40.47	5.19	50.97	5.68	43.93	4.37
14	29.58	.	55.74	9.69	41.22	11.96	53.96	5.61	43.40	1.85
15	29.13	6.36	68.03	.	47.16	10.78	61.41	.	42.58	16.77

Note: Dots (.) indicate that the pseudo-t^2 is not computable because of ties in the hierarchical cluster analysis.

Applying the same reasoning to each year gives four clusters for 2000, 2002 and 2003 and five for 1999 and 2001.

For some years, the choice was not really clear and the cluster trees (or dendrograms) eased our decisions. The cluster tree in Figure 9.2 presents graphical information concerning which observations are grouped together at various levels of similarity for 2003. At the bottom of the dendrogram, each observation would be considered its own cluster. As one climbs up in the tree, observations are combined until all are grouped together, the height of the vertical lines indicating the similarity (or dissimilarity) of two groups. Creating four clusters is tantamount to cutting the tree horizontally where it has only four branches. Since they are among the longest branches, it confirms that the four clusters we formed actually are very dissimilar.

Having determined the clusters, it is interesting to plot the scores one against the other to see how the groups are located. The representation for 2003 is provided in Figure 9.3. MFIs belonging to cluster 1 are located at the bottom-left corner, so that they are relatively ineffective along both dimensions of performance. The MFIs of cluster 2 perform well on

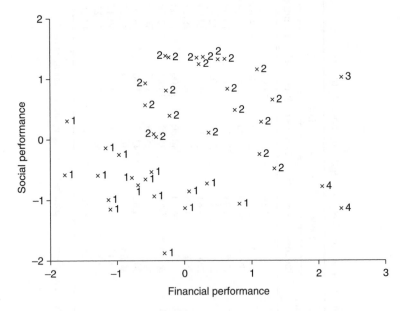

Figure 9.3 Scores and clusters for 2003

Note: Fewer than 45 MFIs appear in the graph because of missing values in the variables included in factor analysis.

the social dimension but not on the financial one. Inversely, cluster 4 is efficient according to the financial dimension but not to the social one. Finally, cluster 3 contains only one MFI, which is very effective on both dimensions. From this plot, one can see that the trade-off between outreach and sustainability is not obvious: in that case, MFIs should be situated along a line going from the top left to the bottom right.

These visual notings are confirmed by the figures contained in Table 9.7 that shows the average scores of the MFIs pertaining to the various clusters found in each year. The composition of groups is not very stable across years, but one could still try to discern some general pattern. For every year, there is one quite large cluster that scores negatively on both performance dimensions, even if it is much smaller for 1999 and 2001. The MFIs pertaining to this cluster are performing relatively

Table 9.7 Mean scores on the two factors, by cluster, 1999–2003

Year	Cluster number	Factor 1	Factor 2	Observations	%
1999	1	0.722	−0.579	11	35.48
	2	−0.213	−1.752	4	12.90
	3	−0.710	0.132	11	35.48
	4	1.226	1.214	4	12.90
	5	−0.667	2.015	1	3.23
	total	0.113	−0.163	31	100.00
2000	1	0.747	−0.204	16	45.71
	2	−0.609	−0.452	15	42.86
	3	−0.770	1.373	2	5.71
	4	1.200	2.335	2	5.71
	total	0.105	−0.075	35	100.00
2001	1	0.885	−0.541	14	37.84
	2	0.664	0.905	6	16.22
	3	−0.774	0.093	14	37.84
	4	−0.441	−1.872	2	5.41
	5	−1.037	2.295	1	2.70
	total	0.098	−0.062	37	100.00
2002	1	0.777	0.029	19	47.50
	2	−0.844	−0.695	15	37.50
	3	−0.499	1.530	5	12.50
	4	1.210	2.916	1	2.50
	total	0.038	0.017	40	100.00
2003	1	−0.742	−0.661	17	41.46
	2	0.716	0.308	21	51.22
	3	1.025	2.347	1	2.44
	4	−0.962	2.197	2	4.88
	total	0.037	0.048	41	100.00

badly on both dimensions. A second cluster manages well concerning the social dimension but scores negatively on the financial dimension, whereas a third one obtains a high score on the financial dimension but performs poorly on the social dimension. If these two groups were containing most of the MFIs of our dataset, we could conclude that some trade-off between outreach and sustainability does actually exist, but this is not the case for every year. Eventually, there is always a very small cluster (sometimes composed of only one MFI) that distinguishes itself from the others by its high scores on both dimensions.

9.5 Assessing what determines performance

The scores ascribed to MFIs through factor analysis will now be used as the dependent variable of an equation. We will thus try to explain why some MFIs perform better than others.

Denoting the performance or score of MFI i on dimension $j = 1, 2$ by s_{ji}, we can posit the following regression model:

$$s_i = x_i\beta_1 + z_{1i}\gamma_1 + \varepsilon_{1i}$$
$$s_i = x_i\beta_2 + z_{2i}\gamma_2 + \varepsilon_{2i}$$

where x_i is a (row) vector of MFI i's characteristics that explain both its social and financial performance, while z_{ji} contains variables that are presumed to affect either its social or its financial performance. Based on the idea that both scores are interrelated by a possible trade-off, we here assume that: $E(\varepsilon_{1i}, \varepsilon_{2i}) = \sigma_{12} \neq 0$, which implies that the equations must be estimated with the seemingly unrelated regressions model (SUR).[2]

Deciding which variable belongs to either the x_i or z_{ji} vectors is not an easy task. We list in Table 9.8 candidate variables which may affect either or both scores. Again, this list is also limited by the number of observations available.

The number of financial services offered by the MFI affects the *scope* of outreach, but one can also presume that it will have an influence on its financial performance, although the direction of this influence is not obvious a priori.[3] The scale of operation (as measured by the size of the portfolio) is related to *breadth* of outreach, but it certainly also has an effect on the financial viability of the MFI, since too small a scale of operation will not be sufficient to cover fixed costs. For the same reason, we also include the number of active clients (*NAC*) in both performance equations.

The number of loan officers per branch is presumed to affect mainly outreach, since MFIs with more loan officers are able to deliver more

Table 9.8   Description of variables used in the SUR model

Variable	Description
Services	Number of financial services offered by the MFI
Scale	Scale of operation (1 = small, 2 = medium, 3 = large)
NAC	Number of active clients in thousands, at the end of the year
Rural	Percentage of rural clients in 2003
Loan officer/branch	Number of loan officers by branch
Ceiling	Interest rate ceiling (0 = no, 1 = yes)
First	Processing time for a first loan (days)
Competitors	MFI has competitors (0 = no, 1 = yes)
Clients/loan officer	Number of clients per loan officer in 2003

credits per client, and therefore this ratio increases both breadth and scope of outreach. We expect that the percentage of rural clients is a factor of *depth* of outreach, since more rural clients are notably poorer than their urban counterparts.[4] Providing credit facilities in rural areas is however usually more costly than in cities, and therefore we also include this variable in x_i. All other variables listed should have direct effects on financial viability, but not necessarily on outreach. The results of the SUR model are given in Table 9.9 below for the year 2003.[5]

A first comment should be made on the SUR method. As can be seen by the value of the Breusch Pagan χ^2 statistic, we cannot reject the hypothesis that the errors are not correlated across equations ($\sigma_{12} = 0$). In this particular instance therefore, OLS could have been used instead of a SUR model (the results of such regressions were very similar). Note also that some coefficients have the 'wrong' sign. The variable services in the social performance equation has a negative and significant coefficient. It has the correct sign in the second equation but is not significantly different from zero.

Also, the variables *NAC* and *scale* have opposite signs in each equation, with all coefficients significant at the 0.05 level. We were expecting these variables to have a similar impact on both scores. We can therefore attempt the following partial explanation. The number of active clients is a *direct* measure of breadth of outreach. Having more clients (with possibly small loans) also implies higher costs per client, which is detrimental to financial performance. The scale of operation is measured by the portfolio size, and could be associated with larger loans. This implies, all other things being equal, that it reduces costs to the MFI, while it is associated with less outreach. The percentage of rural clients has a very sizeable and significant effect on outreach and a negative one

Table 9.9   SUR model of multidimensional performance for 2003

Variable	Factor 1	Factor 2
Constant	1.2902*** (0.3826)	0.8695* (0.5198)
Services	−0.2518** (0.1172)	−0.2332 (0.1444)
Scale	−0.3760** (0.1510)	0.3470** (0.1625)
NAC	0.3457*** (0.1121)	−0.2675** (0.1220)
Rural	0.4941*** (0.1089)	−0.2025* (0.1206)
Loan officer/branch	0.2280** (0.1022)	
Ceiling		−0.3805* (0.2314)
First		0.5670*** (0.1076)
Competitors		−0.9773** (0.3994)
Clients/Loan officer		0.5714*** (0.1126)
R-squared	0.556	0.656
F-stat	9.74	8.8
Breusch-Pagan	0.729	
Observations	39	

Notes: All continuous variables have been standardized: *Loan officer/branch, NAC, Rural, First* and *Ceiling*. Standard errors in parentheses.
*** Significant at the 0.01 level
** Significant at the 0.05 level
* Significant at the 0.10 level

on the financial score, so one should clearly take into account the fact that an MFI has a rural rather than urban clientele in valuing its performance.

Turning now to the variables that were included in the financial performance equation only, we see that all variables have the expected sign and are significant. The number of clients per loan officer has a positive and very significant impact, although quite negligible in value. This variable probably indirectly captures labour productivity or efficiency in the MFI. The number of competitors seems to have a strong negative influence on the financial performance, which seems quite plausible. An interest ceiling has the obvious effect of reducing the capacity to generate revenues from the lending activity, although here, the coefficient is just significant at the 0.10 level. The time requested for granting a first loan has a large and highly significant positive effect on the financial score. It seems therefore that a crucial aspect of financial sustainability could be the scrutiny of loan officers in granting credits.

We also experimented with other variables and specifications. We introduced, for instance, the ratio of the wage rate of loan officers to the minimum wage in the financial performance equation, but it turned out insignificantly different from zero. A similar result is found in Hartarska (2005). We also attempted various specifications to include the number of donors per MFI, the profit status and dummy variable for MFIs being member-owned in the second equation, but none was significant.

9.6 Conclusions

Microcredit is often promoted as an efficient tool to help the poor, based as it is on sound economic principles. Rates of return on small-scale investments can be very high and explain why some people are ready to pay high interest rates in order to finance them. However, market failures and relatively high transaction costs can prevent a substantial part of these investments from being realized through private financial intermediaries, especially in remote rural areas. The aim of MFIs is to fill this gap. As discussed earlier, they can do so either by focusing on the poor and expanding their outreach, or they may prioritize their financial viability.

In this chapter we have tried to provide some new empirical and methodological insights on this important subject. It is quite similar in spirit to Chapter 6 by Flückiger and Vassiliev, where MFIs' 'outputs' are measured and evaluated with respect to resources used in an efficient frontier context, but with different data and an alternative model. Our approach attempts to shed some light on the way the performance of MFIs can be evaluated in a multidimensional context. To this end, we have shown how factor analysis can help construct some synthetic indices of both *outreach* and *self-sustainability*. Several papers have shown how *outreach* itself can be judged upon various criteria. The same is true, though to a lesser extent, for the financial performance. Clearly, some ambiguity can arise as to the choice of variables that should be used to define these indices. One advantage of factor analysis is that no arbitrary weight needs to be ascribed to each variable, as the 'data speak for themselves', in that the weights are computed from the correlation matrix of the chosen variables. One drawback of this technique is that it does not provide information on the absolute level of performance, but it is nonetheless valuable to be able to identify the (relatively) best MFIs of a group.

Cluster analysis was mainly used to better grasp the possibility that some MFIs would form groups across the two scores. The clusters were not very compact and quite unstable across the years, probably also because MFIs come from different countries and are possibly influenced by institutional or macroeconomic factors specific to their countries.

More data, especially from within a few selected countries, could provide a clearer picture of what is going on with our chosen dimensions of performance.

In the last section of this chapter we looked for possible determinants that could explain the positions of the MFIs with respect to both measures of performance. To this end, we estimated a SUR model for the year 2003. Most results were plausible, although we stress that the paucity of the data made it clear that their statistical reliability is rather limited and that they should, for this reason, be considered more for their heuristic value.

Notes

1 Like principal component analysis, factor analysis is a statistical method that attempts to explain a set of multivariate data using a smaller number of dimensions than one begins with.

2 One could also imagine that a system of simultaneous equations, whereby each score enters as an explanatory dependent variable, be estimated via three-stage least squares. We do not pursue this route here, because of our very limited data set.

3 Offering saving deposits, for instance, can be costly to manage, but it is also a source of funds that can prove cheaper than alternatives. See Morduch (1999a) for a discussion on the role of savings.

4 *Scope, depth, breadth,* and *length* of outreach are discussed in Schreiner (2002).

5 Results for the other years can be obtained from the authors. Since the number of observations is smaller for the years 1999–2002, the estimations are not as good. In addition, most of the covariates used in the SUR model were measured in 2003 and are therefore only proxies for the past years.

Part IV
Selected Country Studies

10
Contextual Factors Determining Poverty Outreach and Financial Performance: The Case of Mali

Renata Serra, Fabrizio Botti and
Milasoa Cherel-Robson
Cambridge University

10.1 Introduction

Mali is one of the poorest countries in the world when judged by any of the major indicators. It ranks 174 out of 177 countries in terms of the Human Development Indicator. Both absolute and relative income-based poverty indicators are staggering: the proportions of the population living with less than one and two dollars a day, are 72.3 and 90.6 percent respectively, which are the highest in the world.[1] These figures mask important differences among the poor themselves, which, as discussed below, represent a major challenge for microfinance institutions (MFIs).

Mali's economy is highly vulnerable due to its dependence on primary commodity exports (cotton, cattle and gold) and its lack of diversification, with most of the population occupied in the subsistence agricultural and trading sectors. Insufficient infrastructures and a very high-risk environment, due to harsh agro-climatic conditions, namely the threat of droughts, limit investment opportunities and the potential to attract capital from outside.

Political stability has opened the door to increased donor intervention and funding, and enabled the country to become eligible for international debt reduction under the heavily indebted poor countries (HIPC) initiative,[2] which also released new funding specifically for microfinance development (see Cassimon and Vaessen, 2006). The microfinance sector in Mali is considered to be among the most vibrant and promising in Africa, facilitated by an early regulatory framework, enthusiastic donor support, and a conducive social and institutional environment.

MFIs do, however, face increasing challenges, linked to a slow deterioration of credit portfolios, governance problems and poor definition of roles, the downturn in cotton prices and thus in the incomes of many clients, and a growing competitive environment. In short, the challenges emerge to improve financial performance without abandoning their focus on the poor.

Poverty targeting is a common and pronounced feature of the Malian microfinance industry. It targets particularly vulnerable groups, such as women or rural communities. Like other MFIs in Mali, Nyèsigiso and CVECA, reviewed in the GIAN survey, were created with explicit missions. Nyèsigiso has aimed at women, initially in urban areas, while CVECA has chosen to locate branches in the poorest and most remote areas of Mali, for example, in the Pays Dogon. Measured in terms of average loan balances and the average saving balances, MFIs in Mali effectively succeed in reaching deep, and do so more effectively than most MFIs in West Africa or Africa as a whole (see Table 10.1).

By designing financial products to meet specific needs of women, Nyèsigiso succeeds in reaching out to very poor clients, for example, through credit and saving with education, which is a group lending scheme. This combines loans with education and nutrition training, to serve a relatively poor female segment of clients. The methodology is to induce poor women to self-select into the programme. Credit is offered to solidarity groups of 15–20 women who are jointly liable. Members meet weekly for repayment, and at the same time they get educational, nutritional or business training. Loan sizes are small starting with 25,000 FCFA (38 euros) for a first-cycle loan.

This chapter shows how contextual factors make a difference to the extent to which an MFI can attain the twin objectives of poverty reduction and full cost-recovery. The next section looks at domestic contextual factors. Section 10.3 examines performance drivers from outside of Mali. Section 10.4 concludes.

10.2 Domestic contextual factors: institutions, state and markets

In Mali there is a large unmet demand for financial products, given the inability of the commercial banking sector (nine large and fairly developed banks) to extend operations beyond the cities and the richer cotton-growing South. Low rural population density, low and extremely volatile incomes, and poor quality of infrastructures are among the

Table 10.1 Malian microfinance industry: Outreach indicators (% of GNI ph)

MFI	Active borrowers	GLP (US$)	No. savers	Savings (US$)	Average loan balance per borrower (US$)	Average savings balance per saver (US$)	Women borrowers (%)
Nyèsigiso	27,780	12,169,755	182,571	10,700,240	151	84	50
CVECA	6,585	408,825	2,050	170,231	62	83	39
Kafo Jiginew	94,428	20,959,211	149,109	13,430,012	222	90	28
Kondo Jigima	5,314	3,051,781	49,714	2,374,520	574	48	41
Miselini	11,431	1,026,639	11,431	221,084	90	19	100
Piyeli	4,745	1,206,656	11,118	675,628	254	61	63
Soro Yiriwaso	11,385	692,603	0	0	61	n.a.	100
Total Mali (average)	161,668	39,515,470	405,993	27,571,715	(202)	(64)	60
Total West Africa* (average)	574,983	258,851,781	1,762,458	236,929,906	(406)	(121)	n.a
Total sub-Saharan Africa (average)	2,257,894	703,502,136	5,919,652	685,809,765	(307)	(112)	61

Notes: Data refer to 31/12/2003. West Africa here includes 66 MFIs from nine countries (Benin, Ghana, Guinea, Ivory Coast, Mali, Nigeria, Senegal, Sierra Leone and Togo). n.a. = not available.
Sources: Field work questionnaires, September 2004; www.mixmarket.org; Lafourcade et al. (2005).

main constraints. With 65 per cent of the Malian population residing in the countryside and high rates of urban financial exclusion, there is therefore a high potential for the microfinance sector to grow.[3]

On the other hand, MFI's operational size and lending amount are limited by a low propensity to save in financial assets, due to low income levels, but also a traditional preference to hold savings in physical assets, such as cattle.[4] Women, in particular, appear the most reluctant to confide all their savings to MFIs, preferring to diversify and participate in traditional credit and saving associations (*tontines*). As a result, financial institutions need to offer relatively high interest rates to attract depositors, which, given the cap on lending rates (see below), reduces operational margins. A low propensity to save also implies the need for supplementing MFIs' own funds with other resources, including grants, if operations are to be conducted at a sufficiently large scale to attain financial viability.

Within this context, what has been the role of regulation, the state and other market actors, and how have these affected MFIs' performance?

Regulation

Mali was the first among the eight member countries in the West African Economic and Monetary Union (UEMOA) to apply the PARMEC law[5] and regulate MFIs.[6] A National Action Plan was adopted by all major actors in 1998, and a microfinance association, APIM/Mali, emerged to assist, represent and regulate the microfinance sector. Interest rate ceilings (with maximum lending interest rate at 27 per cent) and a tight deposit/loan ratio, fixing the total amount of outstanding loans at twice the amount of deposit, reduce operational margins. MFIs find it difficult under these circumstances to ensure a sufficient margin (see Chao-Beroff, 1999; and Christen and Rosenberg, 2000).

Early on, the Malian government demonstrated its commitment to microfinance. A sizeable portion (14 per cent) of the US$144 million released by the HIPC Initiative during 2003–04 to income-generating activities was committed to microfinance (Government of Mali, 2002). On the other hand, the government continues its own heavily subsidized microfinance projects, gives rise to unfair competition and market distortions.

Increasing competition amongst established MFIs of different degrees of subsidy dependence, but also from projects funded by the state or donors, prevented the emergence of a level playing field and instead created severe market distortions. Established institutions reacted by moving decisively up-market, as in the case of Nyèsigiso, with financial

Table 10.2 Key data on two selected MFIs in Mali

	Nyèsigiso	CVECA
Main focus	Urban	Rural
Legal status	Co-operative	Village bank
Year of creation	1995	1986
Capital (US$)	1,092,551	49,800
Compulsory deposit requirement	Yes	No
Number of clients	199,204	33,505
Group lending	In some products	No
Staff	Paid	Mostly unpaid

Notes: Figures are valid for 31/12/2003. Exchange rate FCFA/US$ = 522.47 (as of 31/12/2003).
Sources: Fieldwork questionnaires.

products targeted at urban, white-collar employees (*Crédit salaire, Depot salaire, Découvert salaire, Crédit hypothécaire salaries, Crédit à la consommation*). Competition is also manifested by the poaching of qualified staff away from established MFIs. For the CVECA system the practice of having volunteer workers exacerbates staff turnover. Table 10.2 compares the key data relating to these two MFIs.

Mali is also characterized by a relative close relationship between banks, the MFIs and informal finance. One example is the linkage between the BNDA (National Bank for Agricultural Development), the CVECA and village traditional saving and credit associations (*tontines*). The BNDA refinances CVECA, at a low interest rate (8 per cent).[7] BNDA's refinancing is proportional to deposits mobilized: 150 per cent of village bank deposits for the first two years; 200 per cent of their deposits afterward (Nguyen, Ouattara and Gonzalez-Vega, 1999). CVECA offers attractive interest rates on deposits, also for informal credit associations.

10.3 External factors: the implications of subsidy withdrawal

Both Nyèsigiso and CVECA recently experienced a phasing out of donor subsidies. The Canadian Development Agency (via DID) has been Nyèsigiso's main donor; it ended its long-term financial and technical support in 2005, except for ad hoc interventions.[8] Other donors withdrew in 2002, such as Fond Commun de Développement Mali–Canada and USAID/Freedom from Hunger (FFH), as can be seen from Table 10.3.

Table 10.3   Evolution of subsidies, Nyèsigiso, 1999–2003 (US$)

	1999	2000	2001	2002	2003
Investment grant	0	284,806	245,826	168,573	232,757
Operating subsidies	333,712	319,357	348,317	172,349	117,592
Total	333,712	604,163	594,143	340,922	350,349

Source: Union Annual Reports.

Table 10.4   Evolution of subsidies, CVECA Pays Dogon, 1999–2003 (US$)*

	1999	2000	2001	2002	2003
Investment grant	0	0	0	0	24,116[4]
Operating subsidies					
KfW[1]	0	12,569[1]	6,220[1]	0	0
EU	17,226[2]	0	0	0	0
Cash grants	0	0	0	235,422[3]	0
Soft loans[5]	201,908	83,004	87,301	57,420	102,590
Total	219,134	95,573	93,521	292,842	126,706

Notes: * Exchange rate FCFA/US$ = 522.466 (as of 31/12/2003). [1] Operational Deficit Coverage. [2] Urban bank start-up and logistic support. [3] KfW grant conditional on achieving financial self-sufficiency by 2007. [4] Free vehicles value at 31/12/2003. [5] Outstanding BNDA refinancing: duration of 11 months; interest rate 8 per cent.
Sources: Fieldwork Questionnaires and Interviews.

CVECAs witnessed similar donor withdrawals. During the pilot phase (1986–92), KfW (Kreditanstalt für Wiederaufbau) and the Government of Mali shared training costs, project personnel expenses (expatriate advisor, Malian officers and support staff) and vehicles, while village banks covered their operating costs. In a second phase (1993–97), the costs of structural design and training were still covered by donors, but village banks and their clients began assuming part of the project costs, as well as continuing to cover the operational costs. CVECAs achieved autonomy from donors in a third phase (1995–97), when the newly created *Service Commun* started to charge for services provided to network members. Until the withdrawal of a French NGO, village banks also received subsidies in their start-up phase for office construction and equipment. The evolution of donors' support and subsidies from 1999 to 2003 is shown in Table 10.4. In 1997, when the external partner ended its financial support, CVECA was able to cover all its operational cost and achieve financial sustainability, thanks to the longer term effects of the start-up subsidy and cost externalization to community groups. However, that outcome has not been stable as the institutional crisis of 1998–2000 showed. Some village banks were victims of fraud and forced to close down. KfW stepped in with a grant to cover its operational deficit in both 2000 and 2001. On the whole, changes in donor support do seem to have affected the growth of these MFIs and the composition of their client portfolio, as Tables 10.5 and 10.6 show.

Nyèsigiso encountered a steady period of growth during 1999–2003, reflected in the continuous rise in the number of clients, in its activity portfolio, and in the volume of loans and deposits (see Table 10.5). The data available point to a 30 per cent increase in the average loan size for the period 1999–2002. Data from DID's website suggest an even more marked increase in the average loan size, from $365 in 2000 to $669 in 2003.[9]

The CVECA branches in the Pays Dogon, by contrast, has become more poverty focused over the years (see Table 10.6). The loan portfolio shrunk by almost half, parallel to a decrease in short-term deposits. The number of active clients, for example, those who actually borrowed or deposited in the given period, declined significantly.

Nyèsigiso could ensure an expansion of its activities in a period of declining subsidies, because it went slightly up-market, indicated by a decrease in the number of female borrowers and in the proportion of loans to women. Also, the percentage of credits to solidarity groups rather than to individuals declined from 25 per cent to 21 per cent during 2003.[10]

Innovations with product design, such as the Crédit Epargne avec Education (CEE), to ensure poverty focus had mixed results. Nyèsigiso adopted a new policy of requiring more collateral. Training costs that used to be subsidized are now charged to clients to make the product sustainable. This move was not particularly appreciated by the target clientele. During fieldwork focus-group discussion and meetings at two different branches, complaints were repeatedly expressed about excessive pricing.[11] Members confessed that they often sought credit from family and informal lenders in order to pay back CEE loans. The volume of CEE loans decreased from 955,673 FCFA to 766,793 between 2002 and 2003, while the delinquency rate increased from one per cent to 6.41 per cent in the same period.[12]

Generally, the managers of Nyèsigiso quite openly admit their inability, given the increasingly difficult environment for MFIs, to keep up with the poverty reduction objective, which in their view could only be pursued with substantial government or donor subsidies. Nyèsigiso aims

Table 10.5   Outreach measures, Nyèsigiso, 1999–2004

Outreach measures	2004	2003	2002	2001	2000	1999
Personnel	337	327	337	351	347	282
Total clients[a]	n.a.	199,204	159,416	88,425	81,354	69,367
Loans						
Active borrowers[b]	25,423	27,780	9,977	10,516	8,785	7,928
No. loans disbursed	n.a	14,347	9,977	10,516	8,785	7,928
Gross loan portfolio (US$)	8,438,797	12,169,755	10,053,058	8,632,855	7,048,262	6,458,007
Average loan balance per borrower (US$)	332	438	1008	821	802	814
Average loan balance per borrower/GNI per capita (%)[c]	92.2	151	420	356.95	334.16	325.6
Savings						
Voluntary savings (US$)	7,507,669	10,700,240	10,346,710	9,187,070	8,226,019	7,449,593
Number of savers	182,571	127,435	99,522	88,425	81,354	69,367
Average savings balance per saver (US$)	41	84	104	104	101	107
Gender						
Female clients (%)	49.9	43	45	51.8	56.6	n.a.
Female managers (%)	25.1	29.2	27.7	22	30	n.a.
Credit to women (%)	38.5	37.1	39.5	36.5	44.8	n.a.
Efficiency and productivity						
Borrowers per staff member	75	85	30	30	25	28
Savers per staff member	542	390	295	252	234	245
Portfolio quality						
PAR > 90 days ratio %	9.83	3	1.81	2.53	4.09	n.a.

Notes: [a] Due to Nyèsigiso's reporting changes, number of clients refers to MFI members (individuals, groups or associations) until 2001 included, but to the number of individual clients thereafter. [b] Figures for active borrowers are not available for 1999–2002, and thus number of loans has been used instead. [c] Converted into US$ using the World Bank Atlas Method, divided by the mid-year population.
Exchange rate FCFA/US$ = 522.466 (as of 31/12/2003).
Sources: Fieldwork Questionnaires and Interviews; the MIX (www.mixmarket.org) for 2004 figures and DID statistics (www.did.qc.ca) for gender-related data.

at transforming itself into a commercial financial institution that provides services to those who lack access. In order to maintain financial soundness, it plans to target urban sections of the populations, such as civil servants and private sector employees.

Table 10.6   Outreach measures, CVECAs, 1999–2003

Outreach measures	2003	2002	2001	2000	1999
Personnel	658	824	856	817	688
Total clients	33,505	32,413	32,628	30,762	29,007
Loans					
Active borrowers	6,585	6,849	7,031	7,963	7,504
No. loans disbursed	8,638	8,983	9,639	10,294	10,554
Gross loan portfolio (US$)	408,821	378,589	426,295	669,910	765,411
Average loan balance per borrower (US$)	62	55	61	84	102
Average loan balance per borrower/GNI per capita (%)	21.38	22.9	26.52	35	40.8
Savings					
Voluntary savings (US$)	362,808	392,803	604,764	592,021	747,684
Number of savers	2,050	1,878	2,110	2,859	2,155
Average savings balance per saver (US$)	177	209	287	207	347
Gender					
Female clients (%)					
Borrower	39	37	35	29	17
Saver	17	17	15	14	15
Efficiency and productivity					
Borrowers per staff member	10	10	8	10	11
Savers per staff member	3	2	2	3	3
Portfolio quality					
PAR > 90 days ratio %	8[a]	n.a.	n.a.	n.a.	10

Notes: [a] PAR > 30 days ratio for 2003 is 15 per cent according to fieldwork questionnaire data.
Exchange rate (FCFA/US$) used for conversion: 522.466
Sources: Fieldwork Questionnaires and Interviews.

By contrast, the CVECA branches of the Pays Dogon continue to reach potentially vulnerable groups: the percentage of female borrowers went up from 17 per cent to 39 per cent during 1999–2003. However, this seems to have occurred at the expense of growth, and CVECA's operations themselves may be partly under threat following donor withdrawal. The area where donor subsidy cuts hurt most is staff training. Lack of trained staff now limits its expansion and curbs its possibilities to go up-scale. The use of volunteers is only a stop-gap measure as it leads to high staff turnover. CVECA managers, for their part, also suggest that a certain level of continued donor funding may be required if the poverty reduction objective is to be kept over time (Cerise, 1999).[13] According to GIE Guinedou's managers,[14] full financial sustainability will be possible only by attaining significant economies of scale, which would require an increase in number of village banks up to 60. Further expansion of the CVECA system, however, would imply establishing banks in more remote and/or very poor villages. In other words, donor subsidies are required in order to expand the network to a size sufficiently large to reap necessary economies of scale.

10.4 Conclusion

Operating in a challenging physical and economic environment, the wavering longer term stable donor support has led some MFIs to question poverty outreach as a serious strategy. There are signs that some changes, such as the increase in the loan size; the declining volume of, and support for, products targeted to the poor; and the lower proportion of potentially vulnerable members such as women, may be explained by the deliberate effort to reach financial viability. Managers and practitioners openly admit that if an MFI wants to survive in an increasingly competitive environment, it needs to prioritize products and clients that maximize returns.

In the case of CVECA, the phasing out of donor support appears to limit its expansion, growth and, indirectly, its poverty impact. Some strategic moves have even turned out to be counterproductive for the goal of financial sustainability. The move away from the village roots, for example, may, then, have the unintended effect of jeopardizing financial sustainability, because it usually implies an increase in monitoring costs.

The notion of mission drift transpired several times during fieldwork discussions and seems to be well understood by the actors involved. The phasing out of subsidies and the consequent pressure on financial sustainability prompt a reassessment of the MFIs' operational and strategic plans. There may, indeed, be a trade-off between poverty orientation and financial sustainability.

Notes

1 These figures are thus higher than those for Burkina Faso, Sierra Leone and Niger, which have a lower HDI score. Nigeria's population share below the 2$-a-day poverty line is slightly higher than in Mali, at 90.8 per cent, but then the proportion of the very poor is lower, at 70.2 per cent.

2 The HIPC Initiative grants some forms of debt relief to qualifying countries as part of the assistance and reform packages delivered by the World Bank and IMF.

3 Although the microfinance sector provides only 7 per cent of the total volume of credit and 5 per cent of deposits, it assures a more capillary presence in the territory, with a number of counters open to the public amounting to 85 per cent of the total (Bruntrup, 2002).

4 Importantly, cattle ownership is also a way of increasing one's social status in many African societies.

5 The BCEAO, e.g., the central bank of the UEMOA, is the main actor responsible for the microfinance sector, within the framework of the Programme d'appui à la réglementation sur les mutuelles d'épargne et de credit (PARMEC) law, to be adopted by single states.

6 More precisely, the PARMEC law regulates only MFIs with a cooperative structure (e.g., Nyèsigiso), whereas the others need to sign a special agreement with the Ministry of Finance.

7 In case of bank default, the association repays BNDA with funds collected by member contributions.

8 Interview with Mr Réal Deschêsnes, then DID Mali Director, Bamako, 8 September 2004.

9 See www.did.qc.ca.

10 The corresponding figures for previous years could not be obtained due to changes in the way the MFIs records clients since 2002.

11 For instance, out of a loan amount of 50,000 FCFA, CEE clients have to pay a 10,000 FCFA guarantee, 15,000 FCFA for training costs, and 10,000 FCFA to a security fund, which leaves them with only 15,000 FCFA in actual credit to use.

12 Moreover, the intention is to discontinue CEE in Bamako (Interviews with Mr Ely Terra, Nyèsigiso Admistrative and Financial Director, Septmber 2004).

13 A village with an insufficient number of people who can read or write would require very high costs of training for a CVECA to be established, given a CVECA recruits staff from within the village.

14 Interviews with GIE management in Koro, 13–15 September 2004: Mr Moctar Yalcouyé (GIE director), Mr Mallick Tembely (finance and supervision), Mr Daniel Saye (training).

11
Contextual Factors Determining Poverty Outreach and Financial Performance: The Case of Morocco

Saâd Filali Meknassi
Université Mohamed V – Rabat Agdal

11.1   Introduction

This chapter examines the impact of contextual factors on three major Moroccan microfinance institutions: the Zakoura Microcredit Foundation, the Al Amana Association for the Promotion of Micro-Enterprises, and the Foundation for Local Development and Microcredit Partnerships (FONDEP).

The three institutions were selected for different reasons. The Zakoura Microcredit Foundation is the industry leader in terms of the number of active clients. Since it was set up in 1995, it has benefited greatly from financing by banks and its grassroots experience. It has grown rapidly while keeping its initial target population, namely disadvantaged people in urban, semi-urban and rural areas.

In terms of outstanding credits, Al Amana is the largest Moroccan MFI. It was set up in 1997 and started out with a sizeable financial contribution and support from USAID. Rapid growth has been achieved thanks to sound management, technical assistance and a favourable political situation. Its operations currently cover almost all of Morocco and it has over 160,000 borrowers who are mostly organized in groups. In a context of increasing competition, Al Amana has carved itself a niche in rural areas; 134 new branches were opened in 2004 alone.

FONDEP has about a tenth of the number of clients of Al Amana and Zakoura. It is an MFI that targets low-income earners, especially in rural areas, and offers credit as joint liability loans. The trends in targeting clients are shown for the three institutions, alongside comparative MFIs based in Benin, Bosnia and Egypt, in Figure 11.1.

The three Moroccan MFIs reviewed target and effectively reach the very poor: the average loan per active client in relation to the GDP per capita rarely exceeds 20 per cent. At the same time, Al Amana and Zakoura have a level of financial autonomy that is either higher than or similar to that of other MFIs elsewhere, even though these other associations deal with less poor clients (see Figure 11.2). This would suggest that the trade-off can be avoided by scaling up operations of very small and frequent transactions.

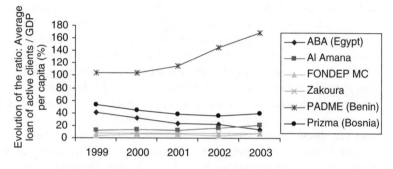

Figure 11.1   Trends in the targeting of clients by MFIs
Source: Data from the GIAN survey.

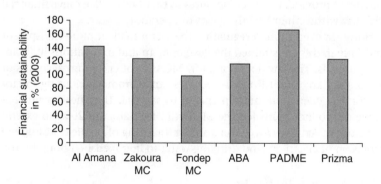

Figure 11.2   Financial sustainability of MFIs in 2003
Source: Data from the GIAN survey.

All three MFIs thus performed successfully in both financial and social terms. This raises the question of the extent to which the specific situation in Morocco may have contributed to this near-optimal positioning of major MFIs on both poverty and profitability scores. Three drivers of performance in particular may have favoured the development of strong microfinance institutions compared with other countries: the institutional context, support by the banking sector and a prudent use of subsidies.

11.2 Institutional context

The microcredit sector in Morocco has been given a legal framework with the promulgation of a law in 1999, Act No.18–97 concerning microcredit.[1] This law created a new type of association, a 'microcredit association' (MCA), which combines the advantages of not-for-profit associations and some of the features of financial institutions. Unlike banks, MCAs are not obliged to have a substantial minimum capital to start with. Also, they can raise the finance needed for loans and receive financial support from both public and private sectors. Microcredit cannot exceed a maximum of approximately US$5600.[2] MCAs can also conduct non-financial activities such as training, advising and providing technical assistance to their clients. During their first five years, associations enjoy tax reductions, such as VAT exemption on credit operations and exemption from customs duty on imported equipment. Moreover, gifts received are tax deductible for company tax and general income tax.

In order to guarantee the transparency of MCA activities, the Act instituted supervisory measures for microcredit activities requiring associations to have an independent annual audit of their accounting. Further, it provides for strict measures so that MFIs will achieve financial viability within their first five years of operation.

However, even though regulating the sector made it more transparent and formal, this constrained the development and innovations of financial products. The law does not allow MCAs to offer savings accounts or to conduct any other financial business apart from distributing microcredit. The clients are quite prepared to say that they need a broader range of products. This led the Moroccan legislators in 2002 to extend the scope of Act 18–97 to cover also the financing of public housing, the provision of electricity and drinking water to impoverished households.

11.3 Support by banks

The banking sector supports the microcredit trade primarily through refinancing facilities. However, only the large MFIs benefit from this

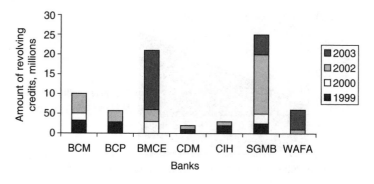

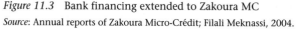

Figure 11.3   Bank financing extended to Zakoura MC
Source: Annual reports of Zakoura Micro-Crédit; Filali Meknassi, 2004.

because of their solid financial structure and results. The support takes place within the same group: the Banque Populaire Group gives decisive support to its subsidiary – the Banque Populaire Foundation for Microcredit – through direct refinancing, and free use of its network of branches, information system and staff training. The same bank also financially supported the Zakoura MC Foundation and Al Amana which are not part of its corporate group. The Société Générale has opened lines of credit at 4 per cent and 4.5 per cent with the backing of a USAID guarantee for up to 42 per cent of its disbursements. The Moroccan Commercial Bank[3] released a guarantee-free US$4 million credit line for the microcredit sector. The Zakoura Microcredit Foundation remains the main beneficiary of finance from national banks, as Figure 11.3 illustrates.

11.4   Subsidies

Subsidies make up over 61 per cent of Al Amana's sources of financing, mainly from USAID, the Hassan II Fund for Economic and Social Development, the Arab Fund for Economic and Social Development (FADES), the Mohamed V Foundation, and CAF America (Figure 11.4). Zakoura did not receive a sizeable subsidy when it started out, but subsequently benefited from grants in its start-up and growth stages. Zakoura MC also developed technical partnerships with international organizations such as UNDP (Microstart), and with national agencies such as the National Water Office (ONEP). An analysis of the breakdown of FONDEP MC's equity shows that subsidies made up 90 per cent of its total equity capital in December 2004 (Figure 11.5).

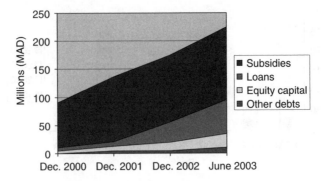

Figure 11.4   Al Amana's sources of financing, 2000–03
Source: PlaNet Rating, 2003.

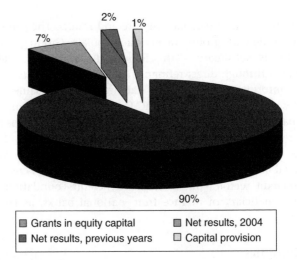

Figure 11.5   Breakdown of FONDEP MC's equity capital, December 2004
Source: FONDEP, 2005.

11.5   Conclusion

Act No. 18–97 on microcredit, while giving countrywide recognition to microfinance, also turned out to seriously constrain the capacity of MFIs to innovate and diversify their products. The very fact that MCAs can only engage in microcredit and must refrain from raising deposits from clients and the general public forces them to turn to bank refinancing or other sources to finance the portfolio growth and go further up-scale. It would be useful for this sector to be able to develop new products that could offer market opportunities for the future, such as micro-insurance, micro-savings, fund transfers and so on. The dominance of the banking system in the approval of credits is illustrated in Figure 11.6.

Financial exclusion in Morocco affects the poor across the board, and at times even people on an average or higher income. Fewer than 20 per cent of the population uses banking services, few villages have a bank branch. Cash remains the most common form of payment. The under-monetarization of the rural economy and the lack of any service providers in the poorest areas might stimulate MFIs to develop new products and a new model for their expansion in rural areas.

It is quite possible that at some point the banks will become more reluctant to refinance the microcredit sector if the MFIs' equity capital falls below 20 per cent of their balance sheet. This shows a need to strengthen intermediation amongst MFIs. Moreover, banks have made it clear that they expect MFIs to share credit risks. The large Moroccan MFIs are considering the feasibility of issuing negotiable documents like commercial papers.

Advocates of microfinance in Morocco and public authorities could consider 'bridging facilities' between the MFIs and banks, in view of the potential increasing demand.

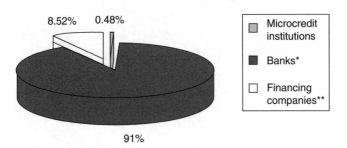

Figure 11.6 Credits approved in Morocco, 2004

Notes: * The only bank credits included are cash advances, property loans and equipment financing. ** The only finance companies included are building societies and leasing companies.

Source: Data from Bank Al-Maghrib, 2004, and FNAM, 2004.

Notes

1 This Act was promulgated by Decree No. 1.99.16 of 18 Chaoual 1419 (5 February 1999) and published in the Official Gazette: No. 4678 – 14 Hija 1419 (1 April 1999). The microcredit sector has come under the supervision of the Ministry of Finance since the promulgation of the Act concerning this sector. The bill on banking currently being considered extends the control of the central bank (Al-Maghrib Bank) to the microcredit sector. To this end, plans are underway to determine the accounting standards and internal controls that are appropriate for this sector.

2 The amount stipulated by law is a maximum amount. The Ministry of Finance fixes the maximum amount for loans in this sector. It is currently 30,000 MAD (US$3380) (the rate of exchange used in this chapter is US$/MAD = 8.87, the average for 2004).

3 Now Attijari Wafa following its merger with Wafabank.

12

Contextual Factors Determining Poverty Outreach and Financial Performance: The Case of Eastern Europe and Central Asia

Justyna Pytkowska
Microfinance Centre for Central and Eastern Europe
and the New Independent States (MFC)

12.1 Introduction

Microfinance in the Eastern European and Central Asian region[1] emerged after the transition from a centrally planned to a market economy, allowing for the development of private entrepreneurship. At the same time vast unemployment forced many citizens to seek economic opportunities and start their own micro-businesses. Some MFIs in the region – probably the great majority – focused on supporting the emerging micro-business sector. Other MFIs saw themselves as complementary actors in reconstruction efforts and post-conflict situations.

In the different sub-regions, different MFI profiles have emerged. Albania and the countries of former Yugoslavia benefited from above average donor support; this is the sub-region with the largest MFIs as well as the most dynamic ones. An important share of the microfinance market is served by microfinance banks and increasingly by down-scaling projects of commercial banks. The competition is becoming an issue leading to client over-indebtedness.

Central and Eastern Europe (CEE), with its rapid economic reforms and integration with the European Union as well as its tradition of small entrepreneurship, has seen primarily the credit union type of MFI emerge, which even survived under the communist rule in the form of employee 'kasas' providing short-term consumer loans to state workers. In Lithuania, Poland and the Ukraine, credit unions provide a wide range of services competitively, even in comparison to banks. The majority of CEE countries are in the upper-middle income stratum and hence they fail to qualify for donor support which penalizes non-bank MFIs with limited capacity for attracting commercial funding.

In the Caucasus there is quite a large number of small MFIs facing serious regulatory constraints. The regulatory environment has been a constraining factor in Central Asia too. Lending by non-bank financial institutions has until recently been limited, resulting in poor market coverage in Central Asia, which has the lowest per capita income of the region. However, newly adopted microfinance laws in Kazakhstan and Kyrgyzstan have caused a rapid increase of the number of MFIs, and banks are increasingly down-scaling.

Lastly, microfinance in Russia and the Ukraine is dominated by credit unions serving micro-entrepreneurs. Due to their high market coverage they serve much larger numbers of clients than any other institutional type. Their major competitors are commercial banks which also have very good network of offices and reach clients in remote areas.

Whatever their niche, practically all MFIs in the entire region pursue a double bottom line: fulfilling their social mission, while ensuring financial sustainability. The most important contextual factors that determine whether MFIs succeed in going up-scale, and thus reach this double bottom line, are access to funding, competition, and legal and regulatory constraints.

- Access to funding – savings collection by non-supervised institutions is not permitted, which creates a problem of finding sources of funds for growth. As donors are shifting their priorities to other regions, MFIs face a problem of availability and affordability of private funds.
- Competition – the success of some microfinance institutions is attracting the interest of commercial banks which have started to offer loans to smaller entrepreneurs.
- Legal constraints – in many countries of the region the regulations concerning financial operations by non-bank institutions are unclear which threatens the existence of many MFIs and hinders their growth.

The chapter discusses results obtained from a sample of 49 microfinance institutions operating in Eastern Europe and Central Asia, 23 of which were non-bank financial institutions (NBFIs) and 26 non-governmental organizations (NGOs), the key data of which are given in Table 12.1.[2]

Table 12.1 Key data on MFIs in Eastern Europe and Central Asia: sample of 49 MFIs

		Number of active borrowers	GNP per capita	Gross loan portfolio/ total assets	Staff productivity	Operating expense ratio	Financial revenue ratio
Return on assets	Pearson correlation coefficient	0.44	−0.35	0.40	0.39	−0.54	0.35
	Significance level	0.001	0.015	0.004	0.006	0.000	0.013

		Depth of outreach	Average salary/ GNP per capita	Gross loan portfolio	Staff productivity	Yield on loan portfolio	
Operating expense ratio	Pearson correlation coefficient	−0.38	Not significant	−0.44	−0.41	0.88	
	Significance level	0.006		0.002	0.004	0.000	

Continued

Table 12.1 Continued

		Number of active borrowers	GNP per capita	Depth of outreach	Percentage of individual loans in loan portfolio	Average loan balance
Financial revenue ratio	Pearson correlation coefficient	0.32	−0.44	−0.31	−0.35	−0.49
	Significance level	*0.023*	*0.002*	*0.03*	*0.018*	*0.000*

12.2 Access to resources

With age, MFIs can grow their client base and go up-scale provided they have sufficient resources to satisfy the demand. The latter is a serious limiting factor as the majority of MFIs are donor-funded and these are becoming scarcer in the region. Many MFIs are starting to look for commercial sources of funds, but it takes time to build such new kinds of relationship as well as account for the higher cost of market funds.

Resource constraints (including the interdiction to collect deposits from the general public) account for the slow and hesitant growth of microfinance institutions in the region and their outreach to people excluded from the banking sector. Outreach here is more limited that in other regions (see *MicroBanking Bulletin*). At the same time the average transaction size is higher here than in other regions; logically, with a given resource basis, MFIs reach fewer clients than MFIs operating elsewhere. Faced with the need to make choices about resource allocation many MFIs also take the easy path and go for higher market segments to begin with which are easier to serve. Furthermore, as MFIs in this region are sustainability-oriented, they concentrate on serving only profitable clients. As yet, there is very little cross-subsidizing of different products that could allow the reaching of vast numbers of less or unprofitable clients.

The legal form, whether NGO or non-bank financial institution (NBFI), does not play a role in the width and depth of outreach. Also, the location of the MFI and its clients in terms of rural or urban areas is not an influencing factor. MFIs with substantial outreach provide more individual loans and their staff is more productive, translating into higher profitability through increased financial revenues, as illustrated in Table 12.2.

12.3 Financial performance

Achieving high returns on assets is more manageable in low-income countries where the MFI can secure higher yields. The biggest driver of positive returns on assets, an indicator of financial self-sufficiency, is cost control, hence an endogenous factor (Table 12.2). Standardized internal procedures and streamlined client service contribute to higher staff productivity. Higher salaries positively influence the productivity of MFI staff in the region without having negative effects on staff expenses.

The scale of operations facilitates cost control. Also, the MFIs which provide larger loans to better-off clients manage to do it at lower unit

Table 12.2 Outreach and profitability

	Age	Total assets	Percent individual loans in loan portfolio	Staff productivity	Return on assets	Financial revenue ratio
No. of active borrowers						
Pearson correlation coefficient	0.40	0.56	0.31	0.41	0.44	0.33
Significance level	0.005	0.000	0.039	0.004	0.001	0.023

cost. On the revenue side, the level of portfolio yields is the biggest determinant as loan portfolio is the major revenue-generating asset. These yields depend very much on the country context – MFIs that operate in poorer countries are able to achieve higher yields because of pent-up demand and MFIs have more flexibility in setting cost-covering interest rates. Furthermore, there is little competition putting pressure on interest rates because of legal constraints which affect the supply of funds to create and develop the microfinance industry.

MFIs that serve poorer entrepreneurs and provide smaller loans set higher interest rates because of higher cost of managing such loans (more frequent meetings with clients, shorter loan duration and therefore more loan cycles throughout the year) and higher risk of non-repayment.

12.4 Social performance

For the majority of MFIs the core target market is unbanked entrepreneurs. In comparison with other regions the average loan balance, as well as the depth of outreach, is much higher. Eastern and Central Asian countries are highly industrialized with considerably high costs of living, so enterprises need to generate more income than in other regions to stay in business. Levels of entrepreneurship are low, and there is a culture of risk avoidance and reliance on the welfare state. Those who start enterprises are usually able to grow them and expect higher loan sizes. Some demand studies carried out by MFIs show that there is more demand for larger, collateralized loans. As poor clients are more costly to serve, MFIs tend to diversify their portfolio to include also better-of clients. This results in higher average loan balance of the institution.

The reasons are three-fold:

- there is a large demand for larger loans among economically active poor;
- in order to diversify the portfolio and therefore reduce the risk, MFIs reach out to clients operating in various sectors of the economy, including production or agricultural processing with demand for investment loans;
- after several years in operations, the MFIs have a group of graduated clients with excellent credit history but also with larger financial needs.

As a result, the deepest poverty outreach, indicated by the low value of the depth of outreach ratio,[3] is observed among MFIs that have a smaller

Table 12.3   Outreach and asset base

		Total assets	Percentage of women borrowers	Capital/ asset ratio	Percentage of individual loans in portfolio
Depth of outreach	Pearson correlation coefficient	0.41	−0.44	−0.37	0.68
	Significance level	*0.003*	*0.002*	*0.01*	*0.000*

		Percentage of group loans in portfolio	Number of agricultural loan products offered
Percentage of women borrowers	Pearson correlation coefficient	−0.40	−0.33
	Significance level	*0.006*	*0.019*

asset base than their counterparts but are able to reach just as many borrowers, serve larger percentages of women clients and are predominantly donor funded. They most often utilize group-based methodologies, as shown in Table 12.3.

Larger MFIs are able to offer a wider range of loan products. Loans for business activities are the predominant form of lending, although agricultural or consumer loans are becoming more popular. This happens in countries where the financial sector is more developed and there are more institutions competing for clients. They offer various loan types in order to search for new markets as well as to satisfy a variety of needs of the existing clients, as better market penetration and higher client satisfaction allows the MFI to distance itself from the competition. More often than not, registered non-bank MFIs have a wider product range than NGOs.

Notes

1   The region of Eastern Europe and Central Asia (EECA) comprises five sub-regions: the Balkans (Albania, Bosnia and Herzegovina, Croatia, Kosovo, Macedonia, Montenegro, Serbia and Slovenia); Central and Eastern Europe (Bulgaria, the Czech Republic, Estonia, Hungary, Latvia, Lithuania, Moldova,

Poland, Romania and Slovakia); the Caucasus (Armenia, Azerbaijan, Georgia); Central Asia (Kazakhstan, Kyrgyzstan, Mongolia, Tajikistan, Turkmenistan and Uzbekistan); and BRU (Belarus, Russia and the Ukraine).

2 In-depth analysis of their financial performance can be found in *2004 Microfinance Sector Development in Eastern Europe and Central Asia* published by the Microfinance Centre for CEE and NIS (MFC) and available at www.mfc.org.pl.

3 Depth of outreach is calculated as average loan balance per borrower divided by GNP per capita. This measure normalized the loan size for different levels of country income making cross-country comparisons possible. Lower values of the ratio mean smaller loans which are associated with deeper outreach to the poor. Higher values mean that the outreach is more shallow as the institution serves clients with larger businesses.

13
Auctioning Subsidies: Chile's 'Access to Credit Program'

Vito Sciaraffia Merino
University of Chile

13.1 Introduction

In 1992, the Chilean government decided to develop microfinance through the Access to Credit Program (PAC) aimed at encouraging formal banking institutions to go down-scale and support microenterprise development. The programme had an original feature: it provided an incentive to formal financial institutions for every approved and disbursed loan. The banks provide credit at their own the risk. The PAC is managed by the Technical Cooperation Service (SERCOTEC), a government agency.

To apply for the subsidy, the financial institution must compete in a tender process. The institution signalling the lowest amount of overhead resources for every credit operation is awarded the tender, provided it meets the targeting specifications. The purpose of the tender is to enhance competition among banks and optimize use of fiscal resources. The subsidy is paid *ex post*, that is, after the micro-entrepreneurs[1] have been financed. The financial institutions can freely determine the interest rates, within the framework of legislation on interest rate ceilings, set by the Superintendency of Banks and Financial Institutions.

To access PAC endorsed loans, micro-entrepreneurs must take the initiative and contact a financial institution. Eligibility criteria for micro-entrepreneurs are:

- Turnover of not more than US$3.5 million p.a.
- Fixed assets (land, equipment, machinery) of not more than US$9.3 million
- Fewer than ten employees working in the microenterprise, including relatives

- The loan must be used to finance investments and working capital
- The minimum loan amount is $240 (UF),[2] the maximum loan amount is $12,000
- No more than three PAC loans per micro-entrepreneur
- The term for repayment of the loan is between six and 48 months.

13.2 Microenterprises in Chile

In 2001 there was a total of 652,445 formal companies in Chile, 82 per cent of which were microenterprises (Comité de Fomento de la Micro y Pequeña Empresa, 2003). A study by the Universidad de Chile similarly estimates the total number of micro-entrepreneurs as close to 600,000 in 2000. The total number of micro-entrepreneurs – formal and informal – amounts to over 1.2 million persons, equivalent to 22 per cent of total employment. Taking also into account wage and unpaid family labour, total employment generated by microenterprises amounts to 2,024,425 workers, which represents 46 per cent of total employment in the private sector and 37 per cent of total employment at the national level. More details are given in Table 13.1.

Estimates can also be made on the probability of a company being part of a certain firm-size category, considering that in a previous period that same company was part of another category (adjusted for sectoral and regional effects). These estimates give rise to a transition matrix for Chilean companies in 1995–2001, the results of which are as follows: of the total number of microenterprises in 1995, 36.72 per cent continued

Table 13.1 Total employment generated by microenterprises, 2000

Employment status	Number of workers			Total employment
	1	2–5	6–9	
Employer	0	125,070	34,425	159,495
Self-employed worker	761,715	306,766	0	1,068,481
Private sector employee or worker	0	511,384	285,065	796,449
Total employment in micro-enterprises	761,715	943,220	319,490	2,024,425

Note: It is important to underline that in the CASEN Survey, category C considers 6 to 9 persons. However, the SII classification considers a company is a microenterprise when it employs up to 10 persons. In this sense, the employment generated by microenterprises is underestimated. *Source*: CASEN, 2000.

to be a microenterprise in 2001, while 40.04 per cent had ceased to exist towards the end of that period. On the other hand, only 4.28 per cent had grown to become a small enterprise, while 0.22 per cent had become a medium-sized company and only 0.03 per cent had become a company. In the case of small companies, 35.35 per cent had remained in the same category in 2001, 25.10 per cent had ceased to exist and 20.74 per cent had moved back to the microenterprise category. Moreover, 4.48 per cent had moved up to the medium-sized enterprise category and only 0.47 per cent to the large company category.

13.3   Has the PAC achieved its goals?

The PAC has two tracks, one via banks and the other via non-banks. Both categories of financial institutions are eligible for the payment of a subsidy for every approved credit disbursed to a microenterprise. The terms and conditions of these tracks slightly differ in that the PAC subsidy to banks is intended for slightly larger client units, compared to the PAC track for credit unions and MFIs, as shown in Table 13.2.

The PAC scheme has been evaluated by the Faculty of Economics of the Universidad de Chile. The evaluation has found a structural impact, in the sense that formal financial institutions have learnt to view micro- and small enterprises as a market. In particular, as a result of the launch of the PAC scheme major financial institutions like Banco Estado, Banefe, Bandesarrollo and Credicoop developed schemes specialized in microenterprises. The PAC programme is acknowledged to have contributed to a certain specialization in microenterprise financing, for three reasons: first, PAC allowed banks to take risks that they would not otherwise have been prepared to take because of the low return on the loans granted to this sector. Secondly, the subsidy enabled formal credit entities to explore these market segments at lower transaction costs than would have been necessary had they to do it on their own initiative. At the same time, it should be acknowledged, though, that for non-banks the PAC may have created a certain subsidy dependence. Thirdly, the interest rate ceiling imposed by the Central Bank filtered out suppliers, at the expense of some potential intermediaries and service providers to microenterprises that withdrew because of the artificially reduced bank margin.

Over the years since 1997 the number of participating financial institutions remained stable, ranging between three and six banks. In interviews, banks signalled that the subsidy was important both to enter this market and to face the start-up costs in the initial period. The

Table 13.2 Comparison of the PAC subsidy: banks and non-banks

Components	PAC subsidy for banks	PAC subsidy for non-banks
Minimum loan amount	$240 $300	$150 $240
Maximum loan amount	$7,500 $12,000	$2,400 $6,000
Minimum loan term	6 months	4 months
Maximum loan term	48 months	36 months
Modality of the subsidy	Absolute (according to the minimum amount provided and with regional differentiation)	Percentage (10% in the last tender); regional differentiation
Maximum subsidy amount	None, in principle	$40,000; regional differentiation
Minimum subsidy amount	None, in principle	$10,000
Resource usage	For investments or working capital	For investments or working capital
Charging commissions and expenses	Not permitted	
Restrictions in the number of subsidized loans	No more than 3	No more than 3
Maximum number of employees	10	5
Average monthly sales	$6,000	$4,200
Maximum value of fixed assets	$15,000	$12,000
Minimum number of years of existence of the enterprise	Not required	Not required

exception is Banco Estado that stated that it would have started to work with this segment anyway; however, the PAC allowed it to do so earlier. Few institutions participate in the programme operating under similar conditions. This could theoretically invite tacit oligopolistic agreements amongst them. However, there is no concrete evidence that this is indeed so. SERCOTEC operates with minimum tender conditions and constant contacts with participating companies, as well as constantly searching for new interested parties.

In terms of depth of outreach, 241,240 subsidies had been granted cumulatively from 1992 to 2003 under both tracks of the PAC, with a growing trend. Moreover, the proportion of PAC-supported loans on all loans distributed by banks and non-banks per year has been steadily growing.

Taking into account that every micro-entrepreneur is entitled to receive the subsidy only three times, these figures stand for a substantial increase in the mass of clients that obtained access to credit thanks to the PAC. In 2004, 35.5 per cent of all micro-entrepreneurs had a loan outstanding with a bank or non-bank and it can be safely assumed that the bulk of this is due to the PAC. According to data of the Banco Estado, there are about one million micro-entrepreneurs, 400,000 of whom are formal. The Banco Estado alone has 200,000 clients. Taking into account the total number of clients of the financial system, the number of micro-entrepreneurs with access to credit would be 300,000, that is, an access to credit of around 30 per cent.[3] That is quite an improvement compared to the beginning of the 1990s, when only around 5 per cent of the micro-entrepreneurs were bankable, or to 2000 with a rate of 20 per cent. That still leaves 700,000 micro-entrepreneurs as eligible credit subjects, but not yet clients. This change can be largely attributed to active government policies in support of microenterprises, such as the PAC programme.

More importantly, there is a very high percentage of microenterprise clients who started off with a PAC product and subsequently graduated to becoming regular bank clients: 98 per cent of Banco Estado clients graduated from the PAC programme, 97 per cent at Banefe and 60 per cent at Bandesarrollo.

In terms of targeting precision, the evaluation compared the amounts tendered for by banks and non-banks with the amount paid out by the state agency SERCOTEC as a subsidy to compensate for microenterprise lending costs. The targeting was also effective in allowing microenterprises to ease liquidity constraints: more than 80 per cent of PAC loans were used for activities directly related to the business.

In terms of impact on collateralization, the evaluation found evidence of a learning process over the last decade as banks started to replace guarantees and securities with field assessments and periodic follow-up. General restrictions as regards lending amounts and terms were lifted as the relationship between the micro-entrepreneur and bank became established. According to Banefe 'in the first nine months, the micro-entrepreneur has access only to credit, but then we prepared a new evaluation and he or she is granted a credit line'. In other words, the financial system has accumulated knowledge and acquired experience to work with the micro-business world.

Despite the PAC subsidy, the interest rate on PAC loans was still comparatively high, as Figure 13.1 shows. Under the terms of the PAC agreement banks were not allowed to charge commissions or other fixed costs. So, either the PAC subsidy did not fully cover the extra transaction costs in lending to microenterprises, or financial institutions topped up the interest rate precisely to make up for revenues foregone because of this restriction.

The PAC was intended to have a demonstration effect: the purpose is for formal credit entities to get to know the average performance of micro-entrepreneurs, but not of each and every micro-entrepreneur. Consequently, in those geographical areas or for those types of microenterprises for which data can be gathered on the viability of microenterprise financing, the subsidy can be phased out. This is the line SERCOTEC is currently following, in that it identifies under-served sectors (a combination of geographical area and type of economic activity) and sets differentiated subsidy amounts. To that extent one can say that SERCOTEC has started to exit the subsidy.

With regard to possible market distortions one can distinguish one related to the size limitation of the loan and another with regard to the

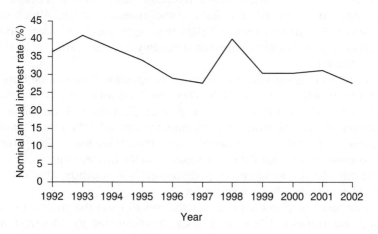

Figure 13.1 Evolution of the interest rate in relation to PAC loans

differentiation between banks and non-banks. The ceiling on loan amounts implies that borrowers do not express their full loan demand. The floor limitation implies a distortion with regard to the outreach of the requested amount, leading possibly to the exclusion of very small entrepreneurs, individual proprietorships and family enterprises with no wage labour. If micro-entrepreneurs in the lower segment with access to the PAC programme compete with those who do not have access to the PAC because of this floor limitation, a distortion will emerge.

The second possible distortion lies in the differentiation between two sets of subsidy conditions for two different types of lending agents, banks and non-banks. This might distort the competition among different types of institutions. The objective should be to create the necessary conditions for generating the sustainable provision of credit to micro-entrepreneurs, and in this sense, efficiency of the providers should be favoured, not the legal status or professional accreditation of a financing agent. While estimates show that some sectors need the subsidy more than others, the central element underlying the subsidy should be targeting the demand side rather than the supply side. SERCOTEC is currently reviewing its policy in this respect. The idea is to look more at the comparative advantage of a certain institution in a certain segment, that is, hence focusing on the demand side, instead of looking at the legal form of a financial intermediary.

With regard to displacement effects, we found that as the PAC centres on credit transactions with individuals who did not have access to formal credit before (at least those transactions about which the Superintendency of Banks and Financial Institutions has knowledge), any displacement, if it occurs at all, would take place in the informal market. Also, loan sharks and commercial house chains that aggressively offer loan products at very steep interest rates could possibly have been affected by the PAC measure.

In terms of good governance of the programme it should be noted that for its administration, SERCOTEC had hired an external company. This delegation led to some, not widespread, deviations from the programme design: for example, companies were found with sales volumes exceeding permitted levels or with more than three loans. There were also errors or missing data in a series of fields that are important for analysis of the programmes's performance. Subsequently, SERCOTEC decided to replace the subcontractor.

Compared to possible policy alternatives to close the credit gap for microenterprises in Chile, the PAC can be considered an efficient strategy. It has a limited time horizon, is incentive-based and focuses on a

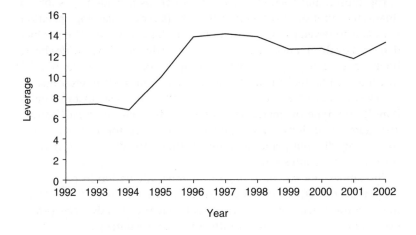

Figure 13.2   PAC leverage over time

root cause of the market gap, namely lender transaction costs. Moreover, the use of a competitive tender process and the payment of the PAC subsidy after the loans had been distributed minimized abuse and market distortions.

This does not mean that this type of a subsidy is a panacea and generally replicable; even in the Chilean context complementary actions to strengthen the PAC could be considered, especially organizing and associating micro-entrepreneurs; this would enable banks and clients to further reduce their operating costs.

The PAC's leverage, that is, how many pesos of credit are generated with every peso of subsidy, is illustrated in Figure 13.2. Efficiency of the PAC has improved over time, reaching a certain level of stability, which once again reinforces the idea of maturity and the need to emphasize targeting or reinforce the programme with other measures.

13.4   Conclusions

The PAC subsidy effectively contributed to the increased provision of finance to micro-entrepreneurs. Clients who passed through the PAC are now effectively considered bank clients. Not only the formal credit sector's knowledge of the microenterprise sector has improved, but there has been a change also in the micro-entrepreneur's familiarity of the formal credit sector.

The subsidy has been clearly an incentive, as it made it possible for financial institutions to cover part of the initial cost to develop operations with and to develop a specialized platform for this sector. The products delivered by the financial institutions were credit, but also provide cheque books, credit cards, sight accounts, mortgage loans and a series of other instruments that had remained out of reach for micro-entrepreneurs.

Development of a special window within financial institutions to handle this type of operation is essential in such an *ex post* subsidy arrangement as long as the microenterprise sector is perceived as something different, and as long as there are differences between microenterprise sub-sectors.

The tender process contributed to market-orientation in pricing and greater overall efficiency. The ceiling on the number of credits per micro-entrepreneur, as well as the fact that the subsidy decreases for every additional credit, are incentives to increase outreach.

Notes

1　Self-employed workers, formal or informal entrepreneurs from any economic sector who produce goods and services on a small scale are eligible for the subsidy, except for agricultural companies that are covered by credit programmes of the Agriculture and Livestock Development Institute (INDAP).

2　The Unidad de Fomento (UF) is an inflation-adjusted unit of account used in Chile; its ISO-4217 code is CLF. The UF was created through Decree No. 40 dated 20 January 1967. Its principal and original use was in mortgage loans, as a way to revalue them according to inflationary variations. Later, use of this unit was widened to all types of bank or private loans, and investments (term deposits or other instruments). As at 1 June 2005, UF1.00 was equivalent to US$29.90.

3　According to Héctor Pacheco, Sub-Manager of Micro- and Small Enterprise Development of the Banco Estado, clients from the different banking institutions cannot be added up as some people are clients of more than one bank, so the numbers should take this aspect into account, registering clients of more than one bank only once.

Part V
Conclusions

14
Policy Implications

Bernd Balkenhol
International Labour Office

In an environment of volatile priorities, and the ad hoc and highly politicized decisions that characterize development aid, donors prefer not to get bogged down in long-term subsidy support for one particular aid sector. This is especially true in microfinance with its claim to make donor subsidies redundant after a few years. The preceding chapters have shown, though, that donor and government subsidies may still be needed for more or less long periods of time, depending on the operating environment of microfinance institutions. The preceding chapters have also shown that there are substantial social benefits associated with the activities of microfinance institutions, whether by way of securing and stabilizing incomes, or by social organization and market broadening. Donors who are ready to acknowledge these benefits should therefore also bring themselves to accept that 'if a programme is shown to be worthy of support year after year, it should get support year after year' (Morduch, 2003, p. 31).

The authors have shown here that public policy in support of microfinance can accommodate a variety of business models, provided that they are based on efficiency, a criterion that underpins both social and financial performance. The following definitions and measurements of efficiency sum up the argument developed so far:

- Most determinants of efficiency across all MFIs fall in two categories: factors that MFI management can influence (like the choice of delivery technique, collateral requirements, graduation lending, etc) and others that it cannot fully control and for which it cannot be held accountable (like client density, scope of clients' viable income generating activities, etc.). A third category of efficiency drivers cannot neatly be attributed to being either management-dependant or

211

exogenous, for example the wages paid to loan officers. Only the first kind of efficiency drivers should and can be used by governments and donors to fix, modify or phase out a subsidy for performance.

- A meaningful qualification of an MFI as more or less efficient requires information on a batch of comparable MFIs positioned similarly on the poverty–profitability continuum. Comparability is based on several criteria: whether an MFI operates in rural or urban areas, whether it is a monopolist or not and whether it faces competition in one or several factor markets. It is also based on similarity of output mixes and production functions (technology, delivery technique like group vs. individual lending, or collateral-based vs. collateral-free lending).

- The level of efficiency may not be immediately visible, but it can be traced and established on the basis of input and output variables, namely number of clients, number of loan officers, number of staff members, administrative expenses (or the subset 'staff expenses'), number of loans and overall loan portfolio.

- Comparisons of the efficiency of MFIs across countries with different operating environments make limited sense. By contrast the country chapters on Mali, Morocco and Chile (Chapters 10, 11 and 13), using a common reference in the regulatory, policy and domestic market environment, better reveal differences in performance and efficiency between MFIs.

- Efficiency measurement of MFIs is always relative to one institution that is closest to the efficiency frontier: the 'best in class'. Linear programming techniques like DEA (discussed in detail in Chapter 6) capture the distance from the frontier and help determine whether or not an MFI is shortening the distance over time. DEA accommodates different production functions in microfinance. Applying DEA systematically across all countries with a certain density of MFIs and repeating this periodically would show which MFI is best in class. This needs to be updated regularly to allow managers of MFIs as well as donors to trace the movement of MFIs towards the efficiency frontier.

- Different production functions define clusters of MFIs; they differ by the degree to which MFI management can influence the quantity and price of labour, capital and other inputs, as well as the quantity and price of the output mix. Cluster analysis and other multivariate techniques as presented in Chapters 8 and 9 show the range of similar types of MFIs in a given country. The results of the survey of 45 MFIs confirm that it is meaningful to constitute clusters of MFIs. Within each cluster there is always one MFI that outperforms others in terms of social impact and financial results. It is 'more efficient' than the other MFIs in its cluster.[1] Cluster formation takes into account the orientation and mission of the MFI, as it groups together distinctly poverty focused MFIs, commercial MFIs and others in between.

14.1 Global donor support to microfinance

The proposed emphasis on efficiency will have far reaching implications for the aid community, given the magnitude of funds flowing to MFIs worldwide. According to the donor consortium CGAP (the Consultative Group to Assist the Poor) the total flow of donor funds to microfinance amounts to between an estimated $800 million and $1 billion per year (CGAP, 2005). Assuming that at the end of 2004 there were an estimated 92 million poor people reached by MFIs, then every MFI client benefited in one form or another from $8–10 of donor grants. Bilateral public aid appears to be the most important channel with a cumulative amount of $97 billion as of 2004, followed by $5.3 billion of public aid through multilateral institutions.[2] International financial institutions are the next substantial source of funds, providing an estimated US$1.56 billion for the outstanding microfinance-related portfolio in 2004 alone (US$701 million of which are direct investments in individual MFIs and US$484 million indirect investments/funds), while international investment funds (social investors) are estimated to have contributed US$637 million in 2004 (of which, US$511 million direct investment in retail institutions and US$126 million in indirect investments/funds). Far behind are international specialized networks of NGOs for which the annual operating budget is indicated, with US$154 million in 2004.

The overall picture of support to microfinance is complex because of the variety of sources and entry points. Broadly speaking, donors consist of bilateral and multilateral aid agencies; international financial institutions, private foundations, charities and social investors. Governments in low-income countries also support microfinance institutions with their own resources. The term 'donors' covers a heterogeneous group of administrations with distinct political agendas (see Table 14.1) and different sensitivities to efficiency in public finance, not just in microfinance, but in development aid and budget management in general.

Moreover, few of the donor institutions can directly influence incentives and sanctions to individual microfinance institutions. A donor agency rarely sits down with the management of an individual MFIs to discuss social and financial performance and efficiency. Instead, it delegates this responsibility to agents such as national apex funds (like PKSF

Table 14.1   Classification of donors by aid approach

Microfinance	Financial sector development	Private sector development/ Enterprise development	Rural/ Agricultural development	Social sector/ Poverty alleviation
		AfDB		
		AsDB		
		Belgium		AfDB
		Canada		Australia
		Denmark		Belgium
		EC		Denmark
		France		EC
		IADB		Finland
		Luxembourg		ILO
		Switzerland		Italy
Australia		United Kingdom	AfDB	Japan
Canada		United States	AsDB	Luxembourg
IADB		UNCDF	France	Norway
IFC	EBRD	UNDP	IFAD	United States
Switzerland	Germany (GTZ)	UNCTAD	Sweden	UNDP
United States	Germany (KfW)	World Bank	World Bank	World Bank

◄——— Financial sector approach   Non-financial sector ———►

in Bangladesh or PPAF in Pakistan), networks of international non-governmental organizations (NGO), multi-purpose programmes and projects, block grants to government agencies and national MF associations.

In order to orient public policy support towards efficiency-based performance in individual MFIs one needs to disentangle this web of discretionary authority over fund use and reporting lines. Who negotiates the exact terms of a soft loan with the MFI? And does a message sent from the donor to the intermediary and from there to the microfinance institution get passed on undistorted and without any bias? Who has discretionary power over aid money and subsidies really?

These are not peripheral issues because aid money going to microfinance can amount to as much as the entire loan portfolios of all microfinance institutions in a low income country. In the case of Madagascar, 11 public bilateral and multilateral donors (leaving aside private aid money) spent US$7 million every year from 2002 to 2004 on microfinance (FMG58 billion at the mean exchange rate of 2004).[3] This was half the outstanding loan portfolio of all MFIs in Madagascar: US$12.1 million (FMG 90 billion) of client member deposits and US$15.9 million (FMG 118 billion) of loans outstanding.

14.2   Weight of subsidies in microfinance

Subsidies in the financial sector are not uncommon, not even in high-income countries where they are hidden behind bank bail-outs, deposit insurance schemes, counter-guarantees to mutual guarantee associations, preferential discount rates and refinancing facilities on soft terms. If market failure in the supply of small-scale financial transactions is not rectified by the market (Stiglitz, 1994), then government intervention can be justified. Whether or not this intervention should be via subsidies is another question. Much would seem to depend on the design of subsidies within government interventions geared to rectify market failure (Valenzuela, 1998).

Subsidies to MFIs range from grants for the start-up capital to credit lines on preferential terms, free technical assistance, free or below market price equipment and fixed assets.[4] In each case, the extent of market distortion and disincentives depends on the intensity, entry point, dosage, timing and phasing-out.[5] Start-up costs, expenses for research and development, the costs of capacity building and creating second tiers, refinancing or technical support infrastructure are generally acknowledged to be 'smart to subsidize' (*Capital Plus*, 2004, p. 14). An example is the Chilean Government's auction of a lump sum to commercial banks to entice them to lend to microenterprises, as detailed in Chapter 13. Other forms of subsidies are considered potentially market distorting. In real life, smart and un-smart subsidies often exist side by side in one and the same microfinance institution.

Of the 45 MFIs reviewed in our GIAN survey every one, without exception, had a donor partner that provided some form of subsidy, some even had several donor partners. Seven MFIs had one donor partner, 15 MFIs two or three and 20 MFIs more than three; two top the list with 12 and 26 donors respectively. Expressed as a percentage of total liabilities, subsidies represent less than 10 per cent in 10 MFIs, between 11 per cent and 50 per cent in 11 MFIs and between 51 per cent and 100 per cent in 12 MFIs. Contrary to expectations the use of subsidies has over the years not decreased for all MFIs. In 14 cases the share of subsidies on total liabilities has increased and in 12 cases it decreased.

14.3   What prompts public policy support to MFIs?

Being in the limelight of the international media and full with human interest stories, microfinance has received donor support often for reasons that have little to do with efficiency or social and financial performance. Convenience is a reason why, in the years immediately following the Micro Credit Summit in 1997, much funding has gone into start-ups or refinancing MFIs. Another reason for continued funding regardless of performance is the familiarity between bilateral donors and NGO networks with head offices in the donor country and global operations and mandate. Their privileged and personalized access to the donor creates a situation where once the donor has decided to fund, for example, the extension of the network in one part of the world, it is difficult to say no to yet another extension elsewhere. Cutting off aid would even reflect negatively on the soundness of earlier funding decisions, so there can be a double bind between bilateral donor agencies and international NGO networks of MFIs.

Up to now the decision on the continuation of funding support has been largely a matter of familiarity, trust and a feeling of sharing the same values. But there are competing claims on limited and often shrinking development aid budgets. Donors and governments therefore increasingly seek a more fact-based foundation for funding decisions. Social and financial performance criteria should guide such decisions. Much work has already been done to develop and apply meaningful performance measurement criteria. As regards financial performance, the catalogue of criteria in the CGAP Consensus Guidelines represents a broad international consensus. In respect of social performance, an international task force set up in 2004 is seeking to arrive at common understanding on how to manage, rate and improve social performance in microfinance institutions.

Having a clear set of criteria for both dimensions of performance in microfinance is one thing, what donors signal about their priorities and expectations to MFIs in real life is another, and this has obviously implications for subsidy dependence. Thirteen MFIs in our sample reported that donors were pushing them towards more emphasis on poverty reduction; 18 MFIs said that their donor partners were prodding them towards greater financial self-sufficiency. The confusion is exacerbated in MFIs that have several donor partners sending out different and conflicting signals. What emerges generally is that donors either go for more poverty impact or better financial performance, but never towards more efficiency within given social and financial performance goals.

This book invites aid agencies and governments to consider efficiency as a more robust and reliable criterion that should guide their decisions on continuing or discontinuing support to MFIs. Efficiency is a criterion that helps discriminate with greater accuracy than financial performance alone between support-worthy and underperforming MFIs, irrespective of the overall orientation of the MFI. An MFI can be more or less efficient in reaching many poor people with small average transactions, as an MFI can equally be more or less efficient if it seeks positive financial results in the shortest term possible. Both are support-worthy as long as they are on or near the efficiency frontier or moving towards it, for a given production function and in a given operating environment.

Efficiency matters for donors in two ways: it is a criteria that can be used to discriminate between performing and underperforming MFIs and thus to guide donor decisions. Inversely, donor decisions and actions themselves influence the level of efficiency in an MFI, whether collectively – as in the case of macro- or meso-level interventions – or targeted at an individual MFI. Whatever they eventually decide to do, donors and governments should at least be conscious of efficiency as an allocation criterion for their funding and of the consequences of their own actions on efficiency in microfinance institutions.

14.4   General effects of public policy on efficiency in microfinance at the sectoral level

Efficiency analysis in banking suggests a number of lessons for public policy and efficiency in microfinance. First, deregulation does not always improve efficiency and productivity, at least not in the short and medium term. In microfinance it is the inverse type of intervention, regulating hitherto unregulated MFIs, that would be expected to enhance efficiency, and is an area that warrants further research. Second, measures to improve management quality and contain problem loans in banking have not had a consistently positive effect on efficiency. For microfinance this underlines the need for compliance with international accounting standards for writing off bad loans, making provisions and reporting in a consistent manner. Third, government measures to break up market concentration are motivated by the fact that financial institutions with more market power charge lower deposit rates and higher loan rates. Monopolistic banks, as is the case with monopolistic MFIs, are more profitable, but this is not necessarily due to greater efficiency (Berger and Humphrey, 1997). Finally, as mergers and acquisitions are likely to play an increasing role as survival strategies for many MFIs, particularly those that cannot tap scale economies, the lessons from banking are that 'profit efficiency improves significantly from mergers of large banks' (Berger and Humphrey, 1997, p. 28).

In microfinance, donor support and the policies that accompany this support affect the efficiency of all MFIs in a country, but also the efficiency of individual MFIs modifying their competitive positions. The most common measures that have a general effect across the board are regulation, monetary and financial market policies and the fiscal treatment of financial institutions. Another example is soft loans with below market rates of interest which affect (negatively) the allocative output efficiency of MFIs.

MFI efficiency is less directly affected by apex funds. Institutions that choose to apply for soft loans from an apex obtain funds at lower costs than MFIs that need to go to the domestic commercial banks for refinancing. It may even be less costly than collecting private deposits. The scope for influencing efficiency in individual microfinance institutions is determined by the composition of their liabilities. Different MFI use commercial loans, soft loans and deposits, but also subsidies and equity to different degrees. Table 14.2 compares the liability side of three selected MFIs: PAMECAS, a financial cooperative in Senegal; AMEEN, a non-bank financial institution in Lebanon; and SEF, an NGO MFI in South Africa.

Depending on the relative weight of the financial resource, an apex can or cannot substantially change the input costs of MFIs that draw on

Table 14.2   Liabilities in three selected MFIs (US$)

	Pamecas (Senegal)	Ameen (Lebanon)	SEF (South Africa)
Equity	6,438,799	1,582,531	1,435,192
Subsidies	1,890,997	585,635	984,840
Deposits	14,723,415	0	0
Commercial loans	0	100,000	0
Soft loans, short term	504,434	4,297,354	1,070,258
Soft loans, long term	517,313	0	0
Total liabilities	22,183,961	5,979,885	2,505,450

its credit lines. By modifying the eligibility criteria an apex fund can further put a certain type of MFI in a more advantageous position in the market.

In most countries MFIs are only subject to regulation if they take deposits from the general public – hence excluding plain NGOs and most cooperatively organized MFIs. NGOs often seek to change legal form to be able to mobilize deposits to reduce the overall costs of inputs. A regulatory environment that makes it difficult to get a banking licence often implies higher input prices, which keeps NGO MFIs from moving closer to the efficiency frontier. Inversely, making this transformation easy without sacrificing depositors' safety will enhance the efficiency of this type of MFI.

Suitable regulation thus broadens the range of both MFI inputs and outputs and increases the number of operators in the market that offer similar output mixes, thus in theory at least enhancing consumer utilities. Whether it enhances the total factor allocative efficiency across the board for these MFIs depends on the technology and labour intensity, but also the methods of wage payment and the degree of competition with other deposit mobilizing MFIs. However, not all MFIs want to collect deposits or become regulated.

Interest rate determination is a key monetary policy instrument that governments resort to for price stability, but also for consumer protection. Interest rate ceilings set a boundary to the profit margin of financial intermediaries. As MFIs in the initial five to ten years need a substantial spread until they get a better grip of their operating expenses, interest rate ceilings can entail operating losses. Interest rate ceilings are a classic example of an exogenous constraint that makes it impossible for an otherwise efficient MFI to break even. Nineteen MFIs in the GIAN sample confront interest rate ceilings, CARUNA and FDL in Nicaragua report interest rate ceilings of 10 per cent, whilst other MFIs operating under regulated regimes confront ceilings of 27 per cent to 36 per cent (San Roque in Bolivia).

Interest rate caps could also imply that some MFIs are obliged to recompose their loan portfolio and move to less costly market segments, thus repositioning themselves on the poverty–profitability continuum. What should matter for a donor is the underlying motivation: if this MFI is fundamentally efficient, the donor should persuade the government to lift the interest rate cap or, as a second best solution, compensate the MFI for the marginal costs incurred in catering to a costly market segment. If, on the other hand, the move is motivated by managerial inefficiency in the MFI, then this may be the time for the donor to reconsider its support. In either case it is obviously crucial for the donor to inform itself about the underlying efficiency in the MFI.

Broad policy initiatives like financial sector reform and liberalization – often in the context of Poverty Reduction Strategy Papers (PRSPs) – in theory should bring new entrants to the financial market and make the supply-side bid down prices, whether MFIs or others. Increased competition means that MFIs need to adjust output prices, output mix and production function; in other words, the allocative output efficiency of MFIs is likely to be constrained, whilst their clients on the whole should be better off. In this scenario there will also be pressure on the factor market 'loan officer', as banks may be tempted to search for staff with experience in small-scale lending, driving up the wage rate for loan officers. However, in practice this does not seem to have happened: commercial banks that have gone down-market and down-scale have done so not because of a policy directive, but on their own initiative. Research by the ILO and others also suggests that in Africa competition in the small-scale finance market has not increased as a result of financial sector liberalization (Korsah, Nyarko and Tagoe, 2001).

At the sector level, governments – and, standing behind them, donors – can enhance the capacity of MFIs through loan officer training. This increases the pool of skilled and qualified staff for all MFIs, enhances staff productivity and motivates MFIs to introduce performance-based salary components. Alternatively an initiative to set up credit bureaux should reduce credit risk and thus financial costs across the market. Again this measure would stimulate overall efficiency *across the board*. Measures to ensure better information about credit risks, protect property rights and improve contract law would lower operating expense in the long term for MFIs that work with clients with assets to pledge; it is not certain, though, that it would change the overall efficiency of other MFIs that cater to a clientele of informal economy operators who want to stay in the informal economy.

In several countries MFIs have formed national associations of MFIs to represent their interests vis-à-vis public authorities and banks. If an individual MFI belongs to a network, then its efficiency will be enhanced, if the national association provides advocacy, information and training services that bring about cost reduction and higher revenues. However, this will not change the efficiency status of the individual MFI compared to other MFIs operating in the same country: meso-level donor aid affects MFIs across the board.

14.5 Support measures affecting the efficiency of individual MFIs

Effects on competition

Donor support addressed at individual MFIs modifies the quantity and prices of inputs and outputs and thus its efficiency. We distinguish here four broad types of support/subsidy measures: start-up grant, operating subsidy, soft loans and capacity building. All of these lower production costs for the MFI, and all leave it to the MFI management to set interest rates at a level that they consider appropriate for the market and for their own financial sustainability. None of these support measures is necessarily geared to artificially lower interest rates below the market level. In addition, we differentiate between quasi-monopolist situations from a competitive market environment.

Few MFIs have come into operation without substantial start-up support, encompassing a lump grant for initial lending operations, plus hardware and expert advice. Subsidies for the start-up of an MFI temporarily give complete latitude in price fixing, unless bound by interest rate ceilings. The MFI takes as given input quantities and prices and seeks to maximize returns, constrained if in competition with other MFIs and unconstrained if alone in the local financial market. Start-up support is a massive subsidy package that includes operating support, meaning that the donor compensates for operating deficits that may occur in the initial phase. At this stage efficiency is not yet very relevant, in the absence of track records and baseline data.

Operating support, for as long as it is available, allows MFI managers to use higher levels of input quantities (loan officer, other staff, commercial loans, deposits) at higher cost levels than would be possible otherwise. Moreover, it allows the MFI to charge lower outputs prices than would otherwise be feasible. This does not make much of a difference if the MFI is a monopolist, but it does make a difference to other MFIs that may compete with it and that do not benefit from the same package of operating support. Thus the tendency of this type of measure is to prolong a situation that MFI managers would argue is a necessary learning period and that competing MFIs perceive as unfair and distorting.

Soft loans modify the quantity and cost of inputs, output mix and output prices. Refinancing on concessional terms gives an MFI a wider spread than would otherwise be available. Among the 45 MFIs surveyed, 25 MFIs – that is, practically all MFIs that are *not* cooperatively organized – received subsidized credit lines (see Figure 14.1). The maturity ranged from

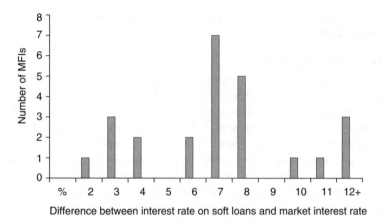

Figure 14.1   The subsidy element in soft loans
Source: GIAN survey results.

one to 11 years with a median of 5 years. Measured by the difference of
the subsidized interest rate to the market rate of interest, 6 MFIs realized
savings of between 2 per cent and 5 per cent on capital costs, 15 MFIs
between 6 per cent and 10 per cent and 4 MFIs of more than 10 per cent.
Looking at the importance of these soft loans for total assets there are 7
MFIs where this was inferior to 10 per cent, in 8 MFI soft loans made up
between 11 per cent and 50 per cent; 5 MFIs used soft loans making up
between 51 and 100 per cent of total assets (see Figure 14.2).

This suggests that subsidies in the form of soft loans are still common
in microfinance and that they are important: in fact, ten of the surveyed
MFIs felt that without subsidies they would have to close down; 34 were
convinced that they would not be able to go up-scale without subsidies
through a better use of human and financial resources. This responds to
the needs of many MFI that feel they do not dispose of both factors of
production in the right quantity and quality: 22 MFIs signal human
resource constraints as their dominating need and 26 MFIs identify
financial resource constraints. This suggests that donor money plays a
critical role in allowing MFIs to combine social and financial goals,
rather than having to choose to go along one or the other dimension.
Again, if the MFI operates in isolation, then this will not have negative
externalities; however, if the MFI competes with other MFIs, then there
is a risk of market distortions and undercutting the operations of competitors, unless donor money is available to all MFIs across the board,

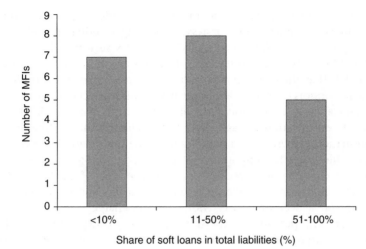

Figure 14.2 The weight of soft loans
Source: GIAN survey results.

for example via an apex. The longer the maturity of such soft loans, the easier it will be for the MFI to expand its output mix and go into longer term, and more revenue-generating lending, which is of potential interest to clients with investment needs, such as the owners of growing microenterprises.

Capacity-building of individual MFIs is another form of subsidy. It comprises staff training, free provision of expert advice, and access to information and advocacy. In-kind support plays a role in MFIs; however, few of the surveyed MFIs reported any significant cash value of equipment, expertise and training: these forms of in-kind subsidies did not account for more than 2 or 3 per cent of liabilities (the exception being the two Pakistan MFIs Kashf and DAMEN where the training received is estimated to be equivalent of 6 and 8 per cent of liabilities). Training is the most common form of in-kind subsidy (29), followed by equipment (20) and expertise/consultants (13). Capacity building affects the technical efficiency of human resource inputs – loan officers, managers and support staff – indicated by productivity ratios such as number of loans/ loan officer, number of clients/staff total and so on. It does not modify the price of these inputs in the short term, although one cannot exclude the possibility that a loan officer whose capacity is enhanced either claims a higher wage or leaves the MFI to join a competitor or a bank.

In general then, subsidies to an individual MFI affect input and output quantities and prices more or less, depending whether the MFI is a monopolist or not. All but four of the 45 GIAN survey MFIs compete with other MFIs, and of these 33 institutions are subsidized. Only two MFIs felt that their market was undercut by a government subsidized scheme. Donors concerned about the best possible effect of their actions on efficiency in MFIs should therefore inform themselves about the market configuration in each case. As this changes all the time, such information gathering is an ongoing task. The case of an MFI from our survey illustrates the importance of the market configuration and its effect on competition. Some 90 per cent of the loans of this MFI are for income generation, offered at between 12.5 per cent and 15 per cent per annum on a declining basis. Moneylenders charge between 30 and 120 per cent per annum for different services, depending on the urgency, purpose, form (cash/in-kind) and the location. Banks charge between 4 per cent (under government sponsored schemes) and 12 per cent in the framework of the self-help group linkage programme. One might think that the government schemes would undercut the MFI, but as it operates in a remote area largely as a monopolist, there has so far not been unfair competition in the local market.

Effects on management

On the basis of our survey data, it is on the whole not possible to establish any link between subsidies and changes in the quality of management of an MFI. However, we have found that MFIs with fixed salaries are likely to be less efficient than MFIs which pay a combination of base salary and a performance-based component. The criteria defined for performance (number of loans, number of transactions, number of clients, total volume, portfolio at risk measures, or a combination of any of these) reflect the orientation of the MFI towards more social or more commercial goals.

Twenty-nine MFIs in our survey use performance-based payment systems, 16 MFIs did not reply to this question. In 12 responding MFIs the performance-based part of the salary makes up 50 per cent and more of the total staff payment. Three MFIs designed the variable part of the salary in a way to induce loan officers to target poverty in clients (by linking the premium to the number and average size of loans), whilst 26 use criteria such as composite indicators of volume, quality and number of transactions. Donors do not seem to have interfered with the payment system. As Table 8.12 in Chapter 8 shows, MFIs with variable pay systems appear to perform better in terms of reaching operational and financial sustainability.

Planning security

Whether operating support, soft loans or capacity building, all subsidies eventually come to an end. Donors, governments or the management of an MFI may have different perceptions of what time horizon is still required for the institution to acquire full autonomy. This is complicated by the fact that competing MFIs with different donor partners may get different signals on the length of the expected adjustment period until full financial sustainability is attained. These possible interferences with competing MFIs make the determination of the optimal point for completely phasing out subsidies all the more challenging, which suggests that some form of common rules for all agents in the market would be useful.

Managers of MFIs are generally under constant stress because of the ad hoc nature of funding decisions by donors. Aid is fickle and follows fashions. It is impossible for managers of MFIs to plan strategically if subsidy support is available for one or two years and needs to be renegotiated all the time. This leads managers of MFIs to diversify their donor partners to reduce the risk of getting dropped unexpectedly. As much as it may give some security having multiple donors, it also increases the burden of multiple reporting and the need to accommodate diverging, or even conflicting, donor expectations: some may want the MFI to emphasize poverty outreach, others full financial sustainability.

This stress is reinforced by the floating nature of clients. Our survey found an astonishing degree of client drop-out.[6] Thirteen MFIs of 37 responding units have drop-out rates between 11 per cent and 30 per cent, ten MFIs have drop-out rates of more than 30 per cent with an extreme value for PortoSol in Brazil, and nine MFIs have drop-out rates below 10 per cent per annum. The reason is either an individual's inability to pay back the loan or the break-up of the group, that is, a mismatch between supply and demand and an ill-fitting delivery technique. In either case the manager of an MFI has to be attentive to the design of the MFI outputs, output mix and pricing in order to keep a stable and growing stock of solvent poor clients. This is not easy, and to have to deal with several donors at the same time does not make the task any easier.

To appreciate the complexities of the dependence of MFIs on public sector support, it helps to consider the case of an MFI in India from the GIAN survey.[7] Over a six-year period it received as cash grants Rp46.84 million (US$1.09 million[8]) for capacity building, that is, training of staff, funding of equipment like computers and consultants but also for product innovation (micro-insurance). It also received 'operational support', that is, cash grants for salaries, printing and stationery expenses and those related to group promotion. 'Operational support' grants are given after the actual expense has been incurred by the MFI. The yearly average of Rp7.8 million of cash grants largely compensated the operating deficit in 1999 (Rp4.4 million), but in 2004 this deficit quadrupled to Rp19.8 million, so the cash grants barely made up for 40 per cent. However, these cash grants came from five different sources and were spread unevenly over the six-year period: nearly 83 per cent came to the MFI in 2003 and 2004 from a public bilateral donor. It is not clear whether this caused or was in turn caused by the rise of operating costs, substantial expansion of the loan portfolio and the doubling of the number of its very poor clients. Whatever the reasons the MFI had at the end of 2004 a very large operating deficit that the donor grant covered for the time being.

This illustrates that the injection of subsidies to cover operational losses can allow an MFI to expand its client base, staff and loan portfolio, but leaves it also in a more vulnerable position financially until it can reap the benefits of scale. Above all, the MFI cannot really expect that the grant will be forthcoming year after year, so it will tend to limit its planning horizon to a few years at most.

This MFI also benefited substantially from four credit lines at below market rates with maturities from five to 11 years and subsidized interest rates of 0 per cent, 2 per cent and 3 per cent. The reference market rate, that is, the deposit rate paid by banks on 90 days deposits,[9] was on average 10 per cent in the period reviewed. The average amount of subsidized credit lines available per year to the MFI was 4315 million Rupees (or a little over $100,000). This represented 64 per cent of total loans outstanding at the end of 2000 and 3.6 per cent at the end of 2004.

Thus the substantial provision of concessional refinancing helped a self-sustaining growth in the loan portfolio. Moreover, the maturities (five to 11 years) appear sufficiently long to give the MFI some planning security, and undoubtedly more so than in the case of cash grants for operating support. This MFI has ambitions: it wants to reach out to 2.2 million poor women by 2009 (from a little over 40,000 at the end of 2004) and boost its loan portfolio by a factor of eight.

So this MFI – like many others – counts on external support including subsidies, without really having the formal guarantees that such donor support will continue to be forthcoming. Because of short planning horizons and different donor priorities, MFIs may feel that it is in their interest to modify their position on the poverty–profitability continuum by changing the output mix of their production functions, rather than to concentrate on shortening the distance to the efficiency frontier in their respective MFI peer group.

14.6 The way forward: how to support the best of class and the others

The CGAP's campaign for better aid effectiveness means that donor agencies are increasingly held accountable for results and need to be able to justify continued support to microfinance. More and more, questions about tangible results and outcomes are being tabled at international conferences and in development aid circles. Consequently donor agencies find themselves confronted with the need to make tougher choices, to discriminate between MFIs that are support- and subsidy-worthy and others that are not, between those that should already be self-financing and those that cannot possibly be so, given an adverse operating environment and context. They might even ponder whether any of their donor money should go into retail institutions at all.

The Donor Guidelines on Good Practice in Microfinance recommend putting the funding relation between a donor and an MFI (CGAP, 2004a, p. 15) on a contractual basis: 'performance-based contracts'. Agreed performance targets, exit strategies and a few core indicators should help to rationalize decisions on renewal or continuation of support. Donors are reminded that they have the responsibility to remain predictable, on time in disbursement and responsive.

In the light of our findings, performance-based contracts should contain efficiency targets distinguishing between areas for which MFI managers can be held accountable, that is, endogenous drivers of performance and other, contextual, factors outside of their influence. In addition, the performance contract could specify the period over which progress should be achieved, with benchmark data established on the basis of the above efficiency indicators and the norms of the reference MFI (best in class). The performance contract should spell out the consequences for failure to progress in efficiency if the MFI management can be held accountable; in other words, the MFI should be able to anticipate the cost of non-compliance, in the form of a reduced or cancelled subsidy.

Most importantly, the contract should signal the rewards and incentives that the MFI can expect if it progresses in efficiency. This accommodates a variety of MFI types in a single country; the more homogeneous the domestic microfinance market, the easier it is to define the rewards and incentives. Ultimately, a more rational and transparent system of allocating subsidies to MFIs should, instead of favouring one type of MFI at the expense of another, gear donor monies towards greater efficiency in each type, working towards a more economical resource use in all MFI configurations, allowing for a broad, competitive and varied supply of financial services to the poor.

Of course, there can still be negative externalities in supporting and subsidizing individual MFIs. This can be controlled, to some extent at least, by choosing the right type, entry point and exit strategy:

- subsidizing the intermediary distorts the market less than, for example, subsidizing the client directly;
- subsidies that come without strings attached are likely to have a greater detrimental effect on the MFI than performance-linked grants;
- regressive subsidies are preferable to linear subsidies;
- subsidies with an exit strategy are preferable to subsidies without limit of time;
- subsidies to international networks ('network support organizations') or apex institutions are less harmful than subsidies to individual MFIs (CGAP, 2004b).

Lessons for coordination amongst donors

To be effective such an efficiency-based approach to the use of subsidies can only work with coordination between those that give subsidies (public and private, bilateral and multi-lateral as well as social investors). On the whole, the record of donor coordination in microfinance is not glorious, but in comparison to other aid sectors the record is not that bad either. In the 1990s the donor community managed to put together a workable coordination framework in the United Republic of Tanzania. Given the continuing commitment of donor agencies, one could test efficiency based performance contracts with MFIs there. All donor and governmental agencies should subscribe to the same principles of transparency and incentive-based support, as non-compliance by one will cancel out any positive externalities of the performance contract applied by all others. The commitments made at the High Level Donor meetings on Aid Effectiveness of 2004 and 2006 in Paris, organized by CGAP, show that donors have become aware of the implications of non-compliance. All that remains to be done is to put these commitments into force.

Notes

1　In other words, this is a departure from the notion of efficiency that equates it with high operating costs (see Christen and Rosenberg, 2000, p. 31). A study by the IMF finds that 'low rates of borrower default combined with high lending rates have not translated into profitability or even the ability to cover costs. The small scale of the loans and the costs of reaching out to clients increase operational expenses, which absorb most of the interest margins'.

2　The figures in this paragraph are derived from CGAP, *Mapping of Funding Flows*, September 2005; I am grateful to Alexia Latortue of CGAP for this information.

3　CGAP idem, p. 31. The exchange rate was in January 2004 FMG 5489 and in December 2004 FMG9287 to the dollar.

4　Grameen Bank received from 1985 to 1996 US$175 million in subsidies, of which US$17 million in form of direct grants, US$82 million as refinancing facilities on concessionary terms, US$48 million as equity not bearing a return to shareholders and US$28 million in the form of not fully entered provisions for loan losses (Morduch, 1999c).

5　Morduch (2000, p. 236) points out the artificiality of the distinction between operational subsidies that balance the end of year accounts *ex post*, and subsidies *ex ante* for key inputs, such as loan resources.

6　Drop-outs are defined differently by different MFIs: many consider a client as drop-out if he /she has no longer any contractual link, claims or liabilities vis-à-vis the MFI. Other MFIs see a client as already a drop-out if a deposits account continues to be kept with the MFI, but there is no longer an outstanding loan balance.

7　The data presented here were collected by M-CRIL on behalf of the ILO as part of the GIAN research project.

8　The exchange rate was 42,2 Rp in 1999 and 43,3 in January 2005.

9　Donor Consensus Guidelines, p. 15.

Annex I

The GIAN survey

The data on the social and financial performance of MFIs were generated in 2004 and 2005 by way of a questionnaire-based field survey. These 45 MFIs operate in Africa, Asia, Latin America, Eastern Europe, the Middle East and North Africa, in 21 countries. Of these MFIs, 26 are listed on the MIX. The survey carried out in the framework of this GIAN research project covers microfinance institutions that had at least 3000 clients, operated continuously between 1999 and 2003 and were able to produce audited financial statements for the entire period.

MFIs in the GIAN survey

	Country	MFI
1	Albania	BESA
2	Benin	PADME
3	Bolivia	CACTRI
4		ECOFUTURO
5		SAN ROQUE
6	Bosnia	PRIZMA
7	Brazil	PortoSol
8		Blusol
9	Burkina	CVECA SISSILI
10		RCPB
11	Egypt	ABA
12		DBACD
13		Al Tadamun
14		Banque du Caire
15	Georgia	CONSTANZA
16	India	SHEPHERD
17		CASHPOR (CMC)
18		AMMACTS
19		BASIX
20		ASA
21	Jordan	MFW
22		Tamweelcom – JMCC
23	Lebanon	Al Majmoua
24		AMEEN
25	Madagascar	OTIV Tana

Continued

Annex I Continued

	Country	MFI
26		ADEFI
27	Mali	CVECA du Pays Dogon
28		Nyésigiso
29	Mexico	CAME
30		Kaxa Taon
31	Morocco	Al Amana
32		FONDEP
33		Zakoura
34	Nicaragua	CARUNA
35		FDL
36	Niger	MECREF de Niamey
37		Mutuelle N'GADA de DIFFA
38	Pakistan	Kashf
39		Development Action for Mobilization & Emancipation (DAMEN)
40	Senegal	ACEP
41		PAMECAS
42	South Africa	SEF
43	Viet Nam	Capital Aid Fund for Employment of the Poor (CEP)
44		Dong Trieu Credit and Savings Fund
45		TYM Fund

Annex II

Multivariate analysis and classification: social and financial performance

Selection of observations and used variables: nominal active variables

15	Variables	50 Associated modalities
M4	Target market (MBB)	5 modalities
S2	Clients organized in groups	4 modalities
S3	Can the MFI receive deposits?	2 modalities
S4	Average deposit as % GDP per capita	6 modalities
S6	% of female borrowers	3 modalities
S10	Explicit poverty focus in the mission statement	2 modalities
S11	Use of poverty criteria to target clients	2 modalities
S12	Are fixed assets required as collateral?	2 modalities
F1	Operational self-sufficiency reached?	3 modalities
F2	Financial self-sufficiency reached?	3 modalities
F3	loan loss provision share (/tot exp)	4 modalities
F4	yield on gross portfolio	3 modalities
F5	Portfolio at risk 90 days (PAR 90)	4 modalities
F6	Write-off ratio	4 modalities
F7	Provisioning at 30 days of delinquency	3 modalities

Clusters by modalities: tree break in 3 clusters

| V. Test | Probability | Percentages | | Global | Modalities: characteristics of variables | | | Weight |
| | | Cluster/Modality | Modality/Cluster | | Modalities | Identifier | Identifier | |

V. Test	Probability	Cluster/Modality	Modality/Cluster	Global	Modalities	Identifier	Identifier	Weight
Cluster 1/3								
5.94	0.000			46.67	CLUSTER 1/3		aa1a	21
		90.91	95.24	48.89	No fixed assets required	S12	S121	22
4.61	0.000	93.75	71.43	35.56	Explicit poverty focus in the mission statement	S10	S102	16
4.01	0.000	92.86	61.90	31.11	Use poverty criteria to target clients	S11	S112	14
3.98	0.000	100.00	52.38	24.44	100% groups	S2	S2_3	11
3.13	0.001	90.91	47.62	24.44	100% women	S6	S6/2	11
2.89	0.002	80.00	57.14	33.33	Write-off ratio = 0–0.5%	F6	F6_1	15
2.84	0.002	73.68	66.67	42.22	Low end [<20%]	M4	M4_1	19
–3.43	0.000	30.30	47.62	73.33	0–99%	S6	S6/1	33

Continued

Annex II   Continued

V. Test	Probability	Percentages			Modalities: characteristics of variables				Weight
		Cluster/Modality	Modality/Cluster	Global	Modalities	Identifier		Identifier	
−4.01	0.000	25.81	38.10	68.89	No use of poverty criteria to target clients	S11	Poverty criteria used to target clients?	S111	31
−4.61	0.000	20.69	28.57	64.44	No explicit poverty focus in mission statement	S10	Poverty focus explicit in mission statement?	S101	29
−5.94	0.000	4.35	4.76	51.11	Fixed assets required	S12	Are fixed assets required as collateral?	S122	23
Cluster 2/3									
3.09	0.001	100.00	100.00	4.44	CLUSTER 2/3			aa2a	2
				4.44	Missing data	F3	Loan loss provision share (/total expense)?	F3/0	2
Cluster 3/3									
				48.89	CLUSTER 3/3			aa3a	22
5.95	0.000	91.30	95.45	51.11	Fixed assets required	S12	Are fixed assets required as collateral?	S122	23
4.14	0.000	72.41	95.45	64.44	No explicit	S10	Explicit poverty	S101	29

		focus in the mission statement?		poverty focus in the mission statement					
31	S111	Use of poverty criteria to target clients?	S11	No use of poverty criteria to target clients	68.89	95.45	67.74	0.000	3.61
33	S6/1	% of female borrowers?	S6	0 to 99%	73.33	95.45	63.64	0.001	3.07
14	S2_2	Clients organized in groups?	S2	0%<S2<100%	31.11	50.00	78.57	0.009	2.39
6	M4_3	Target market (MBB)?	M4	High end [150–249%]	13.33	27.27	100.00	0.009	2.36
11	S6/2	% of female borrowers?	S6	100% women	24.44	4.55	9.09	0.003	-2.79
15	F6_1	Write-off ratio	F6	Write-off ratio = 0–0.5%	33.33	9.09	13.33	0.001	-3.15
14	S112	Use of poverty criteria to target clients?	S11	Use poverty criteria to target clients	31.11	4.55	7.14	0.000	-3.61
11	S2_3	Clients organized in groups?	S2	100% groups	24.44	0.00	0.00	0.000	-3.65
16	S102	Explicit poverty focus in the mission statement?	S10	Explicit poverty focus in the mission statement	35.56	4.55	6.25	0.000	-4.14
22	S121	Are fixed assets required as collateral?	S12	No fixed assets required	48.89	4.55	4.55	0.000	-5.95

Clusters by modalities: tree break in 6 clusters

V. Test	Probability	Percentages			Modalities	Modalities: characteristics of variables			Weight
		Cluster/Modality	Modality/Cluster	Global	Modalities	Identifier	Identifier	Identifier	
Cluster 1/6									
				20.00	CLUSTER 1/6			bb1b	9
3.33	0.000	50.00	88.89	35.56	Explicit poverty focus in the mission statement	S10	Poverty focus explicit in the mission statement?	S102	16
3.26	0.001	40.91	100.00	48.89	No fixed assets required	S12	Are fixed assets required as collateral?	S121	22
2.89	0.002	50.00	77.78	31.11	Use of poverty criteria to target clients	S11	Poverty criteria used to target clients?	S112	14
2.83	0.002	36.00	100.00	55.56	MFI receives deposits	S3	Can the MFI receive deposits?	S3_2	25
2.71	0.003	54.55	66.67	24.44	100% groups	S2	Clients organized in groups?	S2_3	11
2.71	0.003	54.55	66.67	24.44	100% women	S6	% of female borrowers?	S6/2	11
−2.50	0.006	9.09	33.33	73.33	0 to 99% women	S6	% of female borrowers?	S6/1	33
−2.83	0.002	0.00	0.00	44.44	No deposits	S3	Can the MFI receive deposits?	S3_1	20

−2.89	0.002	6.45	22.22	68.89	No poverty criteria used to target clients	S11	Poverty criteria used to target clients?	S111	31
−3.26	0.001	0.00	0.00	51.11	Fixed assets required	S12	Are fixed assets required as collateral?	S122	23
−3.33	0.000	3.45	11.11	64.44	No explicit poverty focus	S10	Poverty focus explicit in the mission statement?	S101	29
−3.40	0.000	0.00	0.00	53.33	Not applicable	S4	Average deposit as % GDP per capita?	S4_5	24
Cluster 2/6				28.89	CLUSTER 2/6			aa2a	
4.74	0.000	65.00	100.00	44.44	No deposits	S3	Can the MFI receive deposits?	S3_1	20
3.98	0.000	54.17	100.00	53.33	Not applicable	S4	Average deposit as % GDP per capita	S4_5	24
3.53	0.000	54.55	92.31	48.89	No fixed assets required	S12	Are fixed assets required as collateral?	S121	22
3.34	0.000	52.17	92.31	51.11	Provisioning at 30 days of delinquency	F7	Provisioning at 30 days of delinquency?	F7_2	23

Continued

Annex II Continued

V. Test	Probability	Percentages			Modalities: characteristics of variables				Weight
		Cluster/Modality	Modality/Cluster	Global	Modalities	Identifier		Identifier	
2.98	0.001	52.38	84.62	46.67	Loan loss≤ 5%	F3	Loan loss provision share (/tot exp)?	F3/1	21
2.87	0.002	60.00	69.23	33.33	Write-off ratio = 0–0.5%	F6	Write-off ratio?	F6_1	15
2.87	0.002	60.00	69.23	33.33	PAR 90 = 0–0.5%	F5	PAR 90?	F5/1	15
−2.61	0.005	5.56	7.69	40.00	No provisioning at 30 days	F7	Provisioning at 30 days of delinquency?	F7_1	18
Cluster 3/6									
				17.78	CLUSTER 3/6			aa3a	8
3.09	0.001	100.00	100.00	4.44	Missing data	F3	Loan loss provision share (/tot exp)?	F3/0	2
Cluster 4/6									
				8.89	CLUSTER 4/6			bb4b	4
3.14	0.001	44.44	100.00	20.00	Loan loss provision = 10% and over	F3	Loan loss provision share (/tot exp)?	F3/3	9
2.99	0.001	40.00	100.00	22.22	PAR 90 = 2% and over	F5	PAR 90?	F5/3	10

Cluster 5/6

				17.78	CLUSTER 5/6			bb5b	8
4.19	0.000	57.14	100.00	31.11	0%<S2< 100% groups	S2	Clients organized in groups?	S2_2	14
2.84	0.002	34.78	100.00	51.11	Fixed assets required	S12	Are fixed assets required as collateral?	S122	23
-2.84	0.002	0.00	0.00	48.89	No fixed assets required	S12	Are fixed assets required as collateral?	S121	22

Cluster 6/6

				20.00	CLUSTER 6/6			bb6b	9
3.19	0.001	66.67	66.67	20.00	Write-off ratio = 0.5–2%	F6	Write-off ratio?	F6_2	9
3.11	0.001	39.13	100.00	51.11	Fixed assets required	S12	Are fixed assets required as collateral?	S122	23
3.09	0.001	53.85	77.78	28.89	Loan loss provision = 5–10%	F3	Loan loss provision share (/tot exp)?	F3/2	13
2.71	0.003	54.55	66.67	24.44	PAR 90 = 0.5–2%	F5	PAR 90?	F5/2	11
-3.11	0.001	0.00	0.00	48.89	No fixed assets required	S12	Are fixed assets required as collateral?	S121	22

Annex III

Multivariate analysis and classification: efficiency, social and financial performance

Selection of observations and used variables: nominal active variables

24	Variables	86 Associated modalities
4	M4 Target market (MBB)	5 MODALITIES
16	S2 Clients organized in groups	4 MODALITIES
17	S3 Can the MFI receive deposits?	2 MODALITIES
20	S4 Average deposit as % GDP per capita	6 MODALITIES
23	S6 % of female borrowers	3 MODALITIES
26	S7 Whether clients can read and sign contracts	4 MODALITIES
31	S10 Explicit poverty focus in the mission statement	2 MODALITIES
32	S11 Use of poverty criteria to target clients	2 MODALITIES
33	S12 Are fixed assets required as collateral	2 MODALITIES
36	F1 Operational self-sufficiency	3 MODALITIES
38	F2 Financial self-sufficiency	3 MODALITIES
41	F3 Loan loss provision share (/total expense)	4 MODALITIES
43	F4 Yield on gross portfolio	3 MODALITIES
46	F5 PAR 90	4 MODALITIES
48	F6 Write-off ratio	4 MODALITIES
50	F7 Provisioning at 30 days of delinquency	3 MODALITIES
52	E1 Client/loan officer	3 MODALITIES
54	E2 Client/staff member	4 MODALITIES
56	E3 % credit officer to total staff	3 MODALITIES
58	E4 Average outstanding loan per active client ($)	4 MODALITIES
61	E5 The operating expenses ratio (operating expense/portfolio) (%)	4 MODALITIES
63	E6 Cost per borrower ($)	5 MODALITIES
65	E7 Loan officer salary/average salary in the banking sector	4 MODALITIES
67	E8 Loan officer salary/minimum wage	5 MODALITIES

Clusters by modalities: tree break in 6 clusters

V. Test	Probability	Percentages			Modalities: characteristics of variables				Weight
		Cluster/Modality	Modality/Cluster	Global	Modalities	Identifier		Identifier	
Cluster 1/6									
				17.78	CLUSTER 1/6			aa1a	8
3.24	0.001	60.00	75.00	22.22	Low end [<20%]	S4	Average deposit as % GDP per capita?	S4_1	10
2.97	0.001	36.36	100.00	48.89	Cost = 0–50$	E6	Cost per borrower ($)?	E6_1	22
2.71	0.003	33.33	100.00	53.33	Yield = 0–25%	F4	Yield on gross portfolio?	F4/1	24
2.62	0.004	55.56	62.50	20.00	Missing data	F5	PAR 90?	F5/0	9
2.57	0.005	32.00	100.00	55.56	Deposits	S3	Can the MFI accept deposits?	S3_2	25
2.46	0.007	42.86	75.00	31.11	Operating expense ratio = 0–15%	E5	Operating expense ratio (operating expense/portfolio)?	E5/1	14
−2.57	0.005	0.00	0.00	44.44	No deposits	S3	Can the MFI receive deposits?	S3_1	20
−3.11	0.001	0.00	0.00	53.33	Not applicable	S4	Average deposit as % GDP per capita?	S4_5	24

Continued

Annex III   Continued

V. Test	Probability	Percentages			Modalities: characteristics of variables				Weight
		Cluster/Modality	Modality/Cluster	Global	Modalities	Identifier		Identifier	
Cluster 2/6									
				4.44	CLUSTER 2/6			aa2a	2
3.09	0.001	100.00	100.00	4.44	Missing data	E9	Processing time for a first loan (group loan or individual loan)?	E9_0	2
Cluster 3/6									
				17.78	CLUSTER 3/6			aa3a	8
3.24	0.001	60.00	75.00	22.22	PAR 90: 2% and over	F5	PAR 90?	F5/3	10
3.02	0.001	54.55	75.00	24.44	Operationally self-sufficient	F1	Operational self-sufficiency reached?	11	
2.62	0.004	55.56	62.50	20.00	Loan loss provision = 10% and over	F3	Loan loss provision share (/total expense)?	F3/3	9
2.57	0.005	32.00	100.00	55.56	Receives deposits	S3	Can the MFI receive deposits?	S3_2	25
2.51	0.006	66.67	50.00	13.33	Broad [20–149%]	S4	Average deposit as % GDP per capita?	S4_2	6
2.46	0.007	42.86	75.00	31.11	Missing data	F6	Write-off ratio?	F6_0	14

−2.57	0.005	0.00	0.00	44.44	No deposits	S3	Can the MFI receive deposits?	S3_1	20
−2.57	0.005	0.00	0.00	44.44	Client/loan officer = 300 and over	E1	Client/loan officer?	E1_3	20
−2.82	0.002	6.06	25.00	73.33	Operationally self-sufficient	F1	Operational self-sufficiency reached?	33	
Cluster 4/6				31.11	CLUSTER 4/6	S3		aa4a	14
4.23	0.000	65.00	92.86	44.44	No deposits	S3	Can the MFI receive deposits?	S3_1	20
3.41	0.000	54.17	92.86	53.33	Loan officer = 2 to 4 x minimum wage	E8	Loan officer salary/minimum wage?	E8_2	24
3.41	0.000	54.17	92.86	53.33	Not applicable	S4	Average deposit as % GDP per capita?	S4_5	24
3.28	0.001	57.14	85.71	46.67	Loan loss provision ≤ 5%	F3	Loan loss provision share (/total expense)?	F3/1	21
3.02	0.001	57.89	78.57	42.22	Low end [<20%]	M4	Target market (MBB)?	M4_1	19
2.59	0.005	60.00	64.29	33.33	Write-off ratio = 0–0.5%	F6	Write-off ratio?	F6_1	15

Continued

Annex III Continued

V. Test	Probability	Percentages			Modalities	Identifier	Modalities: characteristics of variables		Weight
		Cluster/Modality	Modality/Cluster	Global			Identifier		
2.59	0.005	60.00	64.29	33.33	Write-off ratio = 0–0.5%	F6	Write-off ratio?	F6_1	15
2.39	0.009	50.00	78.57	48.89	No fixed assets required	S12	Are fixed assets required as collateral?	S121	22
2.35	0.009	56.25	64.29	35.56	Client/staff [100–200]	E2	Client/staff member?	E2_2	16
−2.39	0.009	13.04	21.43	51.11	Fixed assets required	S12	Are fixed assets required as collateral?	S122	23
−2.77	0.003	0.00	0.00	28.89	Loan officer = 5 to10 x minimum wage	E8	Loan officer salary/minimum wage?	E8_3	13
−2.95	0.002	0.00	0.00	31.11	Missing data	F6	Write-off ratio?	F6_0	14
−3.03	0.001	5.26	7.14	42.22	Loan officer/staff = 0–50%	E3	% credit officer to total staff?	E3_1	19
−4.23	0.000	4.00	7.14	55.56	Receives deposits	S3	Can the MFI receive deposits?	S3_2	25

Cluster 5/6

Cluster 5/6					CLUSTER 5/6			aa5a	
				26.67					12
3.93	0.000	75.00	75.00	26.67	Average loan = $500 and over	E4	Average outstanding loan per active client ($)?	E4_3	12
2.82	0.002	75.00	50.00	17.78	Cost = $200 and over	E6	Cost per borrower ($)?	E6_4	8
2.74	0.003	52.94	75.00	37.78	Client/staff = 8–100	E2	Client/staff member?	E2_1	17
2.71	0.003	100.00	33.33	8.89	Process time = 1–4	E9	Processing time for a first loan (GL or IL) (1e + court)?	E9_1	4
2.50	0.006	66.67	50.00	20.00	Write-off ratio = 0.5–2%	F6	Write-off ratio?	F6_2	9
-2.55	0.005	5.26	8.33	42.22	Low end [<20%]	M4	Target market (MBB)?	M4_1	19
-3.91	0.000	0.00	0.00	48.89	Cost = 0–50$	E6	Cost per borrower ($)?	E6_1	22
-3.91	0.000	0.00	0.00	48.89	Average loan = 0–$200	E4	Average outstanding loan per active client ($)?	E4_1	22

Continued

Annex III   Continued

| V. Test | Probability | Percentages | | | Modalities: characteristics of variables | | | Weight |
		Cluster/Modality	Modality/Cluster	Global	Modalities	Identifier	Identifier	
Cluster 6/6								
				20.00	CLUSTER 6/6		bb6b	9
3.19	0.001	66.67	66.67	20.00	Write-off ratio = 0.5–2%	F6	Write-off ratio?	F6_2	9
3.11	0.001	39.13	100.00	51.11	Fixed assets required	S12	Are fixed assets required as collateral?	S122	23
3.09	0.001	53.85	77.78	28.89	Loan loss provision = 5–10%	F3	Loan loss provision share (/total expense)?	F3/2	13
2.71	0.003	54.55	66.67	24.44	PAR 90 = 0.5–2%	F5	PAR 90?	F5/2	11
-3.11	0.001	0.00	0.00	48.89	No fixed assets required	S12	Are fixed assets required as collateral?	S121	22

Bibliography

ADA (Appui au développement autonomne). 2006. *Transversal analysis of MFI performance in Africa*, 1st edn, July (Luxemburg).

Adams, D. W., Graham, D. H. and Von Pischke, J. D. (eds). 1984. *Undermining rural development with cheap credit* (Boulder, CO: Westview Press).

———. and von Pischke, J. D. 1992. 'Microenterprise credit programs: Déjà vu', in *World Development*, Vol. 20, No. 10, pp. 1463–70.

Al Amana Association Morocco. 2003. *PlaNet Rating*, September (Rabat).

Al-Maghrib Bank. 2005. *Financial Year Report 2004* (Rabat).

Aly, H. et al. 1990. 'Technical, scale and allocative efficiencies in US banking: An empirical investigation', in *The Review of Economics and Statistics*, Vol. 72, No. 2, pp. 211–18.

AMUCCS (Asociación Mexicana de Uniones de Crédito del Sector Social, A.C.). 2000. *Propuesta para construir un sistema financiero al servicio del desarrollo rural* (Mexico).

Banker, R. D. and Moorey, R. C. 1986. 'Efficiency analysis for exogenously fixed inputs and outputs', in *Operations Research*, Vol. 34, pp. 513–21.

Bauman, T. 2003. *Doing pro-poor microcredit in South Africa: Cost efficiency and productivity of South African pro-poor MFIs* (Community Microfinance Network).

Beck, T., and De la Torre, A. 2007. 'The analytics of access to financial services: Introducing the access possibilities frontier', *Financial Markets, Institutions and Instruments*, Vol. 17, pp. 79–117.

———. and Fuchs, M. 2004. 'Structural issues in the Kenyan financial system: Improving competition and access', World Bank Policy Research Working Paper 3363 (Washington, DC: World Bank).

———. and Levine, R. 2005. 'Legal institutions and financial development', in C. Menard and M. Shirley (eds), *Handbook of new institutional economics* (Dordrecht: Kluwer).

———., Demirguc-Kunt, A. and Levine, R. 2000. 'A new database on financial development and structure', *World Bank Economic Review*, Vol. 14, pp. 597–605.

———., Demirguc-Kunt, A. and Levine, R. 2007. 'Finance, inequality and poverty: Cross-country evidence', *Journal of Economic Growth*, Vol. 12, No. 1, pp. 27–49.

———., Demirguc-Kunt, A. and Martinez Peria, M. 2007. 'Reaching out: Access to and use of banking services across countries', *Journal of Financial Economics*, Vol. 85, pp. 234–66.

———., Levine, R. and Loayza, N. 2000. 'Finance and the sources of growth', in *Journal of Financial Economics*, Vol. 58, pp. 261–300.

Bercovich, N. 2004. 'El microcrédito como componente de una política de desarrollo local' (Microcredit as a component of local development policies), Restructuring and Competitiveness Network, Productive and Entrepreneurial Development Division (Santiago de Chile: CEPAL).

Berger, A.N. and Humphrey, D.B. 1997. *Efficiency of financial institutions: International survey and directions for future research*, Wharton School Financial Institutions Center Working Paper 97-05 (Financial Institutions Center, The Wharton School, University of Pennsylvania).

Berryman, M. and Pytkowska, J. 2004. *A review of the Bosnian microfinance sector: Move to financial self-sufficiency* (MIX/MFC).

Boltvinik, J. 2003. 'Tipología de los métodos de medición de la pobreza. Los métodos combinados', in *Comercio exterior*, Vol. 53, pp. 453–65.

Boserup, E. 1990. *Economic and demographic relationships in development* (Baltimore, MD: Johns Hopkins University Press).

Brand, M. 2000. 'More bang for the buck: Improving efficiency', in *The MicroBanking Bulletin*, Vol. 4, pp. 13–18.

——. and Gerschick, J. 2000. *Maximizing efficiency: The path to enhanced outreach and sustainability*, ACCION Monograph Series No.12 (Washington, DC: ACCION).

Brandsma, J. *The Third Microfinance Survey in the Arab World, Preliminary Results.* http://www.sanabelnetwork.org/conference/pdf/Judith_Brandsma.pdf

Bruntrup, M. 2002. *Les associations des institutions de microfinance. Le cas de l'Association Professionnelle des Institutions de la Microfinance du Mali, APIM/Mali* (Eschborn, GTZ, Division 41: Promotion de l'Economie et de l'Emploi).

Cassimon, D. and Vaessen, J. 2006. *Linking debt relief to microfinance: An issues paper*, Social Finance Working Paper 42 (Geneva: ILO).

Campos, P. 1998. 'Encuesta/Las razones del ahorro', in *Reforma* (Mexico).

Capital Plus. 2004. Chicago, MI: Development Finance Forum, Shore Bank Corporation.

CASEN. 1998. CASEN Survey.

——. 2000. CASEN Survey.

——. 2002. CASEN Survey.

Cassimon, D. and Vaessen, J. 2006. *Linking debt relief to microfinance: An issues paper*, Social Finance Working Paper 42 (Geneva: ILO).

Central Bank. *Economic Reports 2003–2004.*

Cerise. 1999. *Les contraintes et les defis de la viabilite des systemes de microfinance en zones rurales defavorisees en Afrique* (Mali: CVECA).

——. 2002. *Gouvernance en Microfinance* (Mali: CVECA).

CGAP. 1995. *Maximizing the outreach of microenterprise finance: The emerging lessons of successful programs*, Focus Note No. 2 (Washington, DC). Available at www.cgap.org/docs/FocusNote_02.pdf.

——. 2001a. *The poverty audit* (Washington, DC).

——. 2001b. *Commercialization and mission drift*, Occasional Paper No. 5, January (Washington, DC).

——. 2002. *Water water everywhere but not a drop to drink*, Donor Brief No. 3 (Washington, DC).

——. 2002. *Supervision Report of the FOSIS-Financial Institutions Program.*

——. 2003. *CGAP Phase III Strategy, 2003–2008* (Washington, DC).

——. 2004a. *Building inclusive financial systems: Donor guidelines on good practice in microfinance* (Washington, DC).

——. 2004b. 'What is a network?', Focus Note No. 26, July (Washington, DC).

——. 2004c. *Assessing the relative poverty of microfinance clients: An operational tool* (Washington, DC).

——. 2005. *CLEAR report: Madagascar* (Washington, DC).

——. SERCOTEC database, 1992–2003 (Washington, DC).

Chao-Beroff, R. 1999, *Self-reliant village banks, mali (Case Study)*, CGAP Working Group on Saving Mobilization (Washington, DC: CGAP).

Charnes, A., Cooper, W. W. and Rhodes, E. 1978. 'Measuring the efficiency of decision making units', in *European Journal of Operational Research*, Vol. 2, pp. 429–44.

——., Cooper, W.W., Lewin, A. and Seiford, L. (eds). 1994. *Data envelopment analysis: Theory, methodology and applications* (Boston, MA: Kluwer).

Cheston, S. and Kuhn, L. 2002. 'Empowering women through microfinance', in S. Daley-Harris (ed.), *Pathways out of poverty: Innovations in microfinance for the poorest families* (Connecticut: Kumarian Press).

Chowdhry, B., Cassell, D., Garnett, J., Milkwick, G., Nielsen, C. and Sederstrom, J. 2005. 'Pricing microfinance loans and loan guarantees using biased loan write-off data', UCLA Anderson School working paper (California: UCLA).

Chowdhury, M., Mosley, P. and Simanowitz, A. (2004). 'The social impact of microfinance', in *Journal of International Development*, Vol. 16, No. 3, pp. 291–300.

Christen, R. 2000. 'Bulletin highlights', in *MicroBanking Bulletin*, No. 4 (Washington, DC), Feb.

——. and Rosenberg, R. 2000. *The rush to regulate*, CGAP Occasional Paper No. 4 (Washington, DC: CGAP).

——., Lyman, T. and Rosenberg, R. 2003. *Microfinance consensus guidelines – Guiding principles on regulation and supervision of microfinance* (Wahington, DC: CGAP).

——., Rhyne, E., Vogel, R.C. and McKean, C. 1995. *Maximizing the outreach of microenterprise finance – An analysis of successful microfinance programs*, Program and Operations Assessment Report No. 10, PNABS-519 (Arlington, VA: USAID/IMCC).

Claessens, S. and Laeven, L. 2004. 'What drives bank competition? Some international evidence', in *Journal of Money, Credit, and Banking*, Vol. 36, pp. 563–82.

——., Demirguc-Kunt, A. and Huizinga, H. 2001. 'How does foreign bank entry affect domestic banking markets?', in *Journal of Banking and Finance*, Vol. 25, pp. 891–911.

——., Dobos, G., Klingebiel, D. and Laeven, L. 2003. 'The growing importance of networks in finance and its effects of competition', in A. Nagurney (ed.), *Innovations in financial and economic networks* (Northampton, MA: Edward Elgar), pp. 110–35.

Clarke, G., Cull, R., Martinez Peria, M. and Sanchez, S. 2003. 'Foreign bank entry: Experience, implications for developing economies, and agenda for future research', in *World Bank Research Observer*, Vol. 18, pp. 25–59.

Comité de Fomento de la Micro y Pequeña Empresa (Micro and Small Enterprise Development Committee), Chilean Government. 2003. 'La situación de la micro y pequeña empresa en Chile' (The situation of micro and small enterprises in Chile).

Conning, J. 1999. 'Outreach, sustainability and leverage in monitoring and peer-monitored lending', in *Journal of Development Economics*, Vol. 60, No. 1, pp. 51–77.

Copestake, J.G. 2003. 'Simple standards or burgeoning benchmarks? Institutionalising social performance monitoring, assessment and auditing of microfinance', in *IDS Bulletin*, Vol. 34, No. 4.

——., Bhalotra, S. and Johnson, S. 2001. 'Assessing the impact of microcredit: A Zambian case study', in *The Journal of Development Studies*, Vol. 37, No. 4, pp. 81–100.

——., Dawson, P., Fanning, J-P., McKay, A. and Wright-Revolledo, K. 2005. 'Monitoring the diversity of the poverty outreach and impact of microfinance: A comparison of methods using data from Peru', in *Development Policy Review*, Vol. 23, No. 6, pp. 703–23.

Cunha, A., Leresche, J.-P. and Vez, I. 1998. 'Politiques sociales et gouvernance: analyser les changements' in *Pauvreté urbaine. Le lien et les lieux* (Lausanne: Réalités sociales), Ch. 6.

Daley-Harris, S. 2003. *State of the Microcredit Summit Campaign Report 2003* (Washington, DC: Microcredit Summit). Vailable at: http://www.microcreditsummit. org/pubs/reports/socr/2003/socr03_en.pdf

Demirguc-Kunt, A., Laeven, L. and Levine, R. 2004. 'Regulations, market structure, institutions, and the cost of financial intermediation', in *Journal of Money, Credit, and Banking*, Vol. 36, pp. 593–622.

Didoni, A. 2003. *Testing for 'monopoly': A case study on commercialization of Peruvian microfinance*, mimeo (Geneva: Graduate Institute of International Studies).

DIPRES. 2002. *Evaluación de Programas Gubernamentales, Notas Técnicas'* (Evaluation of government programmes, technical notes).

Ehlers, T.B. and Main, K. 1998. 'Women and the false promise of microenterprise', in *Gender and Society*, Vol. 12, No. 4, pp. 424–40.

Enjiang, C. 2003. 'Microfinance in rural China', in C. Findlay, A. Watson, C. A. Enjiang and Zhu Gang (eds), *Rural Financial Markets in China* (Canberra: Asia Pacific Press).

Evaluation department MIDEPLAN. 2003. 'Material de apoyo a la planificación social' (Material in support of social planning).

Evans, T.G., Adams, A.M. and Mohammed, R. 1999. 'Demystifying nonparticipation in microcredit: A population-based analysis', in *World Development*, Vol. 27, No. 2, pp. 419–30.

Evers, J. 2000. 'Micro-credit and banks', in *Finance and Common Good*, No. 5, pp. 14–26.

Farrell, M.J. 1957. 'The measurement of productive efficiency', in *Journal of the Royal Statistical Society*, Series A, General, Vol. 120, No. 3, pp. 253–81.

Farrington, T. 2000. 'Efficiency in microfinance institutions', in *The MicroBanking Bulletin*, Vol. 4, pp. 18–25.

Fernando, N.A. 2004. 'Microfinance outreach to the poorest: A realistic objective?', in *ADB Finance for the Poor*, Vol. 5, No. 1.

Fields, G. 2001. *Distribution and development* (New York: Russell Sage Foundation).

Filali Meknassi, S. 2004. *Microfinance – evaluating the Moroccan experience*, Postgraduate dissertation, Centre Monnaie Finance Banque Faculté des Sciences Juridiques Economiques et Sociales, Rabat, Morocco.

Fisher, T. and Sriram, M.S. (ed.) 2002. *Beyond micro-credit: Putting development back into microfinance* (New Delhi: Vistaar Publications; Oxford: Oxfam).

Flückiger, Y. and Vassiliev, A. 2004. 'Evaluating the efficiency of microfinance institutions', paper presented at the Symposium Microfinance and Public Policy, Geneva, IUED, November 2004.

FNAM. 2004. *Chiffres de l'exercice 2004*. Available at http://www.fnam.ma/ rubrique.php3?id_rubrique16

——. and PlaNet Finance. 2004. *Summary of proceedings*, Microfinance Day, 27 May 2004, Rabat. Available at http://www.planetfinance.org/documents/ FR/EV_270504_jdlm_maroc.pdf

Foster, S., Greene, S. and Pytkowska, J. 2003. *The state of microfinance in Central and Eastern Europe and the New Independent State*, CGAP Regional Reviews.

Foundation for Local Development and Microcredit Partnerships – FONDEP. 2005. *Microfinanza Rating*, February (Morocco).

Fouzi, M. 1998. *Le développement des microentreprises en question* (Casablanca: Edition Remald).

Fried, H.O., Knox Lovell, C.A. and Schmidt, S.S. 1993. *The measurement of productive efficiency: Techniques and applications* (Oxford: Oxford Academic Press).

GIAN (Geneva International Academic Network: ILO (International Labour Office); IUED (Institut Universitaire d'Etudes du Developpement); Université de Genève; University of Cambridge). 2005. *GIAN project on efficiency, financial performance and the role of public policy: A study of the conditions for the financial autonomy of microfinance institutions (MFI): Results of studies.*

Gibbons, D. and Meehan, J. 2000. 'The Microcredit Summit's challenge: Working towards institutional financial self-sufficiency while maintaining a commitment to serving the poorest families', mimeo.

Goldberg, M. and Motta, M. 2003. 'Microfinance for housing. The Mexican case', in *Journal of Microfinance*, Vol. 5, pp. 51–76.

Government of Mali. 2002. *Cadre Strategique de Lutte contre la Pauvreté* (Bamako: CSLP).

Grant, W. and Allen, H. 2002. 'CARE's Mata Masu Dubara (MMD) Program in Niger – Successful financial intermediation in the rural Sahel', in *Journal of Microfinance*, Vol. 4, No. 2.

Greeley, M. 2003a. 'Poverty reduction and microfinance – Assessing performance', in *IDS Bulletin*, Vol. 34, No. 4.

——. 2003b. *Sustainability and poverty outreach: Trade-off issues*, Imp-Act Programme, Institute of Development Studies (Brighton: University of Sussex).

Guérin, I. 2003. *Femmes et économie solidaire* (Paris: La Découverte, MAUSS).

Halder, S. and Mosley, P. 2004. 'Working with the ultra-poor: Learning from BRAC experiences', in *Journal of International Development*, Vol. 16, No. 3, pp. 387–406.

Hartarska, V. 2005. 'Governance and performance of microfinance institutions in Central and Eastern Europe and the Newly Independent States', in *World Development*, Vol. 33, No. 10, pp. 1627–43.

Hashemi, S.M. 1997. 'Those left behind: A note on targeting the hardcore poor', in G. Wood and I.A. Sharif (eds), *Who needs credit? Poverty and finance in Bangladesh* (Dhaka: Zed Books), pp. 249–57.

——. 2001. 'Linking microfinance and safety net programs to include the poorest: The Case of IGVGD in Bangladesh', CGAP Focus Note No. 21, May.

——., Schuler, S.R. and Riley, A.P. 1996. 'Rural credit programs and women's empowerment in Bangladesh', in *World Development*, Vol. 24, No. 4, pp. 635–53. Available at: http://www.planetfinance.org/documents/FR/EV_270504_jdlm_maroc.pdf

Hatch, J. 1974. *The corn farmers of Motupe: A study of traditional farming practices in Northern Coastal Peru*, unpublished doctoral dissertation, University of Wisconsin.

Hulme, D. 2000. 'Is micro debt good for poor people? A note on the dark side of microfinance', in *SED*, Vol. 11, No. 1.

——. and Mosley, P. 1996. *Finance against poverty*, Vol. 1 (London: Routledge).

Huybens, E. and Smith, B. 1999. 'Inflation, financial market, and long-run real actitivity', in *Journal of Monetary Economics*, Vol. 43, pp. 283–315.

ILO (International Labour Office). 1976. *Employment, growth and basic needs: A one-world problem*, Report of the Director-General of the International Labour Office (Geneva: ILO).

IMCC. 1994. *Maximizing the outreach of micro enterprise finance: the emerging lessons of successful programs* (draft), for USAID (Washington, DC), Sep.

IMF (International Monetary Fund). 2005. *Microfinance: A view from the Fund*, Monetary and Financial Systems Department (Washington, DC: IMF).

Imp-Act. 2003. 'Microfinance and poverty: Developing systems for monitoring depth of poverty outreach and impact', Report based on a one-day seminar held at Polokwane, South Africa, May, 2003.

——. 2005. *Guidelines to social performance management in microfinance*. Available at: www.Imp-Act.org

Jappelli, T. and Pagano, M. 2002. 'Information sharing, lending and defaults: Cross-country evidence', in *Journal of Banking and Finance*, Vol. 26, No. 10, pp. 2017–45.

Kabeer, N. and Noponen, H. 2005. 'Social and economic impacts of PRADAN's self help group microfinance and livelihoods promotion program: Analysis from Jharkhand, India', *Imp-Act* Working Paper No. 11, March.

Karlan, D. and Zinman, J. 2006. *Observing unobservables: Identifying information asymmetries with a consumer credit field experiment*, mimeo (New Haven, CT: Yale University).

Kerstens, K. and Vanden Eeckaut, P. 1999. 'Estimating returns to scale using non-parametric determinstic technologies: A new method based on goodness-of-fit', in *European Journal of Operational Research*, Vol. 113, pp. 206–14.

Khawari, A. 2004. 'Microfinance: Does it hold its promises? A survey of recent literature', HWWA Discussion Paper No. 276 (Hamburg Institute of International Economics).

Kline, S. 2003. 'Sustaining social performance. Institutionalising organisational learning and poverty outreach at Prizma, Bosnia and Herzegovina', in *IDS Bulletin*, Vol. 34, No. 4.

——. and Matul, M. 2003. *Scoring change: Prizma's approach to assessing poverty and monitoring impact*, Draft, MFC Case-Study Note No. 3 (Warsaw: MFC).

Korsah, K.B., Nyarko, E.K. and Tagoe, N.A. 2001. *Impact of financial sector liberalization on competition and efficiency in the Ghanaian banking industry*, IFLIP WP 01–2, ILO Social Finance Programme (Geneva: ILO).

La Porta, R., Lopez-de-Silanes, F., Shleifer, A. and Vishny, R.W. 1997. 'Legal determinants of external finance', in *Journal of Finance*, Vol. 52, pp. 1131–50.

Laeven, L. and Majnoni, G. 2005. 'Does judicial efficiency lower the cost of credit?', in *Journal of Banking and Finance*, Vol. 29, pp. 1791–812.

Lafourcade, A.L., Isern, J., Mwangi, P. and Brown, M. 2005. *Overview of the outreach and financial performance of microfinance institutions in Africa*, Microfinance Information eXchange (www.mixmarket.org).

Lapenu, C. and Zeller, M. 2002. 'Distribution, growth and performance of the MFIs in Africa Asia and Latin America: A recent inventory', in *Savings and Development*, Vol. 26, No. 1, pp. 87–111.

——. and Zeller, M. 2001. *Distribution, growth and performance of MFIs in Africa, Asia and Latin America*, FNCD Discussion Paper No.114, (Washington, DC, IFPRI).

——., Zeller, M., Greeley, M., Chao-Béroff, R. and Verhagen, K. 2004. 'Performances sociales: Une raison d'être des institutions de microfinance ... et pourtant encore peu mesurées. Quelques pistes', in *Revue Monde en Développement*, Tome 32, 2004/2, No. 126, pp. 51–68.

Lautier, B. 1999. 'Les politiques sociales en Amérique latine: propositions de méthode pour analyser un éclatement en cours', in *Cahier des Amériques latines*, Vol. 30, pp. 19–44.

Levine, R. 1997. 'Financial development and economic growth: Views and agenda', in *Journal of Economic Literature*, Vol. 35, pp. 688–726.

——. 2005. 'Finance and growth: Theory and evidence', in P. Aghion and S. Durlauf (eds), *Handbook of economic growth* (The Netherlands: Elsevier Science).

Littlefield, E., Morduch, J. and Hashemi, S. 2003. *Is microfinance an effective strategy to reach the Millennium Development Goals?*, CGAP Focus Note No. 24 (Washington DC: CGAP).

Love, I. and Mylenko, N. 2003. *Credit reporting and financing constraints*, World Bank Policy Research Working Paper 3142 (Washington, DC: World Bank).

Matin, I. and Hulme, D. 2003. 'Programmes for the poorest: Learning from the IGVGD programme in Bangladesh', in *World Development*, Vol. 31, No. 3. Available at: http://www.bankalmaghrib.ma/Francais/Menu/Anex.asp

——., Hulme, D. and Rutherford, S. 2002. 'Finance for the poor: From microcredit to microfinancial services', in *Journal of International Development*, Vol. 14, No. 2, pp. 273–94.

Mayoux, L. 2000. *Microfinance and the empowerment of women: A review of the key issues*, Social Finance Unit Working Paper No. 23 (Geneva: ILO).

McGregor, J.A., Mosley, P., Johnson, S. and Simanowitz, A. 2000. 'How can impact assessment take into account wider social and economic impacts?', *Imp-Act* Working Paper No. 3, June.

MBB. 2000. *The MicroBanking Bulletin: Focus on efficiency*, Issue No. 4, February.

——. 2002. *The MicroBanking Bulletin: Focus on standardization*, Issue No. 8, November.

——. 2005. *The MicroBanking Bulletin: The scope of funding mechanisms*, Issue No. 11, August.

Mestries Benquet, F. and Hernández Trujillo, J.M. 2003. *Crédito, seguro y ahorro rural: las vías de la autonomía* (Azcapotzalco: Universidad Autónoma Metropolitana).

Meyer, R.L. 2001. 'Microfinance, rural poverty alleviation, and improving food security', in *ADB Newsletter*, Vol. 2, No. 2.

Micco, A., Panizza, U. and Yañez, M. 2007. 'Bank ownership and performance: Does politics matter?', *Journal of Banking and Finance*, Vol. 31, pp. 219–41.

Microfinance Gateway. *The fifty percent solution: Will new government mandates increase the industry's poverty focus or tie its hands?* Available at: www.microfinancegateway.org

Miller, M. 2003. *Credit reporting systems and the international economy* (Cambridge, MA: MIT Press).

Milligan, G.W. and Cooper, M.C. 1985. 'An examination of procedures for determining the number of clusters in a data set', in *Psychometrika*, Vol. 50, No. 2, pp. 159–79.

Mody, A. and Patro, D. 1996. 'Valuing and accounting for loan guarantees', in *World Bank Research Observer*, Vol. 11, No. 1, pp. 119–42.

Morduch, J. 1998. *Does microfinance really help the poor? New evidence from flagship programs in Bangladesh*, mimeo (Harvard, MA: Department of Economics, Harvard University).

——. 1999a. 'The microfinance promise', in *Journal of Economic Literature*, Vol. 37, No. 4, pp. 1569–1614.

——. 1999b. 'The role of subsidies in microfinance: Evidence from the Grameen Bank', in *Journal of Development Economics*, Vol. 60, pp. 229–48.

——. 1999c. *Grameen Bank – A financial reckoning*, Princeton University Discussion Paper (Princeton, NJ: Princeton University).

——. 2000. 'The microfinance schism', in *World Development*, Vol. 28, No. 4, pp. 617–29.

——. 2003. *Subsidy and sustainability*, Paper prepared for GIAN conference on Microfinance and Public Policy, Cambridge University, Nov. 20.

——. 2005a. 'Implementing the Microenterprise Results and Accountability Act of 2004', Testimony for the House International Relations Committee, Subcommittee on Africa, Global Human Rights and International Operations. US House of Representatives, September 20, 2005.

——. 2005b. 'Smart subsidy for sustainable microfinance', in *ADB Finance for the Poor*, Vol. 6, No. 4.

——., Demirguc-Kunt, A. and Cull, R. 2006. *Financial performance and outreach: A global analysis of leading microbanks*, Policy Research Working Paper Series 3827 (Washington, DC: World Bank).

——. and Haley, B. 2002. *Analysis of the effects of microfinance on poverty reduction: Overview* (New York: Robert F. Wagner Graduate School of Public Service).

Mosley, P. and Rock, J. 2004. 'Microfinance, labour markets and poverty in Africa: A study of six institutions', in *Journal of International Development*, Vol. 16, No. 3, pp. 467–500.

National Economic Research Associates. 1990. *Evaluation of the loan guarantee scheme*, Department of Employment Research Paper No. 74 (London: Department of Employment).

Navajas, S., Schreiner, M., Meyer, R.L. and Gonzalez-Vega, C. 2000. 'Microcredit and the poorest of the poor: Theory and evidence from Bolivia', in *World Development*, Vol. 28, No. 2, pp. 333–46.

Nguyen, T., Ouattara, K. and Gonzalez-Vega, C. 1999. *Using village mechanism to expand the frontier of microfinance: The case of Caisses Villageoises in Mali* (Ohio State University).

Nieto, B., Cinca, C. and Molinero, C. 2004. *Microfinance institutions and efficiency*, Discussion Papers in Accounting and Finance AF04–20 (School of Management, University of Southampton).

Nteziyaremye, A. and MkNelly, B. 2001. *Mali poverty outreach study of the Kafo Jiginew and Nyèsigiso credit and saving with education program*, Freedom from Hunger Research Paper No. 7 (Davis, CA: Freedom from Hunger).

Nurske, R. 1953. *Problems of capital formation in underdeveloped countries* (New York, NY: Oxford University Press).

Nussbaum, M. 2000. *Women and human development* (Cambridge: Cambridge University Press).

Olsson, U. 1979. 'Maximum likelihood estimation of the polychoric correlation coefficient', in *Psychometrika*, Vol. 44, No. 4, pp. 443–60.

Parra, E. 1993. *Modalidades de crédito para el sector informal en Colombia* (Credit modalities for the informal sector in Colombia), Aug. (Santiago de Chile: PREAL).

PASMEC (Programme d'appui aux structures mutualistes d'épargne et de crédit, BCEAO). 2005. *Observatory 2003* (Dakar).

Paxton, J. 2002. 'Depth of outreach and its relation to the sustainability of MFIs', in *Savings and Development*, Vol. 26.

PET (Programa Economía del Trabajo). 2002. *Catastro instituciones crediticias* (Cadastre of credit institutions) (Santiago de Chile).

——. 2003. *Crédito a la Microempresa en Chile, Una revisión cualitativa 1991–2001* (Credit for microenterprises in Chile, a qualitative review) (Santiago de Chile).

PlaNet Finance. 2004. *Evaluating the impact of microcredit in Morocco*, Report financed and coordinated by the National Federation of Microcredit Associations.

PlaNet Rating. 2003. *Kafo Jiginew Mali* (www.planetrating.com)

Pytkowska, J. and Gelenidze, Z. 2005. *Georgia Benchmarking Report 2003* (MFC/GMSE).

——. and Bankowska, E. 2004. *Microfinance sector development in Eastern Europe and Central Asia* (Microfinance Centre for CEE and NIS, MFC).

Rahman, A. 1999. 'Micro-credit initiatives for equitable and sustainable development: who pays?', in *World Development*, Vol. 27, No. 1, pp. 67–82.

Recife International Meeting on Urban Poverty. 1996. *Urban poverty, a world challenge. The Declaration of Recife*, Habitat II (Recife).

Regional Micro Credit Summit for Latin America and the Caribbean. 2005. *El rol de las redes de microfinanzas en el crecimiento y expansión del sector en América Latina* (The role of microfinance networks in growth and expansion of the sector in Latin America).

Remenyi, J. and Quinones, B. 2000. *Microfinance and poverty alleviation* (London: Pinter Press).

Rhyne, E. 1998. 'The yin and yang of microfinance: Reaching the poor and sustainability', in *The Microbanking Bulletin*, Vol. 2, pp. 6–8.

Robinson, M. 2001. *The microfinance revolution: Sustainable finance for the poor* (Washington: World Bank).

Roper, K. 2003. 'Refining performance assessment systems to serve sustainability, poverty outreach and impact goals: The case of small enterprise foundation in South Africa', in *IDS Bulletin*, Vol. 34, No. 4.

Sahlins, M. 1976. *Age de pierre, âge d'abondance: l'économie des sociétés primitives* (Paris: Gallimard).

Samanamud Ávila, J., Alvarado Portillo, M. and del Castillo Villegas, G. 2003. *La configuración de redes sociales en el micro crédito en contextos de precariedad laboral: el caso de los confeccionistas en tela de El Alto* (La Paz: Programa de Investigación Estratégica en Bolivia).

SBIF (Superintendency of Banks and Financial Institutions). 2004. 'Leyes y normas de SBIF' (SBIF laws and norms), Chs 7–10, Annex 2.

Schreiner, M. 2002. 'Aspects of outreach: A framework for discussion of the social benefits of microfinance', in *Journal of International Development*, Vol. 14, pp. 591–603.

——. and Yaron, J. 2001. *Development finance institutions: Measuring their subsidy* (Washington, DC: World Bank).

Schrieder, G. and Sharma, M. 1999. 'Impact of finance on poverty reduction and social capital formation: A review and synthesis of empirical evidence', in *Savings and Development*, Vol. 23, No. 1.

Sebstad, J. and Cohen, M. 2001. *Microfinance, risk management and poverty* (Washington DC: USAID).

SEEP. 2002. *Definitions of selected financil terms, ratios, and adjustments for microfinance* (Washington, DC).

SEF (Small Enterprise Foundation). 2003. Six-monthly report to *Imp-Act*. October 2003.

Seiford, L.M. and Thrall, R.M. 1990. 'Recent developments in DEA: The mathematical programming approach to frontier analysis', in *Journal of Econometrics*, Vol. 46, No. 1/2, pp. 7–38.

Sen, A. 1983. 'Poor, relatively speaking', in *Oxford Economic Papers*, 35, pp. 153–69.

——. 1992. *Inequality reexamined* (Oxford: Oxford University Press).

——. 1999. *Development as freedom* (Oxford: Oxford University Press).

SERCOTEC. 2003. 'Cuenta Pública de SERCOTEC' (Public account of SERCOTEC).

——. 2002. 'Orientaciones Institucionales SERCOTEC 2001–2006' (Institutional orientations of SERCOTEC 2001–2006).

Serra, R. 1999. *Creating a framework for reducing poverty: Institutional and process issues in national poverty policy in selected African countries. Mali country study report for the PSPWG of the SPA* (IDS, University of Sussex, Brighton).

Servet, J.-M. 2004. *Inégalité versus pauvreté: Quel rôle peut jouer la microfinance* (Université de Rouen).

——. 2006. 'Performance, impacts et effets des organisations de microfinance', in Servet, *Banquières aux pieds nus* (Paris: Odile Jacob), Ch. 10.

——. and Guérin, I. 2002. *Exclusion et liens financiers: Rapport du Centre Walras 2002* (Paris: Economica).

Sharma, M. 2000. 'Impact of microfinance on poverty alleviation: What does emerging evidence indicate?', IFPRI Policy Brief, No. 2, March.

——. and Zeller, M. 1999. 'Placement and outreach of group-based credit organizations', in *World Development*, Vol. 27, No.12, pp. 2123–36.

SII, Databases of the Internal Revenue Service.

Simanowitz, A. 2003. 'Microfinance, poverty and social performance: Overview', in *IDS Bulletin*, Vol. 34, No. 4.

——. and Walter, A. 2002. 'Ensuring impact: Reaching the poorest while building financially self-sufficient institutions, and showing improvements in the lives of poor women and their families', in S. Daley-Harris (ed.): *Pathways out of poverty: Innovations in microfinance for the poorest families* (West Hartford, CT: Kumarian Press).

Social Performance Task Force. 2005. *Statement of principles. Promoting social performance in microfinance: Toward a 'double bottom line'*. Available at: www.triasngo.org

SOS Faim. 2002. *Zoom micro-finance: Les fonds financiers privés – Bolivie*, No. 7 (Brusells).

Stiglitz, J. 1994. 'The role of the state in financial markets', *Proceedings of the World Bank Annual Conference on Development Economics* (Washington, DC).

——. and Weiss, A. 1981. 'Credit rationing in markets with imperfect information', in *American Economic Review*, No. 71, pp. 393–410.

Sultan, S. 2002. 'Strategies to reach the extreme poor in rural Bangladesh', Paper for *Imp-Act* Thematic Group on Microfinance for the Very Poor, Sheffield University, 28–30 April. Available at: www.imp-act.org

Thannasoulis, E. 2001. *Introduction to the theory and application of data envelopmnt analysis* (Norwell: Kluwer Academic Publishers)

Townsend, P. 2003. 'La conceptualización de la pobreza', in *Comercio exterior*, Vol. 53, pp. 445–52.

Valenzuela, L. 1998. *Overview of MF fraud* (Washington, DC: Microfinance Network, Moving Microfinance Forward).

Von Pischke, J. D. 1991. *Finance at the frontier – Debt capacity and the role of credit in the private economy*, EDI Development Studies (Washington, DC: World Bank).

Von Stauffenberg, D. 2002. *Microenterprise Americas: Latin America's top MFIs* (Lima: MicroRate).

Williamson, S. D. 1987. 'Costly monitoring, loan contracts and equilibrium credit rationing', in *Quarterly Journal of Economics*, Vol. 102, pp. 135–46.

Woller, G. and Schreiner, M. 2002. *Poverty lending, financial self-sufficiency, and the six aspects of outreach*, unpublished paper.

World Bank. 1990. 'Poverty', in *World Development Report* (Washington, DC).

——. 2000–01. 'Attacking poverty', in *World Development Report* (Washington, DC).

——. 2001. *Kingdom of Morocco: Poverty update*, Report No. 21506-MOR, March (Washington, DC).

——. 2004. *South Africa: Technology and access to financial services*, mimeo (Washington, DC).

——. 2005. 'A better investment climate for everyone', in *World Development Report* (Washington, DC).

Zeller, M., and Meyer, R. L. (eds). 2002. *The triangle of microfinance: Financial sustainability, outreach and impact* (Baltimore, MD: The Johns Hopkins University Press).

——., Lapenu, C. and Greeley, M. 2003. *Measuring social performance of microfinance institutions: A proposal*, Social Performance Indicators Initiative: Final Report (Washington, DC: Argidius Foundation and CGAP).

Zohir, S. and Matin, I. 2004. 'Wider impacts of microfinance institutions: issues and concepts', in *Journal of International Development*, Vol. 16, No. 3, pp. 301–30.

Index